THE FATHERS OF THE CHURCH

MEDIAEVAL CONTINUATION

VOLUME 6

THE FATHERS OF THE CHURCH

MEDIAEVAL CONTINUATION

EDITORIAL BOARD

Thomas P. Halton
The Catholic University of America
Editorial Director

Elizabeth Clark
Duke University

Robert D. Sider
Dickinson College

Joseph T. Lienhard
Fordham University

Michael Slusser
Duquesne University

Frank A. C. Mantello
The Catholic University of America

Cynthia White
The University of Arizona

Kathleen McVey
Princeton Theological Seminary

Robin Darling Young
The University of Notre Dame

David J. McGonagle
Director
The Catholic University of America Press

FORMER EDITORIAL DIRECTORS

Ludwig Schopp, Roy J. Deferrari, Bernard M. Peebles,
Hermigild Dressler, O.F.M.

Joel Kalvesmaki
Staff Editor

PETER DAMIAN
LETTERS
121–150

Translated by

OWEN J. BLUM, O.F.M.
Quincy University, Quincy, Illinois

and

IRVEN M. RESNICK
University of Tennessee, Chattanooga, Tennessee

with a preface by

KURT REINDEL
Professor Emeritus, University of Regensburg

THE CATHOLIC UNIVERSITY OF AMERICA PRESS
Washington, D.C.

Copyright © 2004
THE CATHOLIC UNIVERSITY OF AMERICA PRESS
All rights reserved
Printed in the United States of America

The paper used in this publication meets the minimum requirements of the American National Standards for Information Science—Permanence of Paper for Printed Library Materials, ANSI Z39.48 - 1984.

LIBRARY OF CONGRESS CATALOGING-IN-PUBLICATION DATA

Peter Damian, Saint, 1007–1072.
    [The letters of Peter Damian.
    (The Fathers of the Church, mediaeval continuation ; vv. 1–3, 5–6)
    Translation of the Latin letters of Peter Damian.
    Includes bibliographical references and indexes.
    Contents: [1] 1–30—[2] 31–60—[3] 61–90—[5] 91–120—[6] 121–150.
    1. Peter Damian, Saint, 1007–1072—Correspondence.
2. Christian saints—Italy—Correspondence.   I. Blum, Owen J.,
1912–1998.   II. Series: Fathers of the Church, mediaeval continuation ;
v. 1, etc.
BX4700.P77A4   1998   270.3   88-25802
ISBN 0-8132-0702-9 (v. 1)
ISBN 0-8132-0707-X (v. 2)
ISBN 0-8132-0750-9 (v. 3)
ISBN 0-8132-0816-5 (v. 5)
ISBN 0-8132-1372-X (v. 6)
ISBN 978-8132-2640-8 (pbk.) (v. 6)

CONTENTS

Preface, by Kurt Reindel, translated by Uta-Renate Blumenthal	vii
Introduction, by Irven M. Resnick	ix
Abbreviations	xiii
Select Bibliography	xv
Concordance	xxi
LETTER 121	3
LETTER 122	10
LETTER 123	12
LETTER 124	21
LETTER 125	26
LETTER 126	27
LETTER 127	40
LETTER 128	45
LETTER 129	49
LETTER 130	53
LETTER 131	55
LETTER 132	57
LETTER 133	73
LETTER 134	76
LETTER 135	77
LETTER 136	84
LETTER 137	90
LETTER 138	97
LETTER 139	102
LETTER 140	103

CONTENTS

LETTER 141	112
LETTER 142	127
LETTER 143	143
LETTER 144	148
LETTER 145	150
LETTER 146	155
LETTER 147	167
LETTER 148	169
LETTER 149	171
LETTER 150	181

Indices
  Index of Proper Names   187
  Index of Sacred Scripture   191

PREFACE

by Kurt Reindel
translated by Uta-Renate Blumenthal

Father Owen John Blum was born on December 14, 1912, at Indianapolis. He lost both of his parents in an influenza epidemic when he was seven, but a Franciscan Father made it possible for him to attend St. Joseph's Seminary at Teutopolis. He entered the Franciscan order there in 1931, and was ordained to the priesthood in 1938. The following year he joined the Franciscans at Quincy, Illinois, forming a connection that he maintained to the day of his death. He began to study history at The Catholic University of America in Washington, D.C. in 1941 and was influenced by Father Aloysius Ziegler, who first brought St. Peter Damian to his attention. His dissertation, *St. Peter Damian: His Teaching of the Spiritual Life*, was published in 1947 (Catholic University of America, Studies in Medieval History, New Series 10). Fr. Owen subsequently taught at Quincy College, which eventually became Quincy University. From 1963 to 1965, he worked in Washington as one of the co-editors of the *New Catholic Encyclopedia*. Most of all, however, it was the study of Peter Damian that occupied him throughout his career. This outstanding personality of the eleventh century fascinated him. In Fr. Owen's eyes, Damian's writings constituted an all-encompassing *Summa theologica* in letter form, which he endeavored to interpret and whose ideas he tried to publicize with what at times amounted to missionary zeal. For this reason alone he had already planned early on a translation of the texts into English. The chief obstacle to this undertaking was the fact that the works of Peter Damian were only accessible in a reprint by Migne that left much to be desired. Thus, Fr. Owen acquired for his dissertation already a microfilm of one of the main manuscripts transmitting Damian's letters, codex Vaticanus latinus 3797. But this still did not suffice for the translation project, and thus he came to contact the Monumenta Germaniae Historica in Germany. There, the undersigned was engaged in the critical edition of the letters of Damian. Fr. Owen's first visit to Munich in 1956 was the beginning of a close collaboration, which was further deepened during the years 1978 to 1982, when the financial means were found, thanks to the Deutsche Forschungsgemeinschaft, to allow Fr. Owen a research leave in Germany, which he spent at the University of Regensburg. These many years of collaboration represented for the undersigned and his edition of the letters of Peter Damian a great advantage, for in numerous talks and discussions he profited from Fr. Owen's vast knowledge. One result of the collaboration was the publication of the Latin text (*Die Briefe des Petrus Damiani,* ed. Kurt Reindel, Monumenta Germaniae Historica, Briefe der deutschen Kaiserzeit vol. IV, 1–4), the other was the English translation by Owen J. Blum (*The Letters of Peter Damian.* The Catholic University of America Press, The Fathers of the Church, Mediaeval Continuation). At the time of his death on November 1, 1998, Fr. Owen himself had seen through the press volumes one through four (1989 to 1998) of this translation.

INTRODUCTION

by Irven M. Resnick

Letters 121–150, written during the years 1065–71, form the fifth volume in this series. Their number, written over such a brief period, suggests the increasing demands upon Damian for counsel and correction. Once again these letters attest to Damian's concern for his nephew, Damianus, to whom he addressed *Letters* 123 and 138. The first of these contains a lengthy exhortation to guard the virtues of monastic life, with a special emphasis on chastity. Damian exhorts him to fortify himself with the frequent reception of the Eucharist, which provides a safeguard against the snares of Satan. *Letter* 123 also contains an unusual tale attributed to Emperor Stedelandus of Galicia—perhaps Ferdinand I of Castile and Leon (d. 1065)—that sheds some light on tensions that may arise when Christians and Muslims live in close proximity. In this instance, some local Muslims brought a court action to compel three Christian prostitutes to accept their trade, which they had refused. When the women remained recalcitrant despite the court's ruling in favor of the Muslims' complaint, they were sentenced to death. Miraculously, the sentence could not be carried out until the women first received a vision of the Savior, guaranteeing that they would die as holy martyrs.[1] Although *Letter* 125 was not addressed to his nephew, Damianus, it concerns him nonetheless. In it, Damian recommends his nephew to an unnamed abbot, and asks that he receive him as a student for instruction in the liberal arts: the *trivium* and *quadrivium*. Despite Damian's fre-

1. For a discussion of sexual intercourse across the boundaries of religious groups in Spain, with special attention given to the position of prostitutes, see David Nirenberg, "Sex and Violence between Majority and Minority," ch. 5 in *Communities of Violence: Persecution of Minorities in the Middle Ages* (Princeton, NJ: Princeton University Press, 1996).

quent criticism of monks who spend their time discoursing like rhetors in the marketplace, this letter should serve as a reminder that he considered the liberal arts important to the monk's training. His nephew Damianus is named as the recipient for *Letter* 138. In it, Peter Damian confesses his fear that death approaches while he is still caught up in sin. He begs his nephew to pray on his behalf so that he might rid himself of a tendency to lightheartedness and joking, when he knows that only the tears of compunction will benefit him.

In a similar vein, Damian addressed *Letter* 132 to his nephew Marinus, who had received the monks' habit at St. Apollinaris in Classe. Again, he stressed the virtues of chastity and sobriety (in the course of which he displays an expert knowledge of wines) and encourages Marinus to guard his eyes when in the presence of women. This letter presents one of Damian's most comprehensive discussions of the monastic virtues. In it, he also reveals some knowledge of current medical practice, and criticizes healthy monks who waste their time on different medications or in having themselves bled by physicians, with leeches.

This volume also completes the collection of six letters that Damian addressed to the Empress Agnes. In *Letter* 124 he encourages her to conquer her loneliness and includes a moving encomium to the virtue of monastic silence. Employing the bridegroom imagery that Damian used so effectively to describe the solitary's union with God, he reminds Agnes that through silence the Holy Spirit constructs in her a new temple to the Lord. *Letter* 130 repeats these themes, and Damian exhorts the empress to bear the burdens of solitude in imitation of Christ. He exhorts her to meditate on the fleeting vanity of earthly glory, and concentrate on the riches that will be hers in the company of the immortal Bridegroom. *Letter* 144 provides a window on political events of the day. There, Damian regrets having persuaded Agnes to travel to the German court to engage her son, King Henry IV, in an expedition into Italy to defend the Holy See against a Norman advance on Rome, for which Henry was to receive the Imperial crown. Now, Damian has changed his mind and begs the empress to return to Rome. This theme is taken up again in his last letter to Agnes, *Letter*

149. Once more Damian deplores the many visits Agnes has made to the German court, and exhorts her to return to Rome and to the religious life. In a rare autobiographical remark, he notes that nothing could bring him even to walk past the house of his birth in Ravenna except the last illness of his sister, Rodelinda, who had been a second mother to him. This remark provides an opportunity to revise the rather somber picture of Damian's youth, reported by John of Lodi. This letter also fixes the year 1035 for his entry into the religious life at Fonte Avellana.

In other letters in this volume Damian again excoriates twin evils against which he fought, namely clerical marriage or concubinage (Nicolaitism) and simony. In *Letter* 129, addressed to clergy and lay leaders of the Pataria in Milan, he congratulates them for their efforts in the struggle against simony and clerical marriage but warns that their archbishop, Guido of Milan, remains unrepentant. Similarly, in *Letters* 140 and 141, Damian reproaches Duke Godfrey of Tuscany's chaplains, Tudethchinus and John, for the view that those who had bought the office of bishop from lay rulers were not guilty of simony, since they only purchased ecclesiastical estates and not the episcopal rights and dignity. Here, Damian comes closer to condemning lay investiture than in any of his other writings. Damian, however, was keenly aware that proper ecclesiastical procedure should be followed in accusations of simony, and he often had to restrain local communities whose enthusiasm for reform threatened to plunge the Church into disorder. Writing to the citizens of Florence in *Letter* 146, Damian insists that they await the outcome of an investigation by a Roman synod before condemning their bishop Peter for simony. He reminds the Florentines that sacerdotal acts performed by a simonist are valid nonetheless, and cautions them against condemning an innocent man. In this same letter, Damian takes on the Vallombrosan monks of John Gualbertus whose call for revolutionary action threatened to nullify all sacramental functions in Florence. His exhortation to restraint in Florence may be responsible for complaints that Damian was too tolerant of the evil of simony.

This volume also contains letters to other monastic communities, either correcting the relaxed character of their life (*Letter* 142), instituting special fasts (*Letter* 137), or calling upon them to show moderation in the application of the penitential discipline in order not to discourage others from undertaking the rigors of the eremitic life (*Letters* 133 and 139). Of special interest is Damian's *Letter* 131 to the abbot of the Latin rite monastery of St. Mary in Constantinople, praising the monks for their steadfast commitment to the Catholic faith.

Finally, among these letters are several addressed to laypersons. In *Letter* 143, addressed to the Countess Guilla (the wife of Rainerius II, the marquis of Monte S. Maria), Damian encourages the young countess to reform the practices of their estate to relieve the condition of the poor. Both *Letters* 135 and 145 are addressed to the Roman prefect Cencius. In the latter, he praises Cencius for discharging his office with justice and for protecting the poor. But more startling is his commendation of Cencius, who acted as a substitute homilist for Damian in St. Peter's church on the feast of the Epiphany, when Damian's voice failed him. In this letter, Damian articulates a doctrine of the priesthood of all the faithful, for whom preaching should not be an extraordinary function, thus anticipating the second Vatican Council. In the first edition of his works (1606) this notion was thought to be astounding, if not quasi-heretical.

ABBREVIATIONS

Burchard	Burchard of Worms, *Decretorum libri XX*. PL 140.537–1058.
CC	*Corpus Christianorum, Series Latina*. Brepols, 1954– .
CJC	*Corpus Juris Canonici*. Ed. E. A. Friedberg, 2 vols. Leipzig, 1879–1881.
CCCM	*Corpus Christianorum, Continuatio Mediaevalis*. Brepols, 1971– .
CSEL	*Corpus Scriptorum Ecclesiasticorum Latinorum*. Vienna.
DA	*Deutsches Archiv für Erforschung des Mittelalters*
DTC	*Dictionnaire de théologie catholique*. 15 vols. Paris 1903–1950.
FOTC	The Fathers of the Church. New York and Washington, D.C., 1947– .
Gaetani	*S. Petri Damiani . . . Opera omnia*. 4 vols. 1606–1640. Later editions will be cited by year of publication.
Hinschius	Pseudo-Isidore, *Decretales Pseudo-Isidorianae et capitula Angilramni*, ed. P. Hinschius. Leipzig, 1863.
HJb	*Historisches Jahrbuch*
Itala	*Itala: Das Neue Testament in altlateinischer Überlieferung*. Ed A. Jülicher. 4 vols. 1963–1976.
Jaffé	*Regesta Pontificum Romanorum*. Ed. P. Jaffé. 2d ed. Corr. S. Loewenfeld, F. Kaltenbrunner, P. Ewald.

	Graz: Akademische Druck- und Verlagsanstalt, 1956.
LThK	*Lexikon für Theologie und Kirche.* 11 vols. Freiburg, Basel, Rome, Vienna: Herder, 1993–2001.
Mansi	*Sacrorum conciliorum nova et amplissima collectio.* Ed. Joannes Dominicus Mansi. 53 vols. Paris: 1900–1927.
MGH	Monumenta Germaniae Historica
Auct.ant.	Auctores antiquissimi
Capit.	Capitularia regum Francorum
Const.	Constitutiones et acta publica imperatorum
Epp.	Epistolae (in Quarto)
LL	Leges (in folio)
NCE	*The New Catholic Encyclopedia*, 2d ed. 2003.
PG	*Patrologia Graeca.* Ed. J.-P. Migne. Paris 1857–1886.
PL	*Patrologia Latina.* Ed. J.-P. Migne. Paris 1844–1855.
RE	*Real-Encyclopädie der Classischen Alterumswissenschaft.* Ed. Pauly-Wissowa.
Regino	Regino of Prum, *De ecclesiasticis disciplines et religione Christiana libri duo.* PL 132.185–370.
Sabatier	*Bibliorum sacrorum Latinae versiones antiquae.* Ed. P. Sabatier. 3 vols. 1743.
SC	Sources chrétiennes, Paris 1942– .
Vulg	*Biblia sacra iuxta vulgatam versionem.* Ed. Robert Weber. 2 vols. 2d ed., 1975.

SELECT BIBLIOGRAPHY

Sources

Alexander II, Pope. *Epistolae et diplomata.* PL 146.1279–1436.
Ambrose. *De Abraham.* Ed. Charles Schenkl, CSEL 32/1 (1896) 500–638.
———. *De incarnationis Dominicae sacramento.* PL 16.817–846.
———. *De institutione virginis.* PL 16.305–335.
———. *De obitu Theodosii Imperatoris.* Ed. Otto Faller, CSEL 73/7 (1955) 370–401.
Augustine. *De civitate Dei.* Ed. B. Dombart and A. Kalb, CC 47 and 48 (1955).
———. *De diversis quaestionibus LXXXIII.* Ed. A. Mutzenbecher, CC 44A (1975).
———. *De haeresibus.* CC 46, 13/2 (1969) 283–345.
———. *De natura et origine animae.* Ed. Charles F. Urba and Joseph Zycha, CSEL 60 (1913) 303–420.
———. *De trinitate libri XV.* Ed. W. J. Mountain and F. Glorie, 2 vols., CC 50 and 50A (1968).
———. *De utilitate credendi.* Ed. Joseph Zycha, CSEL 25/1 (1891).
———. *Quaestionum in Heptateuchum libri VII.* Ed. I. Fraipont, CC 33 (1958).
———. *Sermones.* Ed. C. Lambot, CC 41 (1961).
Bede. *De temporum ratione liber.* Ed. C. W. Jones, CC 123B (1977).
Benedicti Regula. Ed. R. Hanslik, CSEL 75 (1977).
Burchard of Worms. *Decretorum libri XX,* PL 140.537–1058.
Canones apostolorum, ed. C.H. Turner, in *Ecclesiae occidentalis monumenta iuris antiquissima. Canonum et conciliorum Graecorum intrepretationes latinae* (1899–1939).
Die Chroniken Bertholds von Reichenau und Bernolds von Konstanz 1054–1100, MGH, Scriptores rerum Germanicarum, n.s. 14, ed. Ian S. Robinson (Hanover: Hahnsche Buchhandlung, 2003).
Cicero. *De inventione rhetorica.* Trans. H. M. Hubbell. Loeb Classical Library, 2. Cambridge, MA: Harvard University Press, 1949.
Claudius of Turin. *Quaestiones XXX super libros Regum.* PL 104.623–810.
Collectio Dionysio-Hadriana. PL 67.39–346.
Diogenes Laertius. *De vitis . . . clarorum philosophorum.* Ed. Otto Holtz. Leipzig: Tauchnitz, 1895.

SELECT BIBLIOGRAPHY

Epiphanius. *Adversus haereses* [*Panarion*]. In *Epiphanii . . . Opera*. Ed. G. Dindorfus. 3 vols. Leipzig: T. O. Weigel, 1859–61.
Eutropius. *Breviarium ab urbe condita*. Ed. H. Droysen, MGH Auct.ant. 2 (1879).
Gallia Christiana in provincias ecclesiasticas distributa. Eds. Monachorum Congregationis S. Mauri ordinis S. Benedicti [the Maurists]. 1744; repr. Westmead, Farnborough, Hants, England: Gregg International, 1970.
Gelasius I. *Tractatus*. Ed. A. Thiel, *Epistolae Romanorum pontificum genuinae* 1 (1867–1868) 510–607.
Gennadius. *De scriptoribus ecclesiasticis*. PL 58.1053–1120.
———. *Liber de ecclesiasticis dogmatibis veteris*. PL 58.979–1000.
Gregory I. *Dialogi*. 3 vols. Ed. A de Vogüe, SC 251, 260, and 265 (1978–1980).
———. *Homiliae xl in Evangelia*. PL 76.1075–1312.
———. *Moralia*. Ed. Mark Adriaen. CC 143, 143A (1979); 143B (1985).
———. *Registrum epistolarum*. 2 vols. Ed. P. Ewald and L. M. Hartmann, MGH Epp. 1 and 2 (1891/1899). Ed. D. Norberg, CC 140 (1892) (cites from MGH).
———. *Règle Pastorale*, ed. Floribert Rommel, [French] trs. Charles Morel, *SC* 381–382 (1992).
———. *Sermones de vetero Testamento*. Ed. Cyril Lambot, O.S.B., CC 46, 11/1 (1961).
Horace. *Carmina*. In *The Odes and Epodes*. Trans. C. E. Bennett, Loeb Classical Library 33. Cambridge, MA: Harvard University Press, 1952.
Innocent I. *Epistulae*. PL 20.463–612.
Isidore of Seville. *De haeresibus liber*. Ed. Angel Custodio Vega. Scriptores ecclesiastici hispano-latini veteris et medii aevi, fasc. 5. Madrid: typis augustinianis Monasterii Escurialensis, 1940.
———. *Etymologiarum sive originum libri XX*. Ed. W. M. Lindsay, Oxford (1911).
———. *Quaestiones. In Exodum* PL 83.287–322.
———. *Quaestiones. In Numeros* PL 83.339–360.
Jerome. *Commentariorum in Matheum libri IV*. Ed. D. Hurst and M. Adriaen, CC 77 (1969).
———. *Epistulae*. Ed. I. Hilberg, 3 vols. CSEL 54-56 (1910–1918).
———. *Liber interpretationis hebraicorum nominum*. Ed. P. de Lagarde, CC 72 (1959).
John the Deacon. *Sancti Gregorii Magni vita*. PL 75.59–242.
Juvenal. *Saturae*. Ed. A. E. Housman. Cambridge: Cambridge University Press, 1931.
Leo I. *Epistulae*. PL 54.551–1218.
———. *Sermons*. Trans. René Dolle. 2d ed. SC 22/1-2, 74, 200 (1961–1973).

Odorannus of Sens. *Ad Everardum monachum, de tribus quaestionibus.* In *Opera omnia,* ed. Robert-Henri Bautier, Monigue Gilles, Marie-Elisabeth Duchez, and Michel Hugo (Paris: Editions du Centre National de la Recherche scientifique, 1972).
Petrus Damiani. *Die Briefe des Petrus Damiani,* 4 vols. Ed. K. Reindel. In MGH *Die Briefe der deutschen Kaiserzeit* (1983–1993). (=Reindel, *Briefe*)
———. *Sermones.* Ed. G. Lucchesi, CCCM 57 (1983).
Poenitentiale Egberti. Ed. F. W. Wasserschleben, *Die Bussordnungen der abendländischen Kirche* (1851) 231–247.
Pseudo-Isidore, *Decretales Pseudo-Isidorianae et capitula Angilramni,* ed. P. Hinschius. Leipzig, 1863.
Pseudo-Jerome. *Quastiones hebraicae in librum Regnum et Paralipomenon.* PL 23.1329–1402.
Regino of Prum. *De ecclesiasticis disciplinis et religione Christiana libri duo.* PL 132.185–370.
Turner, C. H., ed. *Ecclesiae occidentalis monumenta iuris antiquissima. Canonum et conciliorum Graecorum intrepretationes latinae.* 2 vols. Oxford: Clarendon Press, 1899–1939.
Victorius of Aquitaine. *Cursus paschalis annorum DXXXII ad Hilarum archidiaconum ecclesiae Romanae.* Ed. Th. Mommsen, MGH Auct.ant. 9 (1982), reprinted by Krusch, *Studien zur christlichen ma. Chronologie. Die Entstehung unserer heutigen Zeitrechnung I. Victorius.* Ersatz der fehlerhaften Ausgagen Mommsens in den M. G. (Aus Abh. Berlin, Jahrgang 1937, Nr. 8, 1938).
Virgil. *Georgica.* Ed. R. A. B. Mynors. Oxford: Clarendon Press, 1990.

Literature

Blum, Owen J. *St. Peter Damian: His Teaching on the Spiritual Life.* Studies in Mediaeval History N.S. 10. Washington, DC: The Catholic University of America, 1947.
Browe, Peter. *Die häufige Kommunion in Mittelalter.* Münster: Regensbergsche Verlagsbuchhandlung, 1938.
Bruyn, D. de. "Une letter inédite de S. Pierre Damian." *Revue bénédictine* 31 (1914–1919) 92–93.
Černik, Peter. "Per la storia del lessico economico medievale: le 'epistolae' di Pier Damiani (1043–1069)." *Studi medievali* 40/2 (1999) 633–80.
Dictionnaire Encyclopédique de la Bible. Turnhout: Brepols, 1987.
Dressler, Fridolin. *Petrus Damiani. Leben und Werk.* Studia Anselmiana 34 (Rome: Herder, 1954).
Duchesne, Louis. *Fastes épiscopaux de l'ancienne Gaule.* 2 vols. (Paris: Fontemoing, 1910).
Fournier, Paul. "Études critiques sur le Décret de Burchard de

Worms," *Nouvelle revue historique de droit français et étranger* 34 (1910) 41–112; 213–221; 289–331; 564–584.

Gilchrist, John. "*Simoniaca heresis* and the Problem of Orders from Leo IX to Gratian," *Proceedings of the Second International Conference of Medieval Canon Law at Boston, 1963*, eds. Stephan Kuttner and J. J. Ryan, Monumenta iuris canonici C1, 1965 (Vatican City 1964) 209–235.

Grundmann, Herbert, ed. *Gebhardt Handbuch der Deutschen Geschichte.* 9th ed. Stuttgart: Union Verlag Stuttgart, 1970.

Jestice, Phyllis. "Peter Damian Against the Reformers." In *The Joy of Learning and the Love of God. Studies in Honor of Jean Leclercq*, ed. E. Rozanne Elder, pp. 67–94. Cistercian Studies Series 160. Kalamazoo, MI: Cistercian Publications, 1995.

Leclercq, Jean. "Simoniaca heresis," *Studi Gregoriani* 1 (1947) 523–30.

Lokrantz, Margareta. *L'opera poetica di S. Pier Damiani.* Studia Latina Stockholmiensia 12. Stockholm, 1964.

Lucchesi, Giovanni. *Clavis S. Petri Damiani.* Faenza, 1970 (=Lucchesi, *Clavis*).

———. "Per una vita di San Pier Damiani. Componenti cronologiche e topografiche." In *San Pier Damiano nel IX centenario della morte (1072–1972)*, vols. 1 (1972) 13–179 (Nos. 1–153) and 2 (1972) 13–160 (Nos. 154–231) (=Lucchesi, *Vita*).

Meyer, Heinz and Rudolf Suntrup. *Lexikon der mittelalterlichen Zahlenbedeutung.* Münstersche Mittelalter-Schriften 56. München: W. Fink, 1987 (=Meyer-Suntrup, *Lexicon*).

Michel, Anton. *Papstwahl und Königsrecht, oder, Das Papstwahl-konkordat von 1059.* Munich: M. Hueber, 1936.

Mittarelli, Johanne-Benedicto and Anselmo Costandoni, eds. *Annales Camaldulensis Ordinis Sancti Benedicti.* Venice: 1756; repr. Westmead, Farnborough, Hants, England: Gregg International, 1970.

Mombritius, Boninus. *Vita s. Silvestri* in *Sanctuarium seu vitae Sanctorum.* New ed. by the Monks of Solesmes [Monachi Solesmenses] 2 vols. Paris: Fontemoing et Socios, 1910.

Neukirch, Franz. *Das Leben des Petrus Damiani.* Göttingen: Gebrüder Hofer, 1875.

Noonan, J. T. *The Morality of Abortion.* Cambridge, MA: Harvard University Press, 1970.

Pelster, Franz. "Der Dekret Bischof Burkhards von Worms in Vatikanischen Hss." *Miscellanea Giovanni Mercati* 2, *Studi e Testi* 122 (1946) 114–157.

Pierucci, Celestino and Alberto Polverari. *Carte di Fonte Avellana* 1. Thesaurus ecclesiarum Italiae 9.1. Rome: Edizioni di storia e letteratura, 1972.

Reindel, Kurt. "Studien zur Überlieferung der Werke des Petrus Damiani I–III." *DA* 15 (1959) 23–102; 16 (1960) 73–154; 18 (1962) 317–417 (=Reindel, *Studien*).

Resnick, Irven M. "Odo of Tournai and Peter Damian. Poverty and Crisis in the Eleventh Century." *Revue Bénédictine* 98.1/2 (1988) 114–140.

Ryan, J. Joseph. *Saint Peter Damiani and His Canonical Sources. A Preliminary Study in the Antecedents of the Gregorian Reform.* Pontifical Institute of Mediaeval Studies. Studies and Texts 2. Toronto: Pontificium Institutum Studiorum Mediae Aetatis, 1956. (=Ryan, *Sources*)

Struve, Tilman. "Die Romreise der Kaiserin Agnes," *HJb* 105 (1985) 1–29.

Werner, Ernst. "Pietro Damiana ed il movimento popolare del suo tempo." *Studi Gregoriani* 10 (1975) 287–315.

Wilmart, André. "Une lettre de S. Pierre Damien à l'impératrice Agnes," *Revue bénédictine* 44 (1932) 125–146.

CONCORDANCE

Since the new edition of Damian's letters in Kurt Reindel, *Die Briefe der Petrus Damiani*, MGH Die Briefe der deutschen Kaiserzeit (München, 1983) has assigned new numbers in chronological order, the old system of number for *epistolae* and *opuscula* is now outmoded. To correlate the new with the old, the following concordance is herewith provided. There is no longer a distinction between "letters" and "works," and *Letters* 171–180 are placed at the end of the series because they are undatable.

MGH (Chronological) Numeration in Earlier Editions

Reindel	Migne Number	Reindel	Migne Number
1	opusc. 2 and 3	27	epist. 6, 24 = opusc. 48
2	epist. 7, 15	28	opusc. 11
3	epist. 3, 2	29	epist. 6, 15
4	epist. 3, 3	30	epist. 4, 4
5	epist. 4, 2	31	opusc. 7
6	epist. 6, 6	32	epist. 4, 13
7	epist. 3, 5	33	epist. 1, 4
8	epist. 5, 12	34	epist. 4, 10
9	epist. 6, 28	35	epist. 5, 6
10	epist. 6, 23	36	epist. 5, 17 = opusc. 8/2
11	epist. 2, 19	37	epist. 6, 7
12	epist. 4, 6	38	opusc. 16
13	epist. 1, 1	39	epist. 5, 9 = opusc. 27
14	epist. 4, 7	40	opusc. 6
15	epist. 8, 4	41	Ad Heinricum
16	epist. 1, 2	42	Ad Odalricum
17	opusc. 10	43	epist. 7, 1
18	opusc. 14	44	epist. 6, 30 = opusc. 51
19	opusc. 8/1	45	epist. 5, 8
20	epist. 7, 2	46	epist. 1, 5
21	epist. 8, 8	47	epist. 4, 14 = opusc. 26
22	epist. 4, 5	48	epist. 2, 1
23	epist. 8, 9 = opusc. 58	49	epist. 2, 5
24	epist. 6, 14 = opusc. 29	50	opusc. 15
25	epist. 8, 7 = opusc. 42/2	51	epist. 7, 14
26	epist. 1, 3	52	epist. 2, 4

CONCORDANCE

Reindel	Migne Number	Reindel	Migne Number
53	Ad Iohannem	97	epist. 2, 2 = opusc. 31
54	epist. 6, 18 = opusc. 46	98	epist. 1, 18 = opusc 24
55	epist. 6, 19	99	epist. 3, 6
56	epist. 6, 27	100	epist. 6, 5
57	epist. 1, 10 = opusc. 20	101	epist. 3, 7
58	epist. 3, 4	102	epist. 2, 15 = opusc. 34/1
59	epist. 3, 9 = opusc. 25	103	epist. 6, 2
60	epist. 1, 7	104	epist. 7, 5 = opusc. 56
61	epist. 1, 6 = opusc. 17	105	epist. 6, 8 = opusc. 21
62	epist. 4, 11	106	epist. 2, 14 = opusc. 33
63	epist. 2, 9	107	epist. 1, 16
64	epist. 7, 9	108	epist. 1, 17 = opusc. 23
65	opusc. 5	109	epist. 1, 19 = Vita Rodulphi et Dominici
66	epist. 7, 19 = opusc. 50		
67	epist. 7, 11 = opusc. 57/1	110	opusc. 9
68	epist. 7, 12 = opusc. 57/2	111	epist. 3, 8 = opusc. 39
69	epist. 2, 3 = opusc. 22	112	epist. 4, 3 = opusc. 18/2
70	epist. 5, 16 = opusc. 42/1	113	epist. 6, 4
71	epist. 7, 4	114	epist. 7, 16 = opusc. 18/3
72	epist. 1, 9 = opusc. 19	115	epist. 4, 16
73	epist. 4, 1	116	epist. 6, 10
74	epist. 4, 12	117	epist. 6, 17 = opusc. 45
75	epist. 2, 8	118	epist. 6, 35 = opusc 55
76	epist. 6, 31 = opusc. 53	119	epist. 2, 17 = opusc 36
77	epist. 5, 5	120	epist. 7, 3
78	epist. 6, 11 = opusc. 44	121	epist. 5, 1
79	epist. 1, 8	122	epist. 1, 11
80	epist. 4, 17 = opusc. 40	123	epist. 6, 21 = opusc. 47
81	opusc. 1	124	epist. 7, 6
82	epist. 2, 12	125	epist. 6, 3
83	epist. 8, 5	126	epist. 2, 20 = opusc. 37/1
84	epist. 5, 7	127	epist. 2, 21 = opusc. 37/2
85	epist. 8, 3	128	Ad Ambrosium et Liupardum
86	epist. 2, 18 = opusc. 52		
87	epist. 4, 9	129	epist. 5, 14 and 5, 15
88	epist. 1, 20	130	epist. 7, 7
89	epist. 1, 21 and opusc. 4	131	epist. 6, 13
90	epist. 2, 13	132	epist. 6, 26 = opusc. 49
91	epist. 3, 1 = opusc. 38	133	epist. 6, 34
92	epist. 6, 16 = opusc. 59	134	epist. 6, 36
93	epist. 8, 13	135	Ad Cinthium
94	epist. 8, 14	136	epist. 8, 12
95	epist. 2, 11	137	epist. 6, 33 = opusc. 54
96	epist. 1, 15	138	epist. 5, 2

CONCORDANCE

Reindel	Migne Number	Reindel	Migne Number
139	Ad Tebaldum	161	epist. 6, 1 = opusc. 43
140	epist. 1, 13	162	epist. 2, 10 = opusc. 18/1
141	epist. 5, 13		and epist. 5, 4
142	epist. 6, 32	163	epist. 5, 3
143	epist. 7, 18	164	epist. 1, 12
144	epist. 7, 8	165	opusc. 12
145	epist. 8, 1	166	epist. 6, 29
146	epist. 8, 11 = opusc. 30	167	epist. 1, 14
147	epist. 5, 10	168	epist. 3, 10 = opusc. 34/2
148	epist. 7, 13	169	epist. 6, 25
149	Ad Agnetem	170	epist. 8, 10
150	epist. 6, 20	171	epist. 8, 15
151	epist. 7, 17	172	epist. 5, 11 = opusc. 41
152	epist. 6, 12	173	Ad Bocconem
153	opusc. 13	174	epist. 4, 15
154	epist. 7, 10	175	Ad Honestum
155	epist. 8, 2	176	epist. 6, 9
156	epist. 2, 6	177	epist. 5, 18
157	epist. 4, 8	178	Ad abbatem A.
158	epist. 6, 22	179	epist. 8, 6
159	epist. 2, 16 = opusc. 35	180	Ad episcopum W.
160	epist. 2, 7 = opusc. 32		

Numeration of Earlier Editions in MGH

Migne Number	Reindel	Migne Number	Reindel
epist. 1, 1	13	epist. 1, 19 = Vita	
epist. 1, 2	16	Rodulphi et Dominici	109
epist. 1, 3	26	epist. 1, 20	88
epist. 1, 4	33	epist. 1, 21	89
epist. 1, 5	46	epist. 2, 1	48
epist. 1, 6 = opusc. 17	61	epist. 2, 2 = opusc. 31	97
epist. 1, 7	60	epist. 2, 3 = opusc. 22	69
epist. 1, 8	79	epist. 2, 4	52
epist. 1, 9 = opusc. 19	72	epist. 2, 5	49
epist. 1, 10 = opusc. 20	57	epist. 2, 6	156
epist. 1, 11	122	epist. 2, 7 = opusc. 32	160
epist. 1, 12	164	epist. 2, 8	75
epist. 1, 13	140	epist. 2, 9	63
epist. 1, 14	167	epist. 2, 10 = opusc. 18/1	162
epist. 1, 15	96	epist. 2, 11	95
epist. 1, 16	107	epist. 2, 12	82
epist. 1, 17 = opusc. 23	108	epist. 2, 13	90
epist. 1, 18 = opusc. 24	98	epist. 2, 14 = opusc. 33	106

CONCORDANCE

Migne Number	Reindel	Migne Number	Reindel
epist. 2, 15 = opusc. 34/1	102	epist. 5, 10	147
epist. 2, 16 = opusc. 35	159	epist. 5, 11 = opusc. 41	172
epist. 2, 17 = opusc. 36	119	epist. 5, 12	8
epist. 2, 18 = opusc. 52	86	epist. 5, 13	141
epist. 2, 19	11	epist. 5, 14	129
epist. 2, 20 = opusc. 37/1	126	epist. 5, 15	129
epist. 2, 21 = opusc. 37/2	127	epist. 5, 16 = opusc. 42/1	70
epist. 3, 1 = opusc. 38	91	epist. 5, 17 = opusc. 8/2	36
epist. 3, 2	3	epist. 5, 18	177
epist. 3, 3	4	epist. 5, 19 = opusc. 28	spuria
epist. 3, 4	58	epist. 6, 1 = opusc. 43	161
epist. 3, 5	7	epist. 6, 2	103
epist. 3, 6	99	epist. 6, 3	125
epist. 3, 7	101	epist. 6, 4	113
epist. 3, 8 = opusc. 39	111	epist. 6, 5	100
epist. 3, 9 = opusc. 25	59	epist. 6, 6	6
epist. 3, 10 = opusc. 34/2	168	epist. 6, 7	37
epist. 4, 1	73	epist. 6, 8 = opusc. 21	105
epist. 4, 2	5	epist. 6, 9	176
epist. 4, 3 = opusc. 18/2	112	epist. 6, 10	116
epist. 4, 4	30	epist. 6, 11 = opusc. 44	78
epist. 4, 5	22	epist. 6, 12	152
epist. 4, 6	12	epist. 6, 13	131
epist. 4, 7	14	epist. 6, 14 = opusc. 29	24
epist. 4, 8	157	epist. 6, 15	29
epist. 4, 9	87	epist. 6, 16 = opusc. 59	92
epist. 4, 10	34	epist. 6, 17 = opusc. 45	117
epist. 4, 11	62	epist. 6, 18 = opusc. 46	54
epist. 4, 12	74	epist. 6, 19	55
epist. 4, 13	32	epist. 6, 20	150
epist. 4, 14 = opusc. 26	47	epist. 6, 21 = opusc. 47	123
epist. 4, 15	174	epist. 6, 22	158
epist. 4, 16	115	epist. 6, 23	10
epist. 4, 17 = opusc. 40	80	epist. 6, 24 = opusc. 48	27
epist. 5, 1	121	epist. 6, 25	169
epist. 5, 2	138	epist. 6, 26 = opusc. 49	132
epist. 5, 3	163	epist. 6, 27	56
epist. 5, 4 = part of opusc. 18/1	162	epist. 6, 28	9
		epist. 6, 29	166
epist. 5, 5	77	epist. 6, 30 = opusc. 51	44
epist. 5, 6	35	epist. 6, 31 = opusc. 53	76
epist. 5, 7	84	epist. 6, 32	142
epist. 5, 8	45	epist. 6, 33 = opusc. 54	137
epist. 5, 9 = opusc. 27	39	epist. 6, 34	133

CONCORDANCE

Migne Number	Reindel	Migne Number	Reindel
epist. 6, 35 = opusc. 55	118	opusc. 8/2 = epist. 5, 17	36
epist. 6, 36	134	opusc. 9	110
epist. 7, 1	43	opusc. 10	17
epist. 7, 2	20	opusc. 11	28
epist. 7, 3	120	opusc. 12	165
epist. 7, 4	71	opusc. 13	153
epist. 7, 5 = opusc. 56	104	opusc. 14	18
epist. 7, 6	124	opusc. 15	50
epist. 7, 7	130	opusc. 16	38
epist. 7, 8	144	opusc. 17 = epist. 1, 6	61
epist. 7, 9	64	opusc. 18/1 = epist. 2, 10	162
epist. 7, 10	154	opusc. 18/2 = epist. 4, 3	112
epist. 7, 11 = opusc. 57/1	67	opusc. 18/3 = epist. 7, 16	114
epist. 7, 12 = opusc. 57/2	68	opusc. 19 = epist. 1, 9	72
epist. 7, 13	148	opusc. 20 = epist. 1, 10	57
epist. 7, 14	51	opusc. 21 = epist. 6, 8	105
epist. 7, 15	2	opusc. 22 = epist. 2, 3	69
epist. 7, 16 = opusc. 18/3	114	opusc. 23 = epist. 1, 17	108
epist. 7, 17	151	opusc. 24 = epist. 1, 18	98
epist. 7, 18	143	opusc. 25 = epist. 3, 9	59
epist. 7, 19 = opusc. 50	66	opusc. 26 = epist. 4, 14	47
epist. 8, 1	145	opusc. 27 = epist. 5, 9	39
epist. 8, 2	155	opusc. 28 = epist. 5, 19	spurium
epist. 8, 3	85	opusc. 29 = epist. 6, 14	24
epist. 8, 4	15	opusc. 30 = epist. 8, 11	146
epist. 8, 5	83	opusc. 31 = epist. 2, 2	97
epist. 8, 6	179	opusc. 32 = epist. 2, 7	160
epist. 8, 7 = opusc. 42/2	25	opusc. 33 = epist. 2, 14	106
epist. 8, 8	21	opusc. 34/1 = epist. 2, 15	102
epist. 8, 9 = opusc. 58	23	opusc. 34/2 = epist. 3, 10	168
epist. 8, 10	170	opusc. 35 = epist. 2, 16	159
epist. 8, 11 = opusc. 30	146	opusc. 36 = epist. 2, 17	119
epist. 8, 12	136	opusc. 37/1 = epist. 2, 20	126
epist. 8, 13	93	opusc. 37/2 = epist. 2, 21	127
epist. 8, 14	94	opusc. 38 = epist. 3, 1	91
epist. 8, 15	171	opusc. 39 = epist. 3, 8	111
opusc. 1	81	opusc. 40 = epist. 4, 17	80
opusc. 2	1	opusc. 41 = epist. 5, 1	172
opusc. 3	1	opusc. 42/1 = epist. 5, 16	70
opusc. 4	89	opusc. 42/2 = epist. 8, 7	25
opusc. 5	65	opusc. 43 = epist. 6, 1	161
opusc. 6	40	opusc. 44 = epist. 6, 11	78
opusc. 7	31	opusc. 45 = epist. 6, 17	117
epist. 8/1	19	opusc. 46 = epist. 6, 18	54

CONCORDANCE

Migne Number	Reindel	Migne Number	Reindel
opusc. 47 = epist. 6, 21	123	opusc. 54 = epist. 6, 33	137
opusc. 48 = epist. 6, 24	27	opusc. 55 = epist. 6, 35	118
opusc. 49 = epist. 6, 26	132	opusc. 56 = epist. 7, 5	104
opusc. 50 = epist. 7, 19	66	opusc. 57/1 = epist. 7, 11	67
opusc. 51 = epist. 6, 30	44	opusc. 57/2 = epist. 7, 13	68
opusc. 52 = epist. 2, 18	86	opusc. 58 = epist. 8, 9	23
opusc. 53 = epist. 6, 31	76	opusc. 59 = epist. 6, 16	92

Letters That Are Not Found in Migne

To abbot A.	178	To Henry	41
To Agnes	149	To Honestus	175
To Ambrose and Liupardus	128	To John	53
		To Odalricus	42
To Bucco	173	To Tebaldus	139
To Cinthius	135	To Bishop W.	180

LETTERS
121-150

LETTER 121

Peter Damian to three archpriests. He defends himself against the charge that he used an incorrect expression in a sermon treating Pope Stephen I,[1] which led his critics to condemn him unfairly for the opinion that the dead cannot derive any benefit from the prayers and good works of the living.

(Lent 1065)

O THE ARCHPRIESTS Andrew, U., and C., venerable brothers in Christ, the monk Peter the sinner sends the affection of fraternal love.[2]

(2) As I lie in bed oppressed by not just a little weariness, do not wonder that I distribute an undistinguished or unpolished letter of rather tired expression, which another brother took in dictation. Rather,[3] because I speak against those who are rustics and untutored (or actually illiterate) it is fitting that I speak to them in a suitably rustic fashion, and heedlessly pour out "whatever pops into the mouth," as they themselves say. Nevertheless, before I come to the matter brought to mind, I shall speak at some length. There was a certain philosopher who, while observing carefully at night the course of the constellations and the motion of the stars, suddenly fell into a pit that, as it is said, was very deep, with a large gaping opening and filled with the obscene squalor of filth.[4]

---

1. Stephen I ruled from 12 May 254 until his death on 2 August 257.
2. Lucchesi (*Vita* no. 195) suspects that the three archpriests resided in the city where Damian had delivered *Sermon* 37. He suggests as a possibility Perugia, where one finds the cloister of St. Salvatore and the Preggio hermitage. In Perugia, the church of St. Stephen was located on the Via dei Priori.
3. On the dictation of the letters, see Reindel, *Studien* 1.52f.
4. On this philosopher, Thales, see also *Letter* 119.68, n. 156. Cf. Plato, *Theaetetus* 174A. Damian must have been citing from another source. Cf. also Diogenes Laertius, *De vitis dogmatibus et apophthegmatibus clarorum philosophorum libri decem* 1.1.34.

This philosopher had a domestic maidservant named Iambi, who freely and even wisely inveighed against her master in iambic meter, which received its name afterward on account of her, and, in a praiseworthy manner, declared of him: "My master," she said, "did not know of the excrement that was under his feet and yet attempted to know the stars." The same thing occurs in our own time[5] as rustics and fools, who knew almost nothing but how to plough up the fields and how to guard the pigs and the enclosures for the various herds, now do not blush to debate the judgments of the holy Scriptures at crossroads and public streets before their fellow herdsmen and before mere girls. Moreover, what is worse to say, during the day they are not afraid to treat the words of the angels while at night they lie in heat between the thighs of women. And in this way they pass judgment on the words of the holy doctors.

(3) Now, your holiness indicated to me in letters that a great scandal has arisen among some people on account of an opinion we expressed in a sermon on the blessed Stephen,[6] namely, that the soul of each individual is later presented for judgment in just that condition in which it departed this world—so that they say that the prayers, offerings, and sacrifices that are offered for the souls of the dead bring them no benefit before judgment. And who should wonder that the same thing that is known to have happened to the very author of the Christian religion should also happen to me, a sinner? For he says: "Unless you eat the flesh of the Son of Man and drink his blood you will not have life in you."[7] And the approximately seventy men[8] hearing this said, "This saying is hard and who can hear it?"[9] And, as Scripture will attest immediately after that, they did not

---

5. See Werner, *Pietro Damiani* 311f.
6. Peter Damian, *Sermon* 37 (CCCM 57.224–231).
7. John 6.54.
8. Damian departs from the Vulg. *multi ergo audientes ex discipulis eius* and instead offers *audientes septuaginta ferme viri dixerunt*. See Meyer-Suntrup, *Lexikon* col. 756, for a discussion of the number 70 as distinguished from the number 72 at Luke 10.1. Also see Jerome, *Epistola* 78.8 (CSEL 55.58) and Isidore, *Quaestiones in Exodum* 1 (PL 83.287BC) and his *Quaestiones in Numeros* 6 (PL 83.341A).
9. John 6.61.

walk with him. Therefore, the sun burned them,[10] for Christ is the sun of justice. In addition, the moon burned them, for I belong to the moon, that is, to the body of Christ, which is the Church.[11] You, however, offering a blessing differently, deign to say to me, "The sun shall not burn you by day nor the moon by night."[12]

(4) Behold, the wise and the prudent men of these parts have progressed so far as to know all the depths of heavenly eloquence, to comprehend all the mysteries of the divine books, and yet, because of one sentence in my sermon, they fall into the dark gloom of blindness. And, if it please them to be heretics, do my friends love me so much that they can not cross over into heresy without me? For whosoever asserts that prayers, oblations, and sacrifices for the dead cannot benefit them, and attempts to affirm this impudently, is actually convicted thereby of being an Arian. Now, Arius insisted during the debates over his error that these works of piety are actually vain and frivolous and will benefit no one in the world to come.[13] Can nimble investigators of the divine words not find many expressions in the fields of the divine Scriptures with which they are able to lay traps and snares for themselves, to become heretics? Moreover, if it please them to find an excuse to withdraw from Christianity, let them judge what the Lord says in the Gospel: "Of that day," that is, the day of Judgment, "neither the angels in heaven know,[14] nor the Son himself, but only the Father."[15] And how can the Son not know the day of Judgment since he, along with the Father, created this very same day, and

---

10. Cf. Mal 4.2.
11. Cf. *Letter* 115.7. See also Reindel, *Briefe* 3.309, n. 13.
12. Ps 120.6.
13. Arius, the heretic. For his teachings, cf. Epiphanius, *Adversus haereses* 75 (PG 42.504–516). Perhaps Damian had his information from Augustine, *De haereticis* 53 (CC 46.323f.; PL 42.39f.); cf. Rowan D. Williams, "Arius, Arianismus," *LThK* 1.981–989; H. Hemmer, "Aérius, Aériens," *DTC* 1.515–516.
14. Damian has *neque angeli sciunt in celo, nec ipse Filius* for the Vulg. *neque angeli caelorum*. See Sabatier 3.149 for *nec Filius* in the old Latin version and with reference to Mark 13.32 *(neque angeli in caelo neque filius)*. And see Jerome, *Commentariorum in Matheum* (CC 77.231; in some Latin codices the words *neque filius* are added). See in addition *Itala* 1.178 for *angeli in celo* and *nec filius*.
15. Matt 24.36.

all times, and all things visible and invisible? Let them also denounce what he says elsewhere: "My teaching is not mine, but of him who sent me."[16]

(5) O Lord Jesus, we are indeed your simple and dull servants and we believe you whatever you say. For we know that you are truth and that you cannot deceive.[17] But how will the wise men of this earth and the very profound and benighted investigators of your divine books be able to find faith in your words? Will they be able to inquire of you with a clever shrewdness, according to their wisdom, how what you have said can be true: "My teaching is not mine"? "If it is yours, how is it not yours? If it is not yours, how will it be yours? Let it be enough, then, that either you assert without doubt that your teaching is yours, and you do not say further that it is not yours or, if you insist that it is not yours, you disavow it as yours now in every respect." And thus one must fear lest they trap you with the clever argumentation of their syllogisms and entangle the author of wisdom in idle talk of captious sophistry.

(6) Furthermore, however, to return now to the history of the book of Kings, the Lord sent to Josiah, the king of Judah, through Holda, the wife of Sellum: "For as you have heard the words of this book, and your heart has been moved to fear, and you have humbled yourself before the Lord, having heard the words against this place and its inhabitants, to wit that they should become a wonder and a curse, and you have rent your garments and wept before me, and I have heard you, says the Lord; therefore I will gather you to your fathers and you will be gathered at your sepulcher in peace, that your eyes not see all the evils that I will bring upon this place."[18] And a little later in the same narrative he adds, "Pharaoh Necho, king of Egypt, went up against the king of the Assyrians to the river Euphrates, and king Josiah went to meet him and was slain at Megiddo when he had seen him."[19] Here the brothers' disparagers, the critics of the works of others, plainly sharpen their teeth. "For the sons of men," as David says, "their teeth are weapons and

---

16. John 7.16. Cf. *Letter* 91.20.
17. See John 14.6.
18. 2 Kgs 22.18–20.
19. 2 Kgs 23.29.

arrows, their tongues a sharp sword."[20] Here, I say, let them belch forth heathen flames from their prattling mouths, vomit up a bitterness of deepest gall, and confound heaven and earth with their clamor, saying: How has the divine voice effectively fulfilled what it promised the king without falsehood? How, truly, has Josiah rested in his sepulcher in peace when he fell under the sword of the Egyptian king by a fortune of war? And thus this prophesy can be applied against them: "They have set their mouth against heaven, and their tongue has passed over the earth."[21]

(7) You, however, my most beloved and harmonious brethren, from whom nothing should be hidden, know without doubt that this is Gregory's view, not ours. Examine carefully the fourth book of the *Dialogues*[22] and there among other statements you will find this: "The Lord says in the Gospel, 'Walk while you have the light.'[23] Also he says through the prophet: 'I have heard you in an accepted time, I have helped you on the day of salvation.'[24] Paul explains this when he says: 'Behold, now is the acceptable time, behold, now is the day of salvation.'[25] Solomon also says: 'Whatsoever your hand can do, do it earnestly, for neither work, nor reason, nor knowledge will be in hell, whither you hasten to go.'[26] David says too: 'Since his mercy is everlasting.'"[27] On the basis of these passages it is truly well-known that each one will be presented for judgment just as he departs this life. In addition, a little later he adds there: "Nevertheless, one must know that no one will be cleansed even of the slightest faults there, unless he deserves to obtain

---

20. Ps 56.5. Damian has *lingue eorum machera acuta* for the Vulg. *lingua eorum gladius acutus*. See Sabatier 2.112, for *machaera acuta* in the old version.

21. Ps 72.9. Damian has *super terra* for the Vulg. *in terra*. See Sabatier 2.146 for *super terram* in the old version.

22. Gregory I, *Dialogi* 4.41.1–3 (SC 265.146ff.).

23. John 12.35.

24. Isa 49.8. Damian has *tempore accepto* for *in tempore placito* and his *adiuvi te* departs from the Vulg. *auxiliatus sum tui*. See Sabatier 2.600 with reference to Ambrose, *De Abraham* 2.10.74 (CSEL 32/1.627) and idem, *De institutione virginis* 15.95 (PL 16.328A), where one finds the same reading.

25. 2 Cor 6.2.

26. Eccl 9.10.

27. Ps 105.1, 117.1.

[this cleansing] there for good acts performed while still in this life."[28]

(8) And let these people hear what this same Gregory says in his *Moralia*, so that they may rave with the furor of a more rabid passion, "Because every wicked person whatsoever actually finds that once he has died he cannot change any longer."[29] Let them cry out, then, and scream and say: If I cannot be changed, what good are offerings, prayers, or sacrifices to me? Let the church close its doors, then, and I will be content thereafter within the walls of my own house. For what good does it do me to enter the churches if I can in no way be changed there? At least, then, let them cease to pursue this little man so bitingly and let them not wish ill-will to be roused up against me so much as against the words' author. Let them tear into Gregory, let them snap at Gregory, and let teeth of bitterest spite strike against him. Let them read him and let them find this in him, and holding over him the censorious rod of judgment, let them cast back at him the decrees of damnation he deserves and, like ones utterly mad, let them sharpen their teeth on him and seize him, just as mangy dogs do, for instance, by biting. Let them hear what other things this same Gregory says, "As often as the hand reaches for food for the sake of immoderate eating, just so often is the fall of our first parent repeated."[30]

(9) I certainly do not exaggerate how harsh this is, since I have no doubt that it is clear to any one reading it. And he wrote so many things of this sort, which we have omitted for the sake of conciseness, in order not to pass beyond the limit of epistolary brevity, which is a loathsome thing to do. But these people love me so much that they read me only and, intent upon me alone, they condemn all the books of the holy Scriptures. And those who have barely learned how to run through the alphabet syllable by syllable are made judges over me and do not fear to pass judgment on me. Far be it from either the blessed Gregory, illustrious and distinguished doctor of the Church, or from us who are humble and poor, who only desire

28. Gregory I, *Dialogi* 4.41.6 (SC 265.150).
29. Gregory I, *Moralia* 14.20.24 (CC 143.712).
30. Gregory I, *Regula pastoralis* 3.19.62 (SC 382.376).

to follow in his footsteps as far as is fitting, to forbid that sacrifices or prayers be offered to God almighty without cease for any of the dead whatsoever, even if they were the gravest sinners, and thus to forbid that they be assisted by the devotion of the living faithful. And indeed those who understand this statement this way err, just as night wanderers do, and reach out to touch the wall with a hand like one who sees very poorly. For the purpose of solving this question we are unwilling to be their teacher because, on account of their heart's arrogance, they refuse to be disciples.

(10) You however, most beloved brethren, call down the compassion of God almighty upon me your servant. Moreover, commend me to lord Drudo[31] and his brother and to the viscount and the other noble men of our monastery and hermitage. May God almighty guard you with his protection and grant to you a portion with his elect priests.

31. On Drudo, see Lucchesi, *Vita* no. 195.

LETTER 122

Peter Damian reports to Pope Alexander II on his illness and begs the Pope to take under his protection the bishop of Orleans and his church against the godless men harassing him.

(Beginning of 1065).[1]

O LORD ALEXANDER, bishop of the highest See, the monk Peter the sinner offers his service.

(2) Your blessedness should know, venerable father, that the bishop of the church of Orleans came to me here[2] and, finding me lying down on a small pallet, begged for the aid of my intercession because he hoped that I have some influence over you. Making his escape at last, though not without great tribulation, from the many calamities and pressures that are brought not only upon him but also upon his church by wicked and depraved men, he deduced that the best course, after having spurned the aid of this deceitful world, would be to seek a remedy only from the Apostolic See, to rush to your holy footsteps, and to fly to the shady bower of the holy Roman church just as if to the harbor of the safest port, safe from the many storms of a wave-driven sea and from the rocks and whirlwinds.[3] Naturally, as this church has assisted all in distress through the privilege of a divine office, let it receive him also with maternal

---

1. Lucchesi dates this letter to 1065 (*Vita* no. 194), in contrast to his *Clavis* 32, which dates it to summer 1064.
2. Among a list of forty-three bishops at the Roman synod of 1065 Harro, Bishop of Orleans, subscribed to a privilege of Alexander II. See Alexander II, Pope, *Epistolae et diplomata* 27 (PL 146.1308D). See also *Gallia Christiana in provinciis ecclesiasticas distributa 8*, ed. by the Maurists (1744; repr. 1970), col. 1438f., where Bishop Hadericus is listed for the years 1063–1067. On the bishopric of Orleans, see also Duchesne, *Fastes* 2.457ff.
3. Ryan, *Sources*, no. 201, p. 105, refers to Gelasius I, *Tractatus* 2.10 (Thiel 1.529); Jaffé 669. At *Letter* 48.4 Damian describes the Roman See as *unicus et singularis portus*.

piety and defend his church from an invasion of violent and wicked men.

(3) On this account, I humbly beseech your grace, I humbly beg the brotherhood of my friendly opponent the lord archdeacon[4] and of your other holy associates, that for love of us you deign to come to the assistance of this brother who earnestly requested my assistance and that you strive to temper justice's severity with respect to him, insofar as it is not displeasing to God.

(4) Moreover, since you deem it worthy to know how things are with me, for almost seventy days I have barely been able to lie down or to sit, much less to stand, except with great difficulty. What more, shall I say that I feel a loathing for wine, making my stomach nauseous, since I shudder in horror at various kinds of honeyed and colored drink? But I do not emphasize these things too much because, while I ask for a sigh and compassion from the fraternal love of others of my brotherhood, from the highest of my friends (to wit, from the lord archdeacon), I do not doubt that this must elicit laughter.

(5) Moreover, make a decision, I beg you, concerning the already mentioned bishop, so that almighty God will take delight at the judgment of your wisdom, and let him grow cheerful once the womb of the apostolic See is spread out over him just like the womb of maternal piety.

(6) Since I do not have our seal at the present time, I enjoin my nephew Damianus[5] to take possession of this with the surety of a seal.

---

4. The reference here is to Hildebrand, archdeacon of the Holy See.
5. The nephew who later succeeded to the priorate of Fonte Avellana, and showed great interest in its library.

LETTER 123

Peter Damian to his nephew, Damianus. He exhorts him to follow a pure life and recommends to him the frequent reception of the Eucharist.

(July/August 1065)

O MY DEAREST SON DAMIANUS, the monk Peter the sinner offers the affection of paternal love.¹

(2) Because the carrier of these letters is anxiously preparing to depart, I am not able to write the things that must be sent in a polished, ordered manner of composition, and I want you to consider the sense of what is true rather than to lie in wait for the elegant artificial finery of words. Meanwhile, therefore, as I am unable to be present for a reason known to you, it suffices that I have written to you simply what the Apostle commanded Timothy by letter, to a contemporary, as it were: "Until I come," he said, "attend to reading, to exhortation, and to doctrine."² He had certainly already said these things to him: "Be an example of the faithful in word, in conduct, in love, in faith, in chastity."³

(3) And though I remain silent, in the meantime, concerning the other virtues that are enumerated now in the letter, may you strive to guard chastity, which I placed last, not only in your bodily members, but also let it reign and flourish especially in the deepest recesses of the heart. Indeed there is no virtue that endures harsher struggles in the flower of adolescence than the one that ardent desire assails, just as if we have begotten it in a surging fire's furnace of titillating allurement. But although it is not appropriate for us to consider this topic more

---

1. Damian also addressed *Letters* 138 and 158 to his nephew.
2. 1 Tim 4.13.
3. 1 Tim 4.12.

LETTER 123

fully, because there is not enough leisure to do so, owing to so much haste, it does not displease me to remark succinctly and rather hurriedly here upon what the empress Agnes—who indeed was once crowned with a golden diadem but who now is more blessedly and incomparably more eminently joined in marriage to the eternal king—reported to me yesterday at the time of vespers, when evening light was falling, as the merit of a distinguished example restores your mind more than repetitive prolixity of speech. Besides, while the aforementioned bride of Christ and daughter of the blessed Peter is nourished delightfully in a discussion of all the virtues, purity dwells still more readily upon an examination of chastity and modesty.

(4) Whence it happened that while we were discussing some things concerning the salvation of souls in shared communications and especially as we were twirled about like little flowers of verdant chastity in one's hands, she declared this right in the middle. After the victorious emperor Otto, she said, seized the kingdom of Italy from Berengar, he sent into exile in Germany his two captured daughters.[4] To be sure, since they bore the appearance of a pleasing countenance and the dignity of the race of kings in their bodies' remarkable beauty, many leading princes of the kingdom of her highness, Adelheid,[5] began vehemently to insist that they were worthy to join in a bond of betrothal with maidens of such elegant form. One of the young girls, assuredly—since they condemned all the suitors with equal disdain and felt a loathing for mortal marriage with the sternness of a holy pride—placed over her breasts two young chickens and hid them between her garment and flesh until they had completely putrefied. And when she saw men coming to speak with her, she secretly loosened her garment and she rejoiced that a stench wafted up to the noses of those addressing her. And since those coming to speak with her suffered this injury to their noses each day, finally the deluded solicitude of those seeking to obtain her ceased, and the Virgin of Christ guarded the integrity of her body inviolable by means of this

---

4. Otto I forced Berengar of Ivrea into vassalage in 951–952.
5. Otto married Adelheid, queen of Italy. See *Letter* 102.23 and n. 49.

simulated putrefaction of another's flesh. Thus it happened that afterward both of the sisters chose the nun's rule and, until the end of their lives, they guarded blamelessly the monastic manner of life.

(5) On account of this, O my son, one should be ashamed to succumb meekly even in thought to the vice of inordinate desire, when you observe the weaker and fragile sex triumph with such glory. And so that, like an overseer, you may be able to drive out the raging beast from your legal domain, if I may put it so, be content, brother, to fortify yourself with the reception of the prized Body and Blood of the Lord.[6] Let the hidden enemy see your lips reddened with the Blood of Christ, which causes him to shudder with horror, terrified, and soon he will flee into the den of his dark places, quaking with dread. For what you receive under the visible species of bread and wine he understands, whether he wishes to or not, to be the reality of the Body and Blood of the Lord.

(6) In addition, however, this same venerable queen told me then that previously in the church of Worms, when from neglect the eucharist had been reserved for too long a time in a box, later only flesh was found there. So when with inquisitive eyes many people turned their attention to it, they judged it to be, without a doubt, nothing other than true and solid flesh.

(7) Moreover, Rainaldus,[7] the venerable bishop of the church of Como, a truthful witness, explained while he was present what had happened to him a little earlier. There was a priest, he said, in the church that I serve, with God's authority (and, unless I am mistaken, he is still alive today) who had so little and so poor an acquaintance with the teaching of the alphabet that it was clear that he was hardly able to read a bit of writing syllable by syllable. Nevertheless, constrained by very great poverty, he was compelled to celebrate mass in whatever way he could. Sometimes, when he carried to the sick the eu-

---

6. In the MSS. *quanti* is found instead of *iam quotidie,* which appears in the Gaetani edition. Therefore, here Damian no longer provides evidence for daily communion in the Middle Ages. Cf. P. Browe, *Die haüfige Kommunion im Mittelalter* (Münster, 1938).

7. For Rainaldus, bishop of Como, see also *Letters* 104.19 and 124.2.

charist of the sacred office, without fail a little bit of the Lord's Blood remained behind in the chalice, as he was certainly negligent and indolent. He discovered this when returning to the church, but hindered by squeamishness he was unwilling to receive it himself, and so then he washed the chalice and plunged it into a marble laver in which there was holy water. And, O great sign of divine power! it happened that what was poured out of the chalice suddenly turned that part of the laver blood red, namely, where two large drops of Blood were squeezed out. But neither these drops nor others next to them, which seemed to be very small, could be washed off or cleansed no matter how much effort was applied, nor could the redness of the Blood imprinted on it be removed in any way. Since, then, that purple Blood adhered so tenaciously to the stone vessel, how much do we suppose the power of heaven claims for itself the right of legitimate power over a Christian breast? So dearest son, you should not defer to guard yourself often with these heavenly sacraments, with which you keep away from yourself arguments of diabolical cunning and clever artifice. Therefore, stand always girded and constantly firm on the battle line, and be not unaware that an unfailing adversary struggles tirelessly against you.

(8) Meanwhile, as I say these things, it brings me to remember that Hildebrand the archdeacon of the Roman church reported on the same events that were recalled above by the queen and the bishop to those present. I saw, he said, two holy and not ordinary monks and became well acquainted with them. To be sure, they dwelled in individual cells at a monastery that had been constructed in a place called Aachen. One of the two, who also seemed to be the more uneducated, was named Marinus, the other, however, by his proper name was called Romanus. Marinus hardly passed a single day in which either he did not see the devil in some apparition or hear him in a dream, since the ancient enemy often chanted the psalms with him, and concelebrated with him the offices of divine praise. Truly, sometimes the author of darkness transfigured himself into an angel of light, and commanded him, as if declaring a law, "Beware," he said, "since you have been found

worthy to see and to speak with an angel of God, it is unseemly that you speak with people about anything." Actually, just as if he had received the command by divine providence, he withdrew himself utterly from all conversation with his brethren and constrained himself under an unyielding rule of silence. When Romanus, first his brother and then later the abbot of the monastery, vehemently insisted that he speak with them, and he refused to reply, the abbot, violently breaking down the doors of the cell, chastised the indiscrete brother with deserved blows, and thus compelled him to resume the power of speech. Then he added an admonition: "The ancient adversary," he said, "the enemy of all good works, tempted you into self-imposed silence for this reason, so that you would lose the fruit of fraternal support, and so that those who ought to have been supported by you would not have the aid of your consolation." And in this way the brother, who had sinned not out of malice but from ingenuousness, very quickly recovered his mind and, once he had rejected the devil's suggestion, he humbly assented to the admonitions of the pious father.

(9) But while I challenge you, my son, to rid yourself of the snares of the ancient enemy, I do not omit what the aforementioned queen reported she heard from the mouth of the blessed Leo IX, pontiff of the Roman church.[8] Now the aforementioned pope said, "My aunt," he said, "when she became a nun, was placed in a monastery of men. And there, living in her own cell with a certain pygmy (that is, a woman of short stature), she patiently and humbly discharged the offices of daily praise. But on a certain night, when she rose prematurely for the celebration of the divine offices, and, as she was wont to do, she called out to her companion, again and again, and the latter did not respond at all because she had fallen into a deep sleep, finally, having been aroused to anger, she did not attend to what she was saying. 'Devil,' she said, 'get up.' At her voice immediately the devil approached, appearing in the likeness of the one who was sleeping, and he began to chant the psalms at the same time by repeating the verses together with her. And

---

8. Leo IX ruled from 1049 until his death in 1054.

when, with their singing uninterrupted, they came to that place in the psalter where one says, 'Let God arise, and let his enemies be scattered, and let those who hate him flee before him. As smoke vanishes, let them vanish,'[9] and the rest, the evil spirit immediately paused and did not presume to say those verses. The holy woman, since she wondered at what was before her, became greatly afraid, and foolishly not suspecting what it was, she made over herself the sign of the cross and immediately the evil spirit disappeared. And the one who had been the holy woman's companion for chanting the psalms revealed who he was by hiding herself deceitfully.

(10) "During the night hours the vile spirit brought the corpse of some man who had been hung for his crimes to this venerable matron and, in order to strike terror in her, if I may put it thus, procured a present of this sort for himself. As soon as it became known to the abbot of the place and to the brethren of the community what the most wicked enemy had made for himself, he brought it to pass that all the brothers would pour out prayers in common over that wretch, with resolute prayers. Later it was revealed to someone by divine providence that mercy attended him, because of the brothers' prayers. And thus certainly the ancient enemy was deceived for, as he plotted to mock the living, he was forced to bear the loss from among the dead."

(11) Examples of this sort of diabolical temptation are placed before you for this reason, so that you would be shrewdly vigilant against the snares of the enemy, the adroit deceiver. And while it delights you to hear about the victories of those who wrestle with the enemy, do not allow yourself to relax in the idleness of languid inactivity.

(12) But now let these things suffice. Commend me to the brothers. Advise the lord prior[10] on our behalf not to grow cool in the fervor of his wonted piety and compassion, but rather advise him that he should not fail to insist upon hospitality for

---

9. Ps 67.2–3.
10. The prior of Fonte Avellana in 1067 (?), as well as in 1068/69, was named Baruncius/Baroncius. See Pierucci/Polvari, *Carte* nos. 24 and 27.

guests and upon support for the indigent, so far as domestic affairs allow.

(13) But I also provide an appropriate example to him, which I confess will be rather beneficial for that of which I want to persuade him. For, as the same queen Agnes said above, there was also a certain man in parts of Germany who traveled over a trail[11] of narrow passes, the rugged places of the mountains, and the shade of the forests, out of a fondness for hunting. Here, as he ran about anxiously hither and thither and sought out the dens of wild beasts with an effort of excited curiosity, he found two women, to wit a mother and a daughter, who were wandering miserably through the mounds of wintry hoar-frost and the deep drifts of the snow. To be sure he was directed by compassion, and he said to his companion who alone followed him, "Let us lift these women onto our horses, one on each horse, and carry them to the dwelling-places of men, because otherwise they will perhaps be exposed to the jaws of wandering wolves or without a doubt they will die from the extreme power of the cold." The companion utterly refused and fretted that this could cause them harm. The master said to him, "If you are loath to do so," he said, "I will carry both of them alone, and I will eagerly bear this harm you mention." And when he had placed one behind and one in front, with himself sitting in the middle, at last his companion—who was confounded and goaded by stings of conscience—left one to his master and himself took hold of the other to carry her. And so then they carried them through very difficult places and through long tortuous routes, not without grave danger, until by chance they found a mill-house on the way and they left them there. Moreover, the master did more, and bestowed a garment on each one of them, with which to temper somewhat the power of the cold.

(14) Here, after a short time, he became a monk and then he was led to death with growing unease. Then, speaking to the brothers who were standing near him, he began to cry out with great reproach, "Do you see the crowd of demons beyond number, which has surrounded me on all sides, which does not

---

11. Reading *a via saltuum* for *avia saltuum*.

cease to assail me and to look upon me with terrible eyes?" And although the brothers pressed on with uninterrupted prayers of psalmody, nevertheless he continued to be afraid, with fits of trembling, when finally the companion who had been on the hunt with him, as was said, called out to him, as he was standing nearest to him: "Do you not see," he said, "that woman whom you and I together brought to the watermill, holding in her hands the garment that then I gave to her, swinging it and violently driving out all the demons from this house?" And a little bit later, thanks be to God, they were all cast out and actually disappeared from before my eyes, thanks to this woman's influence. And thus he died with the security of a well-founded hope, and the fruits of compassion that he exhibited when alive, he found offered to him when he was dead. Now it often happens that one light of a good work bursts forth from among the many dark places of carnal actions, which guides a person to a good end and to a haven.

(15) For this reason I do not think it unprofitable to add what Stephen,[12] a prudent and honest man, chaplain to this same queen, recounted. Now, he said that Stedelandus,[13] the emperor of Galicia, told of what one person observed, while another reported it afterward. There were, he said, three harlots who had devoted themselves to the obscene, foul acts of houses of ill-repute and, if I may speak in this way, by a shameful pandering they were prostituted to anyone passing by. But although the kingdom had a mixed population of both Christians and Saracens together, the women exposed themselves wickedly to Christians, yet they refused utterly to be the consorts of the Saracens. And since these Saracens felt insulted

---

12. On Stephen, see Dressler, *Petrus Damiani* 166; Lucchesi, *Vita* no. 197; and Struve, *Romreise* 21, n. 103.

13. Stedelandus cannot be positively identified. The editors of the *Annales Camaldulensis* note that Mabillon considered *Stedelandus* to be a scribal error for *Fredelandus,* and they suggest that this may in fact be Ferdinand I of Castile and Leon (d. 1065). See *Annales Camaldulensis Ordinis Sancti Benedicti,* eds. Johanne-Benedicto Mittarelli and Anselmo Costandoni (Venice: 1756; repr. Westmead, Farnborough, Hants, England: Gregg International, 1970) 2:322. For Ferdinand I, see "Ferdinand Ier," in *Biographie Universelle Ancienne et Moderne,* new. ed. (Paris: Madame C. Desplaces, 1855) 13:532–533.

that they were despised for this foul transaction, and their people complained that they suffered injury, at last they dragged the women before the ruler's tribunal and vehemently demanded that they consent to intercourse with them too, just as they do with Christians. But as they could not in any way prevail upon them for this sinful act, whether by threatening them with fearful things or by offering them enticements, after the ruler's judgment was delivered they were condemned to death. What more? As soon as the executioners[14] approached, they struck their bared necks with gleaming knives, but they could not even cut the surface of the skin with their empty blows.

(16) Meanwhile, because these women eagerly wanted to die but they were unable to kill them, they delivered them up to imprisonment. One night the Savior appeared to one of the two, who was a bit stronger than the other, and said to her, "Do not be afraid. Today I will put an end to your struggle and I will receive you in the delight of my glory with the crown of martyrdom." And on the next day they were led before the tribunals of judgment and, after questioning them again, the same sentence was applied nevertheless. Their mind was unchanged, and they refused the embraces of the Hagarenes[15] just as they had done before. Therefore, the executioners, since they had determined that they had no power over their necks, immediately cut their throat with a sword, and thus martyrs were made of harlots.

(17) But seeing that already the pen is brought out longer than I had decided at the beginning, the quill has to be checked and the limit of epistolary brevity must be imposed. Finally, I implore the compassion of divine piety to infuse you with the strength to guard chastity as inviolable among the rest of the virtues and the signs of all those of holy religion, and to safeguard the vessel of your body in sanctification and honor. Since he is the one who says in the Song of Songs, "I am the flower of the field, I am the lily of the valleys,"[16] so just as he deigned to become the son of the Virgin for you, let him make you bloom with flowers of chastity.

14. *Spiculatores*, which seems, in this instance, related to *spiculum*.
15. A common term for Muslims, after Hagar, the mother of Ishmael.
16. Cant 2.1.

LETTER 124

Peter Damian to the Empress Agnes. He offers her consolation in her unfamiliar loneliness, through which she can be safeguarded by the true sense of communion with the Holy Spirit. Containing a moving encomium to the virtue of monastic silence, this letter abounds in the bridegroom imagery Damian often employed to describe the solitary's union with God.

(1065/1066)[1]

TO HIS LADY, THE EMPRESS AGNES, the monk Peter the sinner offers service.

(2) I think, venerable lady, that because the lord Rainaldus, bishop of the see of Como, the holy woman Ermensinde,[2] your former relation, and I also, your servant, have departed from you to our own places, your mind now wavers and, just as one deprived of the solace of us all, it deplores the fact that it has remained alone. Perhaps the severity of very long silence is a burden, and it is tedious now that the presence of others for conversation is wanting, whom often, when they were present, you avoided, as you needed a more remote place for a refuge. For often we tolerate what is offered freely, and enjoy what we obtain with greater difficulty. We consider of little value what is abundant, and we eagerly desire what we perceive to be lacking.

(3) Truly, may your pious mind, which burns ardently with the fire of divine love kindled by all prayers, never pine away because of the absence of human society. Rather, as much as it considers that earthly solace is wanting, so much more may it trust in the nearness of the paraclete, the Holy Spirit. Thus,

---

1. Lucchesi, *Vita* no. 197, dates this letter from August 1065; Struve, *Romreise* 22, argues for the end of 1065 or 1066.
2. For Ermensinde, Agnes's sister-in-law, see *Letter* 104.2, and n. 7.

when our Savior declared he was about to take himself to the Father after the glory of the resurrection, and he perceived that the minds of the disciples were not a little disturbed on account of this, immediately he added, "Because I have spoken these things to you, sorrow has filled your heart. But I tell you the truth, it is expedient for you that I go, for if I do not go, the paraclete will not come to you. But if I go, I will send him to you."[3] If, then, the illuminator of minds could not flow into apostolic breasts with full diffusion unless Truth itself, which was about to send him to them, remove his corporeal presence from their eyes, how much more necessary is it that one who is simply human remove himself from the crowd of people, to become capable of achieving the gift of heaven? And thus when the human mind is freed from the presence of people, it merits the entry of the Holy Spirit.

(4) Therefore, do not count the absence of those who abided with you a loss. Instead, let the occasion for salvation, the profit of perfection and the propensity of our merit be counted as increased, because when the din of human conversation ceases, through silence the temple of the Holy Spirit is constructed in you. For this reason the sacred history attests that for the construction of the Israelite temple, "there was neither hammer nor axe nor any tool of iron heard in the house of the Lord when it was being built."[4] Indeed, the temple of God grew through silence, because when the human mind does not focus itself on outer words, the building of a spiritual edifice rises up to the sublime summit, and rising up, the more it is lifted to the heights, the more it is prevented from focusing on external things, enclosed in the protection of silence, for, "The guardian of justice is silence."[5] And Jeremiah says, "It is good to wait with silence for the salvation of the Lord, it is good for a man when he has borne the yoke from his youth. He shall sit solitary and be silent, because he has taken it up upon himself."[6] Plainly, when the solitary is silent he raises himself above himself, because when the human mind is everywhere encompassed by the

---

3. John 16.6–7.
4. 1 Kgs 6.7. Damian substitutes *domo Domini* for the Vulg. *domo*.
5. Isa 32.17. Damian substitutes *custos* for the Vulg. *cultus*.
6. Lam 3.26–28.

cloisters of silence it is led up to the highest places of the air, it is carried off to God through heavenly desire, and is kindled in his love through the ardor of the spirit. And, just like a living fountain, when it does not allow itself to be poured out hither and thither on rivers of words, it achieves the heights on rising waves.

(5) Therefore, let the temple of your breast grow now through silence, let the edifice of spiritual virtues rise up in you as if made of celestial stones, where the heavenly bridegroom, whom you love with all your heart, shall rest delightedly just as if on his marriage bed. Remember then what the Apostle says, that "another foundation no one can lay but that which is laid, which is Christ Jesus. If any one has placed upon this foundation gold, silver, precious stones, wood, hay, stalks, of whatever sort it shall be, fire will reveal it."[7] What must one understand by gold, silver, and precious stones if not the strength and jewels of the virtues? What else but the weakness of vices is indicated by the wood, hay, and stalks? Make certain, then, that the edifice that is in you be not made from weak material, which can be subject to the flames, and which will be dashed by the blowing force of the wind. Plainly, a voracious flame easily can consume wood, hay, and stalks whereas gold, silver, or precious stones do not know how to submit to fire. And certainly the same Apostle says, "Taking the shield of faith, in which you may be able to extinguish all the worst fiery darts."[8] Let the fire, then, which the hidden enemy sends, find the precious metals of the virtues in you, not the stalks and kindling of the vices. Let not a weak and rotten material fall meekly to the raging flames, which the cunning ambusher blows at you, but let the rigor of an impenetrable and robust solidity stand against him, so that the power of the Most High, which overshadowed[9] the virginal womb, may also guard your mind in the perpetual verdure of vernant modesty, and not—may it be avoided!—allow it to be burned by vapors of spiritual wickedness.

(6) Console yourself therefore, venerable lady, and expel

---

7. 1 Cor 3.11–13. Damian substitutes *posuerit* for the Vulg. *superaedificat, stipulas* for *stipulam*, and *quale cuiusque fuerit* for *uniuscuiusque opus manifestum erit*.
8. Eph 6.16. Damian substitutes *nequissima* for the Vulg. *nequissimi*.
9. Cf. Luke 1.35.

from your heart all the tedium of harmful sadness. Let Christ be the one with whom you converse, let Christ be your companion and table guest. Rather, let your pleasures be Christ himself, let him be a meal of daily refreshment,[10] let him be aliment of the most profound sweetness for you. Read together with him, chant the psalms continually with him, and finally prostrate yourself with him on the floor when about to say a prayer. Raise yourself up with him, when you are about to sleep let the bed receive you with him, let sleep come upon you with him. Let his modest and virginal embrace draw you close, so that what Isaiah said may be truly fulfilled in you: "And the bridegroom will rejoice over the bride, and your God will rejoice over you."[11] And you as a special bride will be able to say what the bride says in the Song of Songs: "My beloved shall abide between my breasts."[12] Now it happens that a person's heart is situated between the breasts. Therefore, the beloved abides between the breasts of the bride when Christ is loved with the entire heart by any faithful soul. Your holy soul says, then, to the bridegroom, "Behold you are fair, my beloved, and comely. Our bed is flourishing."[13] For he is the one "beautiful above the sons of men."[14] And because you have condemned the royal insignia on account of his love, despised imperial rank, he will be your crown, he himself will be for you above the purple, and he will prepare for you beautiful jewels of perfect glory. Thus, rightly, you ought to sing with the prophet, "The Lord has clothed me with a garment of salvation, and with a robe of gladness he has girded me, as a bridegroom decked with a crown, and as a bride adorned with her jewels."[15]

(7) Here he will console you for the absence of human soci-

---

10. This is the only time in Damian's letters that he seems to advise daily communion, a rare occasion of such advice in the eleventh century. Cf. *supra*, Letter 123, n. 6; cf. also Browe, *Die häufige Kommunion*.
11. Isa 62.5.
12. Cant 1.12.
13. Cant 1.15.
14. Ps 44.3.
15. Isa 61.10. Damian substitutes *vestimento* for the Vulg. *vestimentis*, *letitie* for *iustitiae*, *sponsus decoratum* for *sponsum decoratum*, and *sponsa ornata* for *sponsam ornatam*.

ety, here he will suffice for you in place of speech and command over all. Here, like another Elkanah, but far more preeminent, truly he will say, not "Anna," but Agnes, "why do you weep, and why do you not eat, and why is your heart afflicted? Am I not better for you than ten children?"[16] And since Elkanah means God's zeal, God's zeal, the redeemer's love, will comfort your mind in every weary moment of bitterness and difficulty, so that you throw yourself on him in every moment of adversity you suffer, take refuge under his shade from the pain of human persecution, and rest sweetly secure in his embraces. He who has deigned to suffer for you storms and shipwreck on worldly billows will offer himself to you as a refuge of the most profound quiet.

16. 1 Sam 1.8.

LETTER 125

Peter Damian to an abbot. He recommends his nephew to him as a student.

(Late summer or Fall 1065).[1]

OUR] HOLINESS CONCLUDED that he has been utterly obliterated, or, if I may put it this way, scraped clean from the most intimate wax tablets of my breast. Rather, there are those who dwell with me in service to Christ and who assemble with me for his love who witness how often your name is in my mouth with benediction, and how often I celebrate in public your angelic community.

(2) In addition, I ask your holiness's compassion for this youth, namely, my sister's child, to provide for him from your paternal piety both a teacher and sustenance and, receiving him as yet rude and untutored, or like a Jacob resting completely upon a staff,[2] to return him to us later with the twins of the trivium and quadrivium as a wife. Look upon my image in this boy, then, observe the appearance of my countenance in this one, and whatever the cost of piety is toward him charge not to him but rather to me.

(3) Oh, would that I could send to you what I wrote to the holy ones of Cluny or the many other things that I produced on various themes after my return from Gaul. May God omnipotent guard you, venerable father, and keep watch for a long time over the safety of your servants, and make me see the angelic appearance of your countenance as if present before me.

---

1. This fragmentary letter is missing the name of an addressee. Gaetani identified the recipient as Hugh of Cluny, although this identification remains uncertain. All one can say with certainty is that it was sent to a French or Burgundian abbot, since Damian's nephew studied in Gaul. Another possibility is Adraldus of Bremen, abbot of Fruttuaria.

2. Cf. Gen 32.10.

LETTER 126

Peter Damian writes to Alberic of Monte Cassino, providing an answer to the many questions he raised on the interpretation of the Bible. These questions arose particularly from a reading of the Old Testament, and Damian's Christocentric mystical and allegorical interpretations reveal a great deal concerning his approach to the text and his method for resolving apparent contradictions.

(1065)[1]

TO ALBERIC, VENERABLE BROTHER, the monk Peter the sinner, greetings in the Lord.

(2) The old history records that when the sons of Joseph, namely, Ephraim and Manasseh, demanded more extensive lands for their possession they received this response from Joshua, commanding them to cross over the mountains, to clear the dense growth of the forests, and in this way to obtain by their own hands a larger lot for themselves.[2] Moreover, a little later he said to the seven tribes, "How long are you indolent and slack and do not go in to take possession of the land that the Lord the God of your Fathers has given to you?"[3] You too, brother, as you urge and demand from me that certain little questions be solved for you, must then be directed to the mountains of the doctors [of the Church] and the forests of the Scriptures, where, sweating from uninterrupted labor, you may clear away the trees of the woodland that are growing wild, avoid the knotty trunks of doubts, and cultivate for yourself fallow lands just as with the hands of your own effort.

(3) Thus, the soil of celestial eloquence will have to be weeded with the mattocks of your own subtlety, so that you will not

---

1. Dated 1065, following Lucchesi.   2. See Josh 17.18.
3. Josh 18.3.

suffer hunger while waiting for nourishment from the hands of others, but rather soon shall live with great pleasure in a surfeit of spiritual delights, bringing forth the abundance of a rich crop by your own labor. Nevertheless, in the meanwhile, as your fruits are absent, let ours—I shall not say storehouse, nor what is even less, cask, but merely the very small measure of a bushel—succor you, and may your need be tempered in some way by our little crop. There is indeed a certain mean between living splendidly and perishing utterly from the poverty of hunger. Certainly, you want me not only to explain what you seek to know but even to convey you to the heights until ignorance thus perish, so that forgetfulness not steal upon you thereafter.

(4) Proceed, then. How is it, you ask, that it is said, "Saul was a child of one year when he began to reign, and he reigned two years over Israel"?[4] Some think it should be understood in this way: that at the beginning of his reign King Saul had a one-year old son, namely, Ishbosheth,[5] who cried still like a tender one-year old infant, and for two years after the death of his father Ishbosheth ruled over Israel. But seeing that this interpretation is rejected by learned men, let us seek out another. Blessed Jerome certainly teaches that this is to be understood in this way, that he was innocent, just like a one-year old boy, when he began to reign, and he remained in the simple state of this same innocence for two years.[6] But the one who was then a child of humility later was made a slave through pride.

(5) You inquire, further, who were the Cherethites and Pelethites, who are said to have been David's warriors?[7] One reads in the book of Numbers that the Lord said to Moses, "Gather for me seventy men from the elders of Israel, men you know to be the people's elders and masters. Bring them to the door of the tent of the covenant, and let them stand beside you there, and I will take some of the spirit that is on you and put it on them so that they might share with you the burden of the people and you will not have to bear it alone."[8] And from their

---

4. 1 Sam 13.1. 5. Cf. 2 Sam 2.8.
6. See Pseudo-Jerome, *Quaestiones hebraicae in librum I Regum*, PL 23.1337C.
7. See 2 Sam 15.18. 8. Num 11.16–17.

stock came forth two clans, one of which was called the Cherethites and the other the Pelethites. And "Cherethites" means "giving judgment" and "Pelethites" means "punishing," so that those whom the one judges, delivering a death sentence, the other punishes by imposing the sentence.[9]

(6) Then you add: Why are David's sons, who were no more related by blood to the sons of Aaron than the other tribes are known to have been, called priests? But know this, that as venerable priests and teachers were established over the people, sometimes princes or teachers are designated by the word for priest, as is found elsewhere: "Ira the Jairite was David's priest,"[10] that is, teacher. So too when it is said, "David's sons were priests,"[11] one should understand this as if it were saying that they were their brothers' teachers, or certainly were princes among the others, as the old translation has it. For where the new edition says, "David's sons were priests," the old one reads, "David's sons were princes in the court of the king."[12]

(7) Furthermore, you claim that you do not understand what is written: "There was also a third battle in Gob against the Philistines in which Adeodatus, the son of the forest, a weaver of the Bethlehemites, slew Goliath the Gathite."[13] But certainly this can easily be understood. For "Gob" means "pit"[14] and just as one who is cast into a pit of lions is placed in peril, so David offered himself, as it were, to the lions' teeth[15] when, about to do battle, he threw himself upon Goliath's rage. And David is himself properly called "given by God,"[16] seeing that he was chosen by God for the kingdom. He is even called the son of

---

9. These etymologies are also found in Claudius of Turin, *Quaestiones XXX super libros Regum* 4.18 (PL 104.818C).

10. 2 Sam 20.26.

11. 2 Sam 8.18.

12. Acc. to Reindel, the old edition is the LXX, and the new is the Vulg. He also directs attention to a similar note in Claudius of Turin's *Quaestiones*, already cited.

13. 2 Sam 21.19.

14. See Pseudo-Jerome, *Quaestiones hebraicae in librum II Regum*, 23.1361A.

15. Cf. 1 Sam 17.34.

16. *Adeodatus*. Cf. Pseudo-Jerome, *Quaestiones hebraicae in librum II Regum*, PL 23.1361A.

the forest, because we know that he was brought forth from woodland pastures,[17] where he pastured the sheep. Nor is David called a weaver without good reason, since his mother belonged to the people of Bezalel,[18] who built the tent of the covenant in the desert, which he covered with some finely wrought damask weave.[19]

(8) Nor is he said improperly to be from the Bethlehemites, since David took his origin from Naomi and Ruth and they had come from Bethelehem during a time of famine,[20] and they later returned to this same Bethlehem when it was flourishing with abundance. The following passages declare that without doubt David was himself this same Adeodatus, with all the others added to them, when it is said, "These four were born of Arapha in Gath, and they fell to the hands of David and his servants."[21] Of course I could explain what this signifies mystically, except that it is clear that the brevity due a letter prevents me. Yet all these refer to Christ, according to a mystical understanding. For he himself is that "given by God," of whom it is said in Isaiah, "A child is born to us, a son is given us."[22] Not incongruously is he called a son of the woodland, seeing that he deigned to be born according to the flesh of the Jews, who bore no fruit of a spiritual seed, just as wild trees that are not planted in a garden but arise in the woodland have come forth sterile. Thus one reads, "A voice crying out in the desert,"[23] that is, among the unfruitful Jewish people.

(9) Our Redeemer is also rightly said to be a weaver because he devotes himself to the task of weaving now as he clothes himself with his faithful and weaves garments of justice with them. The Apostle says of these garments, "So that he might present the glorious Church to himself, having neither stain nor wrinkle."[24] And the prophet says, "You shall wear them all just as a jewel."[25] And the psalmist rightly sings of Christ's faith-

17. 1 Sam 16.19.
18. 2 Chr 1.5.
19. Exod 36–38.
20. Ruth 1.1.
21. 2 Sam 21.21.
22. Isa 9.6. Note that Damian's *puer* departs from the Vulgate's *parvulus*.
23. Isa 40.3.
24. Eph 5.27. Again, Damian's text departs slightly from the Vulg.
25. Isa 49.18.

ful, "Let your priests be clothed with righteousness."[26] And according to Ezekiel the Lord hastens to the soul that he has most becomingly arrayed with spiritual garments, but she has deserted him when she is polluted with the uncleanness of adultery: "I have clothed you," he says, "with embroidered garments and I have shod you with blue-violet shoes and I have girded you with fine linen and clothed you with fine garments and I have adorned you with jewels."[27] And, a little further on: "And you have been clothed with linen and damask and many colors."[28] Why then is it remarkable if our Redeemer is called a weaver, when he clothes the soul, which is assigned to him by right of betrothal, with the finely woven splendor of virtue? For he is himself the Wisdom of God, of whom Solomon says, "she has sought out wool and linen, and has toiled at the counsel of her hands,"[29] whose fingers have grasped the spindle, all of whose servants are clothed with two cloaks,[30] whose flesh, moreover, has been made a coverlet in the Passion, but at the Resurrection his garment is the same linen and royal purple.[31]

(10) He is even rightly called a Bethlehemite because it is well known that he was born of the Virgin in Bethlehem. When it is said that the third war was in Gob, this means that the true David, the savior of Israel before the law and under the law and later, in evangelic grace, always has had faithful warriors with whom he fought against the Philistines, that is, against evil spirits. Therefore, at this third war David came to Gob, which means "pit," because just as the stronger prevailed over one who was well armed,[32] our very Redeemer even descended by himself into hell. Therefore, he says through the psalmist, "They have cast me into the lower pit, in dark places and in the shadow of death."[33] There he struck Goliah of Gath, because when he snatched the souls of the elect from the halls of Gehenna he wounded the ancient enemy, who exercised despotic rule over them, with a joyful wound.

26. Ps 131.9.
27. Ezek 16.10–11.
28. Ezek 16.13.
29. Prov 31.13.
30. Cf. Prov 31.19, 21.
31. Prov 31.22.
32. Luke 11.21.
33. Ps 87.7. Damian's *tenebris* departs from the Vulg. *tenebrosis*. See Sabatier 2.175, with reference to the Roman Psalter, p. 216.

(11) You also ask why this discrepancy appears in the sacred Scriptures, that in the book of Kings one reads that David at one and the same time purchased from Ornan the Jebusite the threshing floor and the oxen, which had to be offered as a sacrifice, for only fifty shekels of silver,[34] whereas in the book of Chronicles it is reported that he gave 600 shekels of gold for the threshing floor alone.[35] But without any doubt one must know that in the book of Kings one reads that David purchased only the oxen for fifty shekels of silver, but the text is altogether silent concerning how much he paid for the threshing floor. On the other hand, the book of Chronicles is silent concerning the oxen but asserts that the threshing floor was purchased for 600 shekels of gold. One easily sees this if the order of the words in each book is carefully examined. Now, this is the word order in the book of Kings: "Therefore, David purchased the threshing floor and the oxen for fifty shekels of silver."[36] One must divide it in such a way that Scripture says first, "David purchased the threshing floor," but does not explain for how much. Then this should follow: "and the oxen for fifty shekels of silver." In the book of Chronicles, one reads, "Therefore, David gave Ornan 600 shekels of gold of just weight for the site, and built there an altar to the Lord."[37] Thus, the two passages divide themselves so that one enumerates the price for the oxen and the other the price for the threshing floor alone. Certainly, there is a difference between the things for which the amount of the price is fixed, but the Holy Scriptures do not contradict one another.

(12) In addition, you reckon that this text should be considered, which reads, "There was, moreover, a battle there spread over the face of the entire earth, and the forest took toll of more of the people that day than did the sword devour."[38] These are blessed Jerome's words concerning this passage, from the book of the *Hebrew Questions*:[39] "The Hebrews affirm that this forest," he says, "which one reads took toll of more

---

34. 2 Sam 24.24.
35. 1 Chr 21.25.
36. 2 Sam 24.24.
37. 1 Chr 21.25–26.
38. 2 Sam 18.8.
39. Pseudo-Jerome, *Quaestiones hebraicae in librum II Regum*, PL 23.1357D.

people than the sword devoured, was really the ferocious beasts that were in the forest, by which many more were taken than shall have been devoured by the sword." Here the interpretation of the Hebrews, as it is called, was true, however it seems to us that all the mad and senseless men who were traitors along with Absalom crashed into the boughs standing in their way, having been blinded once God abandoned them. And this is the reason why one should say that there were more destroyed who fell to the forest consuming them than were devoured by the the sword cutting them to pieces. Certainly one does not doubt that it should be understood in this way if what follows from the pen is considered even in a superficial way. For after it says, initially, "the forest took toll of more of the people that day than did the sword devour" it adds immediately after, "It happened that Absalom encountered David's servants, riding on a mule. And when the mule went under a thick and large oak his head was caught in the oak and while he hung between the heaven and the earth, the mule on which he rode passed on."[40]

(13) Moreover, you ask what happened to the ark of the Lord and the tent of the covenant, which were fashioned in the desert. Just as a lack of information imposes almost no constraint concerning this matter, so the information we have contributes almost nothing useful. Nevertheless, just as Scripture's authority has handed down, one finds that the tabernacle, as well as the ark and the incense-altar, were hidden by the hands of the prophet Jeremiah on Mount Abarim, where it is known that Moses is buried.[41] If one pays careful attention to the beginning of the second book of Maccabees, this information is clearly disclosed. It says, "It was in this writing that, after a divine message had been given to him, the prophet commanded that the ark and the tent of the covenant should go with him until he came up to the mountain on which Moses went up and saw God's splendor. And coming there, Jeremiah found a cave-dwelling and he carried the ark and the tent of the covenant

---

40. 2 Sam 18.8–9.
41. Num 27.12; Deut 34.1.

and the incense-altar into it, and then blocked the entrance."[42] Thus Jeremiah, as was said, hid these three mysteries on the aforementioned Mount Abarim. Our curiosity does not presume to inquire whether he did something else with these things afterward, or whether they really remained undisturbed there, because Scripture never makes any mention of it.

(14) You ask that this passage in Isaiah also be explained for you: "I struck him on account of the sins of my people and gave a wicked man for a burial-place and a rich man for his death."[43] It is, as it seems to us, to be understood this way. The Father almighty struck down the Son on account of the sins of his people because he determined that he must suffer the gibbet of the Cross in order to remove our sins. The Son was handed over by the Father for this purpose, that the slave become free. Just as the Apostle says, "Who did not spare his Son, but handed him over for all of us."[44] The innocent one was beaten with blows for this reason, so that the sinner, healed from the blackness of his wounds, might rejoice. Just as the same Isaiah says, "He was himself pierced for our iniquities, crushed for our crimes, by his stripes we are healed."[45] But our Redeemer deigned to suffer on account of two peoples, namely, for the Gentile and Jewish peoples. One of these is called wicked, whereas the other is rightly said to be rich. And indeed the Gentile people was the wicked, because while serving idols it had neglected the piety of divine service. In Greek, this piety is called *theosebia*. The Jewish people was truly the rich one, because when it received the sabbath, circumcision, the new moon, and all the rituals of the divine law, it overflowed with abundant riches as if from a heavenly treasure house. Paul rejoiced that the recently converted Corinthians abounded with these riches when he says, "I give thanks to my God always for you in the grace of God, which is given you in Christ Jesus, that in all things you are made rich in him, in all utterance and in

---

42. 2 Macc 2.4–5.
43. Isa 53.8–9. Damian reads "wicked man" [impium] for the Vulg. "wicked" [impios].
44. Rom 8.32.
45. Isa 53.5.

all knowledge, so much so that nothing is wanting to you in any grace."[46] Therefore, our Savior, by the death that he took upon himself, revived the two peoples of the Father from death, namely, the Gentile people who previously had wickedly served demons, and the Jewish people who, although cleaving to the letter that kills and unaware of the vivifying spirit,[47] nevertheless possessed the riches of the divine law.

(15) Next, you ask what the meaning of this is in the prophet Jeremiah: "Shall not both good and evil proceed out of the mouth of the Most High?"[48] This question is nearly the most renowned in the entire Church. For many ask it and, often repeated, it runs out of the mouth of many people. But this question is easily resolved, even if not by us, but confidence may be taken from the one who, bestowing it, opens the book and looses its seals.[49] The Father almighty even handed the innocent Son over to the hands of the wicked, yet nevertheless he did not stray from the right path of justice, seeing that he determined that justice would overflow because he permitted him to be subject to a time of injustice. Just as one reads in the book of Wisdom: "Since you are just," it says, "justly you order all things; and yet you condemn a man who ought not to be punished."[50] Therefore, the Father permits the Son to suffer death, nevertheless he does not command the murderers to murder him. Otherwise, when they ascribe a work of impiety to the author of piety, they would have been guiltless.

(16) Therefore, God granted power to the persecutors of Christ, but he did not command the persecutors to slay him. This is why the prophet first spoke, saying, "To destroy a man wrongfully in his judgment, the Lord has not approved."[51] Indeed, God would destroy a man wrongfully in judgment if he ordered an innocent man to be condemned. But it is one thing to condemn, it is something else not to snatch one away from the punishment of condemnation; it is one thing to urge one on to raging, sacrilegious impulses, and something else again

46. 1 Cor 1.4–7.
48. Lam 3.38.
50. Wis 12.15.

47. Cf. 2 Cor 3.6.
49. Cf. Rev 5.5.
51. Lam 3.36.

never to restrain him from the madness of a rage he has conceived. This is why he adds there, not in the way of approving but of reproving, "Who is he who commands a thing to be done when the Lord does not order it?"[52] He says, "when the Lord does not order it," but not "when the Lord prevents it." God, then, did not command the persecutors to crucify our Savior, because he found nothing in him that ought to be punished. Nevertheless, he did not prevent them from crucifying him, because in no way did he free the one about to suffer, for the sake of the world's salvation, from the hands of the wicked. And then correctly he added, "Shall not both good and evil proceed from the mouth of the Most High?"[53] Indeed, goods would proceed if he were to snatch him from the punishment that was inflicted on him, but evils if he were to find a fault in him for which he ought to be judged subject to punishment. Therefore, neither goods nor evils proceed from the mouth of the Most High in Christ's Passion, because the Father neither frees him from the law's power nor condemns him by the law's justice, because even though he does not find him to be a sinner nevertheless for the sake of the world's salvation he does not snatch away the innocent man positioned for suffering. He sees that he is guilty of no sins, nevertheless he does not free him from the hands of the wicked, so that as the innocent man undergoes punishment the sinner is turned to forgiveness. And when the one who does not have to do so releases the debts of us all who, bound together, were held under the interest of the old bond, all are rendered free from the law once the obligations have been annulled.

(17) I have often had doubts about something that, nevertheless, you do not ask, namely, why David, while he lived, dealt kindly with Joab and Shimei, with whom he was very angry, whereas when he was near death he ordered Solomon, who succeeded him in the rule of the kingdom, to destroy them. He said, "You know what Joab the son of Zeruiah has done to me, what he did to the two captains of the army of Israel, to Abner the son of Ner and to Amasa the son of Jether, whom he slew

52. Lam 3.37.
53. Ibid.

and shed the blood of war in peace."⁵⁴ And a little after this he adds, "Do therefore according to your wisdom and do not let his hoary head go down to hell in peace."⁵⁵ He also said this about Shimei, "You have also with you Shimei the son of Gera the son of Jemini of Bahurim, who cursed me with a grievous curse when I went to the camp."⁵⁶ Then, after other things had come in between, he added, "You shall bring down his grey hairs with blood to hell."⁵⁷ Why is it that David, when he was dying, condemned them but spared them while he was alive, when actually the order of reason would demand that when alive he should exact vengeance from traitors or from any enemies, but when dying he should deal with them compassionately?

(18) But one must know that the kingdom of David, who was weakened by as many persecutors and troubles as he was afflicted with adversities and needs, along with his companions in war, indicates this present age in which Christ is afflicted with his members and in which the Church is rent by many trials. The kingdom of Solomon, who surpassed all the standards of royal merit in riches and glory, rose above all the dignities of princely empire, announces the glory of the future life in which Christ, who is truly a peace-maker, quietly enjoys with his members eternal things and feasts solemnly at the feasts of the heavenly banquet.

(19) Therefore, our Redeemer, although he is one and the same, now is a David, and then will be a Solomon, because he does not cease to fight against the devil through his members just as if with a strong hand, and then certainly he will not cease to fight against the senseless controversies of the spirit and of all flesh with his body, which is the Church, so that truly he will reign peacefully in eternal tranquility. Now, as if another David, he is oppressed by the burdens of calamities among his elect, is driven by the pressures of various persecutions and adversities, is weakened by tribulations and troubles, whereas later just like another Solomon he will obtain the extraordinary abundance of immortal riches. Now David, fleeing from before Absalom,

54. 1 Kgs 2.5.
55. 1 Kgs 2.6.
56. 1 Kgs 2.8.
57. 1 Kgs 2.9.

leaves behind in his house ten concubines whom Absalom wickedly defiles in incest,[58] because our Redeemer, when cast out from the Jewish city, hastens to the desert places of the Gentiles, and leaves the Jews behind in the house of the Law, not marching along manfully but living in a womanly manner. Not inappropriately, the ten concubines indicate the Jews, because while they meekly guard the Decalogue of the Law they do not deserve to reach the chaste bed of marriage but rather, banding together without the ring of faith, they choose a union with concubines. Wantonly Absalom corrupted them, because an evil spirit corrupts the reprobate souls of the wicked just as if prostituting them. It is written of them that later David "went not to them, but they were shut up until the day of their death living in widowhood."[59] They lost the man concerning whom the prophet Isaiah says, "seven women received one man."[60] Solomon says about them that they are seven hundred queens.[61] And the seven received the one whom the ten lost. The Holy Church, filled with the sevenfold gift of the Spirit, has united with the heavenly bridegroom. The synagogue, which received the Decalogue, lost this bridegroom and remained a widow because, while it has stood unmovable in the home of customary ritual and legal ceremonies, it refused to go out into the desert places of the Gentiles with king David.

(20) Therefore, when David was still alive he tolerated those he condemned in the end because Christ, the judge of the human race—whom David signified—now spares mercifully those upon whom he imposes a sentence of just condemnation at the end of the age. Therefore, first David displays mercy, whereas Solomon judges with justice. Since our Redeemer is one and the same now, as if another David, he tolerates with equanimity the depraved acts of the reprobate whereas later, just like another Solomon coming in his glory he cuts them down as if having brandished the sword of his judgment. This balance of divine reckoning is frequently found in the expressions of this

---

58. Cf. 2 Sam 15.16.
59. 2 Sam 20.3.
60. Isa 4.1. Damian has *accaeperunt* for the Vulg. *apprehendent*.
61. 1 Kgs 11.3.

same David, just as here he says, "Mercy and judgment I will sing to you, O Lord."[62] And, "God loves mercy and truth. Mercy and truth have met each other."[63] Thus, to be sure, as long as mercy is set before truth, like another David he is set before Solomon, so that those whom David piously endures by mercy Solomon justly condemns by judgment. And one should know that those who perform evil acts are actually indicated by Joab, who committed a murder with his own hands, and those who speak wicked things are prefigured by Shimei, who so greatly cursed the king. For both those who act wickedly and those who devote themselves to false and reprobate statements will be condemned without doubt in the reckoning of the Last Judgment, just as this same David said, "You hate all the workers of iniquity; you will destroy all who speak a lie."[64]

(21) But now we enjoin silence upon the pen, so that this letter not pass beyond the limit of epistolary brevity, and in order that we not be proved ignorant while we struggle to teach you answers to the questions.

62. Ps 100.1.
63. Ps 83.12; 84.11.
64. Ps 5.7.

LETTER 127

Peter Damian to Alberic the Deacon of Monte Cassino. Two further questions from Alberic are taken up here, and in the course of his answers Damian demonstrates his knowledge of contemporary computation. From his own words, this letter can be dated for the exact day of the week on which it was written. As on other occasions, Damian here expects the imminent end of the world.

(Wednesday of Holy Week, 23 March 1065)

O MY DEAR BROTHER ALBERIC, the monk Peter the sinner sends greetings.

(2) You tell me, my dear friend, that you are not sure why the writings, not only of the Old Testament, but also of a great many of the doctors of the Church assert that a man matures for ten months in his mother's womb, but do not say that he comes forth in nine months. Lest I go too far afield, it will suffice for me to cite just one text. For Solomon says in the book of Wisdom, "I too am a mortal man like all the rest, descended from the first man, who was made of dust, and in my mother's womb I was wrought into flesh during a ten-month space compacted in blood from the seed of her husband and the pleasure that is joined with sleep. When I was born, I breathed the common air."[1] Now, both John the Baptist and the very author and creator of nature, Christ himself, were born within the period of nine months in such a way, that they did not reach over, even for a single moment, into the tenth month. For John, according to the Scriptures, was conceived on the twenty-fourth of September, and was born on the twenty-fourth of June. Our Savior, however, was conceived in the

---

1. Wis 7.1–3.

womb of the Virgin on the twenty-fifth of March, and for the salvation of the world was born on the twenty-fifth of December. In these two conceptions and births, of both the servant and the master, we find nine months so fully taken up, that the tenth month had not even begun. If you think carefully about both periods of time, however, you will find that the Lord remained in his mother's womb two days longer than John. Therefore, since there is not the slightest ambiguity that most men are born within the space of nine months, how is it that the doctors [of the Church] say that they remained in the womb for ten months?

(3) But so far as we know, among the ancients months were computed to have only thirty days. The norm, however, that is now observed, stating that some months have thirty days, others thirty-one, derives from the disposition of Romulus, who founded the city of Rome.² Now, since Romulus came from a coarse and rustic background, when establishing the new government he had begun, he assigned the beginning of each month to the day on which one could observe the rise of the new moon, thus fixing the day of the kalends as that on which the new moon first appeared. But since it was apparent that sometimes the moon rose later, at other times earlier, it happened that when it appeared later, the preceding month had more days, and when earlier, it had fewer days. And thus it was that some months had thirty-one days, while others could count only thirty days. Consequently, we may conclude that this rule is still observed by us in reckoning the months, derived from its original institution.

(4) But because the older saints, as it seems to me, did not observe this rule of the pagans, they assigned only thirty days to each month. Therefore, it will suffice for me to cite the text of just one doctor. St. Augustine says, "It has taken forty-six years to build this temple. Are you going to raise it again in three days?"³ When this number is multiplied by six, this is the amount of time the Lord remained in his mother's womb. For, forty-six

2. Cf. Bede, *De temporum ratione* 12 (PL 90.348–349).
3. Cf. John 2.20.

times six makes two hundred and seventy-six. And this number of days completes nine months and six days, which is reckoned as ten months in the case of pregnant women."[4] In these words, then, it is undoubtedly shown that only thirty days are assigned to each month. And if thirty days are multiplied by nine, we arrive at two hundred and seventy. In two hundred and seventy the number thirty is found nine times, which, according to the blessed doctor's statement, completes nine months. But the six days that are the remainder, are considered to be the tenth month. Hence, since in our time there are seven months that have thirty-one days, there were some days among the ancients that exceeded nine months, and taking the part for the whole, they computed them as a tenth month. Hence, since there were fewer months for the amount of time, they were considered more when it came to counting, so that as we now say there were nine, taking the part for the whole, they then would say that there were ten. In the meantime, let this solution to your question suffice for you, until you happen to hear a better one from those who are knowledgeable.

(5) You also have doubts about the Lord's passion and resurrection, which this year are in total agreement with events just as they happened when the Lord was crucified. You ask whether this is a rare or frequent occurrence. Some will say that they never saw this happen, while others contend that it occurred often in their lifetime. But since you strive to be a student of the truth, you should fear to accept such variety of opinion, lest you be led into error in the midst of these conflicting statements.

(6) You should be aware, however, that as far as I can gather from the tradition of writers who preceded us, this event of the Lord's passion, occurring at the very time on which the Lord hung on the cross, happened in the same way only once, and is now repeated for the second time. For, in the year 533 after the Lord's passion, the feast of Easter occurred in the same month on the same day and moon, and in the same epact, that on the

---

4. Cf. Augustine, *De trinitate* 4.5.9 (CC 50.172); idem, *De diversis quaestionibus LXXXIII* 56 (CC 44.4.95–96).

first occurrence was the fifth, on which it had occurred in the first year of the original resurrection of the Lord. And this year it happens in the same way, so that all things concur. For as then when the Lord suffered, it was the month of March, the date was the twenty-fifth of March, the day of the week was Friday, and the moon was the fourteenth, it afterwards happened in the very same way in 533, and occurs again this year, which is 1065. Four learned men arranged the Easter chronology, namely, Hippolytus,[5] Eusebius,[6] Theophilus,[7] and Prosper.[8] After these came Victorius,[9] born in Aquitaine, a most exact computist, who, when requested by Saint Hilary,[10] the bishop of Rome, carefully restored the plan, and with searching investigation composed his chronology.

(7) And so, he produced a list of years covering five hundred and thirty-two years, so that in 533 the feast of Easter would occur in the same month, on the same date, day of the week, and moon, and in the same epact on which it had been celebrated in the first year, that of the Lord's passion and resurrection. And this year, too, in which we now live, we see the passion of the Lord, which will be celebrated tomorrow, returning to the same arrangement. In that this year, therefore, repeats the first series of events during the passion and resurrection of the Lord, it undoubtedly agrees with the calculation of Victorius that I mentioned above. In the meantime, however, while the subject might be more clearly explained, let us be satisfied, dear brother, with the present resolution of both questions.

(8) Yet I would like you to know, that after this feast of Easter

---

5. Hippolytus of Rome (fl. early 3d c.); cf. Clemens Scholten, "Hippolyt v. Rom," *LThK* 5.147–150.

6. Eusebius of Caesarea (265–339); cf. Timothy D. Barnes, "Eusebius v. Caesarea," *LThK* 3.1007–1009.

7. Theophilus of Alexandria (345–412); cf. Michael Fiedrowicz, "Theophilus v. Alexandrien," *LThK* 9.1471–1472.

8. Prosper of Aquitaine (390–455); cf. Domingo Ramos-Lissón, "Prosper v. Aquitanien," *LThK* 8.644–645.

9. Victorius of Aquitaine (mid-5th c.); cf. Rosemary Nürnberg, "Victorius v. Aquitanien," *LThK* 10.773. See Victorius's *Cursus paschali annorum 532*, ed. Th. Mommsen (MGH Auct.ant. 9.666–735).

10. Hilary (pope 461–468); cf. Georg Schwaiger, "Hilarius, Papst," *LThK* 5.103.

has come and gone, it will occur again in the same way ninety-five years from now, everything agreeing with this year's celebration, namely, as to the same month, date, day of the week, and moon, and with the fifth concurrent day, but in a leap year, with the same epact and turning of the nineteen-year cycle. After this fifth epact in leap year, in two hundred and forty-seven years from now the feast of Easter will occur in the same way. And later it will happen three times that Easter will likewise always occur in ninety-five years, everything agreeing with what we said above. But in this fifth epact that we have now, after the first passion of the Lord Easter will never occur again, excepting only the one of which Victorius spoke, and the one now repeated for the second time. And from then on it will never happen again that all these things will be in agreement, that is, month, date, day of the week, and moon, and with the same epact and turn of the nineteen year cycle, except for the year 533 when all was the same.

(9) But since the world is now coming to an end, it is superfluous to go through long calendars of calculations and to produce volumes for the ages.

LETTER 128

Peter Damian to the hermits, Ambrosius and Liupardus. He writes to congratulate them on their purpose to live and be buried at Fonte Avellana. He is especially edified by Liupardus of Piacenza, who, after leaving the secular world, had also withdrawn from a wealthy monastery to enter the hermitage. Ambrosius, formerly of Milan, may well be the same monk to whom he addressed *Letter* 81, *On the Catholic Faith*. Included here is also a formal attestation by Damian and his whole community, granting burial rights at Fonte Avellana even to those hermits who, because of ill health, had been compelled to live outside the hermitage.

(ca. 1065)

O THE BROTHERS, sir Ambrosius and Liupardus, the monk Peter the sinner, in the bond of undivided charity.

(2) Let us give thanks to God, the author of all goodwill, who inflamed your hearts with the fire of such a noble spirit, that while alive you should never wish to live outside the hermitage, nor in death to be buried away from it. Since long ago, moreover, he persuaded the minds of the people of Israel to exchange the horrid conditions of a barren desert for the fertile fields of Goshen, endowed with the beauty of abundant grass,[1] he also impelled you to abandon the bountiful living of those noble cities, Milan and Piacenza, to scorn their riches, and like starving men invited to a royal banquet to come to the poverty of a strict life in the hermitage. And so, despising the pleasures of carnal desire, you have bravely seized upon the arduous regimen of this solitary life. Boldly condemning the attractions of carnal desires, you have seized upon the difficult

---

1. Cf. Gen 46.28–47.6.

practice of this solitude, which especially amazes me where you are concerned, brother Liupardus, since after the renunciation of the world you abandoned riches and, moreover, a monastery accustomed to the most splendid luxuries. It is an easy thing, indeed, to change one's mind as if one were changing his clothes, to alter one's spirit along with one's habit. But it is more rarely the case that as one perseveres in this order, he turns his back on affluence to which he was accustomed. It is surely difficult to find one who, while not altering his garb, has exchanged rich fare for poverty, indulgence in a softer life for discipline under a monastic rule. Fervor engendered by a heavenly inspired audacity has ignited the natural disposition of you both, as your blessed spirit bravely takes itself in hand, violently tearing you away from the world, as if it were bringing back to a triumphant Christ the bountiful spoils of war.

(3) And as you also show your concern for being buried in this place, you give a clear indication that you have built the immoveable foundation of your home, not on a patch of shifting sand, but rather on a rock; so that while as mortal men you have decided to live for Christ in poverty, as wealthy men you may later rise in glory on the day of Judgment. Abraham, moreover, bought a burial plot from Ephron the Hittite,[2] Jacob made his son Joseph swear that he would bury him alongside his grandfather,[3] and Joseph himself had his brothers vow that they would take his bones with them when at length they departed from Egypt.[4] And indeed, for this purpose they chose for him a burial place in the promised land,[5] since they had no doubt that at some later time the coming of the heavenly Redeemer would happen there. Nor were they unaware that afterwards as Christ performed the mysteries of human redemption there, he would especially hallow that region with his precious blood. Therefore, these venerable patriarchs greatly desired to be buried in the land where they knew Christ would be crucified. Similarly, you too wish to rest here after your death, in the place where you determined to carry the cross in imitation of Christ. For it is here that Christ is daily crucified in his mem-

2. Cf. Gen 23.16.
3. Cf. Gen 50.5.
4. Cf. Gen 50.24.
5. Exod 13.19.

bers where, by participating in his sacrifice, we offer the allegiance of our spirit, and by the restraint imposed by this severe life, we immolate our flesh by depriving it of its selfish desires.

(4) Since you request that when some severe illness befalls you, you not be taken, as is customary, to a monastery where you will receive the gentle treatment of a less strict life, but that fraternal charity permit you to remain here until your death: Wherefore, I the monk, Peter the sinner, with the common consent of the older and younger brothers declare, decree, and by force of an unalterable decision confirm, that any sick brother who is able to abstain from eating meat, not be compelled against his will to go to some other monastery, but be permitted to spend his confinement to bed in this hermitage, with every kindness and zealous care shown to him. But if it is absolutely necessary, and his sickness requires him to eat meat, let him be brought to the countryside to the cells or churches that are under the jurisdiction of this hermitage, where, as is evident, after all that is necessary has been done for him, with God's help he may either regain his strength and recover, or, after all the duties of human solicitude have been discharged, he be brought back to the hermitage where he spent his life, there to receive the burial he deserves. But should anyone presume to breach the ordinance that we have decreed, after leaving this life let him be found guilty of violating this judgment.

(5) Here then, my dear brothers, I have paid the debt you asked for, I have weighed out the coin your holy request demanded, and as you wished, have confirmed your petition in writing. Henceforth, therefore, serve God without worrying about this old concern, throw off this idle sorrow from your mind, and with your whole being rejoice in the sweetness of your expectation of heaven. For the devil is the instigator of sadness, while the Holy Spirit is the author of spiritual joy. And so, as you have planned, establish your roots in this house, and let their growth reach up to heaven, so that your tree, as the prophet says, "may strike root under ground and yield fruit above ground."[6] Daily keep your graves before your eyes, filled,

---

6. Isa 37.31; cf. also 2 Chr 19.30.

as it were, with your own remains, and constantly meditate on the last day of your lives. Thus, when it comes, like a sudden thunderbolt it may not strike you down as you yawn in idleness, but like something that is well known, with which you are familiar, it may shine on you as someone eagerly awaited, by whose help you may come to the end of your exile in a foreign land and enter the splendor of your father's house.

LETTER 129

Peter Damian to the priests Rodulfus and Vitalis, to the deacon Arialdus, and the layman Erlembaldus, leaders of the Pataria in Milan, and to others. He congratulates his co-workers in the struggle against simony and clerical marriage. Their efforts are still needed, since the unrepentant archbishop, Guido of Milan, has returned to his old ways. Yet, they should not despair, since the Church of Milan has overcome similar adversities in the past.

(Between the end of 1065 and early 1066)

O THE HOLY BRETHREN Rodulfus,[1] Vitalis, and Arialdus,[2] and to Erlembaldus[3] and the others fighting with insuperable faith for the forces of Christ, the monk Peter the sinner sends greetings in Christ.

(2) I give thanks to almighty God, my dear friends, that as news of your deeds has spread, I often hear that you have persisted in the holy enthusiasm that was given you by the grace of the Holy Spirit, and have fought with unceasing fervor against the enemies of ecclesiastical discipline.

(3) For the evil forger never stops building his cursed workshop within the confines of the Church, never leaves off striking coins with the blows of his hammer, turning out the money of hell. The heresy of the Nicolaitans, moreover, which, as we collaborated with you, seemed to have been rooted out, still puts forth new growth, and by the wild emergence of noxious weeds, now chokes Christ's ripening grain that is nearing golden-hued maturity. Hence, we prostrate ourselves before the Lord, complaining and lamenting as we say, "Lord, was it

---

1. Cf. C. Violante, "Patarines," *NCE* 10.940–942.
2. Cf. Jörg W. Busch, "Arialdus," *LThK* 1.967.
3. Cf. Jörg W. Busch, "Erlembald," *LThK* 3.795–796.

not good seed that you sowed in your field? Then where has the darnel come from?"⁴ And to this we add: "Shall we go and gather the darnel?"⁵ But he replies at once with these consoling words: "Let them both grow together till harvest; and at harvest time I will tell the reapers: 'Gather the darnel first, and tie it in bundles for burning; then collect the wheat into my barn.'"⁶

(4) Now, since God can undoubtedly do all things, he is surely able to rid the field of the church of Milan of every plague of heresy and keep unharmed the fruit of its verdant faith. But he wishes to test the constancy of his faithful followers, to see how forcefully they resort to arms, how bravely they engage in hand-to-hand combat, and finally, with what untiring spirit they fight against the devil and his accomplices. For, it is in his power to resist their teacher, Simon, who once opposed his apostles, that he not rise into the air, but allow him to be lifted up to some degree, that he might be forced to fall to the ground, thus promoting God's greater glory and his utter disgrace.⁷

(5) Consequently, my dear friends, as you struggle against the twofold battlefront of the devil's legion, do not let up, do not grow weary and basely lose heart. But like true sons of Benjamin, who was called "the dexterous son,"⁸ fight with your accustomed bravery, using both hands, and with the sword of God's word decapitate the two-headed monster. Indeed, remember Jesus, from whose mouth came forth a sharply honed two-edged sword,⁹ who while cutting down all that was before him, overthrew the cruel and barbarous enemy. But if, perhaps, a growing number of evil spirits seems to be attacking you, confidently cry out with Elisha, "Those who are on our side are more than those on theirs."¹⁰

(6) What more need I say? I refer to the statement of the

---

4. Matt 13.27.   5. Matt 13.28.
6. Matt 13.30.
7. Cf. Acts 8.9–31; see also the apocryphal *Acta Petri*, on which cf. D. Doré, "Apocryphes du N.T.," in *Dictionnaire Encyclopedique de la Bible* (Turnholt: Brepols, 1987) 118.
8. Cf. Jerome, *Nom. Hebr.* 3.24 (CC 72.62); see also Judg 20.16. For Benjamin as "the dexterous son" or "the son of the right hand" see also Gen 35.18 and *Letter* 159.4–5.
9. Cf. Rev 19.15.   10. 2 Kgs 6.16.

Apostle, "If an angel from heaven should preach a gospel at variance with the gospel I preached to you, he shall be held outcast."[11] But note that those who formerly were held fast by the snares of the Nicolaitans and of the simonist heresy, now heap up damnation for themselves, and after violating their sacred oaths are guilty of perjury, so that what John says in the Apocalypse may be truly fulfilled in them: "Let the evildoer go on doing evil and the filthy-minded wallow in his filth."[12] But on the contrary may what follows be realized in you: "Let the good man persevere in his goodness and the holy man be true to his dedication."[13]

(7) It was always the rule and something innate in the Church of Milan that it should have men of diverse belief, such as Auxentius[14] and Ambrose. Like a rabid dog the former would bark at the faithful, while the latter drove him out with the evidence of the Old and New Testament, employed like a two-pronged fork. The former provided them with error as their drink, laced with the poison of vipers; the latter poured out the purest water drawn from the heavenly spring. The former plunged into hell his followers, who were fed on virulent milk and seduced by cunning deceit; but with the sweetness of apostolic doctrine the latter lifted them up to the rewards of heavenly glory. The former brought on the gloom of blindness for those who believed in him, while the latter provided for those who obeyed his episcopal commands the splendor of the true faith and the light of eternal grace. Wherefore, I am pleased to proclaim in his honor the praise I wrote for this occasion: "O Ambrose, golden star!"[15]

(8) May almighty God, my dear friends, with the keys of blessed Peter the apostle open for you the gate of the kingdom of heaven, and by the prayers of your bishop, blessed Ambrose,

---

11. Gal 1.8.   12. Rev 22.11.
13. Ibid.
14. The Arian bishop of Milan (+375). His successor was Ambrose; cf. Wilhelm Geerlings, "Auxentius," *LThK* 1.1304.
15. MSS G1 and P1 here insert the following: "Look at the end of this book among his other hymns." Damian's hymn in honor of St. Ambrose is found in MS V1, fol. 366r; ed. in M. Lokrantz, *L'opera poetica* no. 36, p. 123; Lucchesi, *Clavis* 139.

indulgently cleanse you from all the filth of the spirit of darkness. May he allow you to remain steadfast in that inviolable truth with which you began, and established on the rock of apostolic faith, resist all the errors of perverse doctrine. May he grant you so to live through all misadventure as you pass through this life, that you may be worthy to dwell with him, who is the author of life, and to rejoice without end in the heavenly Jerusalem. Amen.

LETTER 130

Peter Damian to the Empress Agnes. Since he finds it impossible to visit her, Damian exhorts the empress to bear the difficulties of her solitude in imitation of Christ. What she must endure is trivial compared with the indignities he suffered. She should meditate on the fleeting vanity of earthly glory, and concentrate on the riches that will be hers in the company of the immortal Bridegroom.

(End of 1065 or early 1066)

TO HIS LADY, THE EMPRESS AGNES, the monk Peter the sinner offers the attention of a servant.

(2) Because I am at such a distance from you, and find it impossible to be with you at this time, I am indeed filled with sorrow and daily lament your absence. In the meantime, however, before I can again visit you, I advise you to be patient and not find it burdensome to bear the harshness and difficulties that come your way, and out of love for the heavenly Bridegroom, to put up with solitude or even with the absence of necessary things. For since Christ endured the cross for you, why should you wonder that you must undergo poverty for love of him? If he whom powers and dominations serve in heaven, suffered spittle, scourging, and abuse, blows and slaps in this world, why is it such a great thing for you, who are earth, to abandon the empty display of imperial honor, and give yourself to him, not as the queen of the world, but something that is much more glorious, as the servant girl of the eternal king? Remember what the Apostle says, "Let us then go to him outside the camp, bearing the stigma that he bore. For here we have no permanent home, but we are seekers after the city that is to come."[1] What a happy exchange! In place of dross you are giv-

1. Heb 13.13–14.

en gold, for darkness you receive light, and for earthly honors the prize of heavenly glory. For as the prophet says, "All mankind is grass and all their glory lasts no longer than the flower of the field. The grass withers, the flower fades, but he who keeps the word of the Lord endures forevermore."[2]

(3) You should also recall that he who today is clothed in purple, is tomorrow put into the grave. One who today rules over men, tomorrow rots away and becomes the food of worms. Today he is girt with royal attire, but tomorrow his lifeless body is wrapped in tattered rags. Today he is crowned in splendor, seated in dignity on a kingly throne, but tomorrow his fetid remains shrivel away in the grave. And so, my lady, carefully think about these and similar things, and with Jesus now patiently endure the hardships of this life, that when he appears who is to be your judge, you may properly go out to meet him like one of the wise virgins with lighted lamps,[3] and in place of purple that will fade with time you may receive the robe of immortality. And in exchange for a crown, fashioned of earthly metal, may you wear that diadem made in heaven adorned with precious stones.

2. Isa 40.6–8.
3. Cf. Matt 25.1.

LETTER 131

Peter Damian to abbot M—— and to the Latin monks of the monastery of St. Mary in Constantinople. He rejoices that, although they are living among foreigners speaking a strange tongue, they have not abdicated from the Catholic faith. The kingdom of heaven is open to all lands and to all languages. After exhorting them to live according to the *Rule* and to follow in the footsteps of the Fathers, he bids them consult with their messenger, Peter, about his answer to their question.

(1065–1071)

O SIR M——, the venerable abbot of the monastery of St. Mary in Constantinople,[1] and to the other brothers, the monk Peter the sinner sends greetings in the Lord.

(2) Let us rejoice, my dear brothers, because while living among foreigners in a land speaking an alien tongue, you have not, as I learned from reports that came my way, been exiled from the Catholic faith and good works. Therefore, "as fellow citizens with the saints and members of God's household,"[2] you are not abandoning your own home, so long as you live within the confines of the holy Church and strive to walk the line of an upright way of life. Obviously, the court of heaven is open equally to residents of any land on earth, and where the values of true belief and a holy lifestyle are the same, diversity or variety of language does not stand in the way. For wherever a servant of God may live, it behooves him to divest himself of worldly and carnal deeds, and as one dead to this world, with untiring steps always to tread the path of virtue.

(3) This is why the fingers and toes of King Adonibezek's

---

1. Perhaps Abbot Maurus. Cf. Reindel, *Briefe* 3.437, nn. 1–2.
2. Eph 2.19.

hands and feet were cut off,[3] to clearly demonstrate that all secular deeds and advancement should be cut away from us. Adonibezek is interpreted to mean "the lord of destructive power."[4] To whom else does this refer but to the devil? Surely, he is the lord of destructive power, the author of violence and madness, just as our Lord, on the contrary, is said by the prophet to be "the father for all time, the Prince of peace."[5] And as Scripture relates, this Adonibezek said, "I once had seventy kings, the fingers and toes of whose hands and feet were cut off, picking up the scraps from under my table. What I have done to others, the Lord has done to me."[6] Therefore, what are we to understand by the seventy kings but the nations speaking seventy languages, the extremities of whose hands and feet the evil spirit has cut off? By so doing, he does not allow every people to lead good lives, nor walk in the path of justice. But our Redeemer cut off the extremities of both hands and feet of Adonibezek, that is, the enemy of the human race, when he restrained his chosen ones from performing evil deeds and from living sinful lives.

(4) And so, my dear friends, do not allow this tyrant to rule over you, him, you can be sure, whom the sword of divine justice has mutilated. Therefore, enrich your spirit with the power of your desire for God. With fervent effort yearn for the glory of the heavenly kingdom, carefully repress all enticements to carnal pleasure, and always progress toward God by observing the monastic life in the footsteps of the holy Fathers. And thus, as you strive to keep on the path of justice, you will come to the author of justice and of all holiness himself.

(5) My dear brothers, may almighty God rescue you from the hands of your ancient enemy, from pilgrims convert you into fellow citizens, and bring you within the walls of the heavenly Jerusalem, where there is no diversity of language or purpose. On the question, however, about which you wished to consult me, be sure to inquire of your messenger, brother Peter, and observe whatever he shall orally report to you.

3. Cf. Judg 1.6
4. Cf. Jerome, *Nom. Hebr.* 31.8 (CC 72.98).
5. Isa 9.6.
6. Judg 1.7.

LETTER 132

Peter Damian to his nephew, Marinus. Drawn by family affection, Damian paternally advised the young religious at whose investiture as a monk at St. Apollinaris in Classe he had personally officiated. His advice to Marinus stressed the virtues of chastity, sobriety in food and drink—in the course of which he appears to give evidence of an expert knowledge of wines—and the custody of the eyes when in the presence of women. He should practice sincere confession of his sins, selectively imitate the good example of others, and avoid hypocrisy and the distracting influence of worldly affairs in his conversation. Instead of bragging about the gentility of his ancestors, he should seek nobility in his profession as a follower of Christ. This letter is perhaps Damian's most comprehensive discussion of the virtues proper to the monastic life.

(1065–1071)

THE MONK PETER THE SINNER to the boy Marinus, greetings in the Lord.

(2) The raw recruit is easily defeated in his first taste of combat in battle, unless he uses beforehand the good offices of the drillmaster and is carefully instructed. You, too, who only recently swore your oath and joined the army of God, who in professing this holy purpose enrolled in the junior auxiliary of the armed forces, know that in preparing yourself for service in spiritual combat, you need to be more fully trained, in that you have engaged to do battle in a heavenly division rather than an earthly one. Of which truly the Apostle says, "Although we walk in the flesh, we do not fight according to the flesh. The weapons we wield are not those of the world, but are divinely potent."[1]

1. 2 Cor 10.3–4.

(3) Moreover, because you are related to me by blood, since you are my nephew,² I think that care for your welfare more urgently depends on me by reason of your tender years, which need another's help, and this seems to be the case because the duty of close relationship demands it. For, since the Apostle is of the opinion that he who is promoted to the office of bishop must have children who are submissive in all chastity,³ in the catalogue of virtues appropriate to a future bishop he lists his children's purity and obedience.⁴ Although you are not my son, you can still not rightly be considered as someone exempt from my care, since you are related to me through my brother. This is especially so, since I myself invested you with the monastic habit and therefore not without cause may I consider myself absolved from giving you advice.

(4) First of all, my dear son, with great vigilance strive to preserve chastity and abstain from every sin of deadly impurity, that according to the Apostle, "you may learn to gain mastery over your body, to hallow and honor it."⁵ This is, indeed, the moral purity without which no one will see God. Preserve the garment of your body in spotless condition, that at the marriage feast of this great king it may not be found soiled by the filth of wanton lust.

(5) May chastity always abide in your body, always in your mind, that its lilies may shine brightly from your undisciplined flesh, as from a piece of plow land, and that its root may also remain undamaged and possessed of all its vigor. Should carnal pleasure entice you, and temptations to impurity arise, quickly have recourse to the weapons suggested by the Apostle,⁶ and like an eager soldier take up the sword of the Gospel.⁷ With Christ as your leader, you will easily be able to cut down the fierce lines of the barbarous enemy. One thing is important: that sobriety should daily be your sole companion, and it

---

2. Cf. Neukirch, *Leben* 115, no. 144. He considers Marinus to be a nephew, and refers to *Letter* 153.73, where Marinus is again called *fratruelis*. This word may also be translated "cousin"; cf. Lucchesi, *Vita* no. 154.
   3. Cf. 1 Tim 3.4.　　　　　　4. Cf. Titus 1.6.
   5. 1 Thess 4.4.　　　　　　　6. Cf. Eph 6.13–17.
   7. Cf. Luke 22.49.

should never be allowed to part from your company under the influence of prurient gluttony. When the visceral passages are filled with juices engendered by food, then undoubtedly the fires of passion tend to burn more fiercely. Now this disorder is warded off by dryness, and when the humor of a weakened body diminishes, this disease grows powerless for lack of moisture. Clearly, just as fire is opposed to water, so lust is opposed by cold. Therefore, when the stimulant of food deserts the natural warmth of the body, the fervor of lust will also be extinguished.

(6) And so, I would not have you longing for sumptuous foods, nor freely indulging in wine, nor at times daring to discuss the variety of its color and bouquet: this one is made worse by the thin Lagean[8] wine, while a strain of earthy frailty weakens the other. This variety, moreover, is red like the Thasian,[9] and the other glows with the golden hue of the Mareotic.[10] Bah, this vintage is flat, it has been baptized! I surely expected to be served wine, but it seems that very little wine was mixed with this water. To this wine the Aminean[11] vine makes a real contribution, but Rhaetic[12] almost surpasses it. You should not wish to know about the bouquet of Argitis,[13] or the wine of Rhodes,[14] or what lively sweetness Tmolian[15] produces when blended with purple Precian[16] and Psithian.[17] For these are all tokens of philosophizing gluttony, the occasion for the abomination of drinking to excess.

(7) Therefore, in taking food, moderation lessens its roughness, and small portions will improve its commonness. Nor does it suffice to restrain gluttony when faced with more elegant foods, unless one has learned moderation in using those that are ordinary. For at times one can be guilty of gluttony when partaking of everyday food, just as you can take pleasure

---

8. Cf. Virgil, *Georgics* 2.93; Isidore, *Etymologies* 17.5.16.
9. Cf. Virgil, *Georgics* 2.91.
10. Cf. Virgil, *Georgics* 2.91; Isidore, *Etymologies* 17.5.25.
11. Cf. Virgil, *Georgics* 2.97.   12. Cf. Virgil, *Georgics* 2.96.
13. Cf. Virgil, *Georgics* 2.99; Isidore, *Etymologies* 17.5.23.
14. Cf. Virgil, *Georgics* 2.102; Isidore, *Etymologies* 17.5.15 and 17.
15. Cf. Virgil, *Georgics* 2.98.   16. Cf. Virgil, *Georgics* 2.95.
17. Cf. Virgil, *Georgics* 2.93.

in having intercourse with a deformed prostitute. To be sure, one who customarily fills his stomach with a small portion of dry bread, is not likely to be a judge of choice foods. He who fears drinking water until he has had his fill, will not try to overindulge when drinking wine. Hence, if you wish to live by the rules of sobriety when confronted with delicacies, be careful not to loosen the reins of gluttony with regard to simple foods. For why must we seek out delightful foods, which obviously are very expensive, since they have no taste before they enter the mouth, and after they are swallowed, make no difference to the stomach that they enter? Therefore, our entire journey toward pleasure, which we pursue so ambitiously, is summed up on the fingers of one hand: whoever desires Christ and eats of that bread that came down from heaven,[18] will pay little attention to precious foods that are the material from which dung is made. For what is not perceived by the senses after one's appetite is sated, should be for you the same as bread and vegetables. And if gluttony does not satisfy itself, but only the stomach, why does it choose something that is more delicious, since it is all the same to the stomach?

(8) Therefore, lest purity be imperiled by shipwreck, let sobriety be the mistress of your body and keep a steady helm amid the hazards of this uncertain life. Also be on your guard against thoughts you ought to dispel, because you should not be more earnest in restraining the lustful movements of your body than in protecting your mind from shameful thoughts and imaginations. I once knew a brother in Christ who followed this strict norm of constant custody over his mind, that as soon as some suggestion to impurity crept up on him, he would promptly say to himself, as if he were ready to travel, "Come, let us go to the circus." Then, in his imagination wandering through all the cemeteries and graves, he would carefully examine the matter and corruption of decaying bodies, the crawling worms and the rot of decomposing flesh. And as he thought that this flesh, once in its prime so full of vitality, was now subject to such disaster, he concluded that his body too would be in the same condi-

---

18. Cf. John 6.33.

tion that he now observed. Such meditation puts an end to lustful thoughts, because it holds up corruption to our view; nor is there any room for passion when the mind dwells on the grave. Oh, how often did this brother apply a red-hot knife or blade to his genitals, as if it were a cautery, so that at the crackling sound of frying flesh, he seemed to smell in vivid fashion the stench that rose to his nose.

(9) When at times it becomes necessary, and you are unable to avoid speaking with a woman, always glance to the side as if you were looking at someone else, act as if you were not there, speak as if you were a long way off, stop your conversation and look down to the floor, so that you would be unable to say whether her complexion was pale or ruddy. Once, as the blessed Romuald returned from a meeting with the countess of Sibylla, he is reported to have slyly said to his disciple who accompanied him, "What an elegant and beautiful face this woman has, if only she had not unfortunately lost one eye." And the disciple replied, "You are mistaken, master," he said, "for as I carefully observed her beautiful face, I saw nothing at all wrong with her eyes." Then at once the master severely corrected him: "And who," he said, "taught you to look at a woman's face?" At that, the disciple was aware that he had been taken in, was ashamed of what he had said and asked pardon, and firmly promised that from then on he would be more cautious.

(10) In fact, our crafty adversary is a painter. Yet, while he can easily cause us to remember things we had once seen, he can hardly produce on the walls of our mind the images of things that are unknown to us. So, if you would wish to advance to the heights of perfection, you must henceforth make every effort to be instructed in all the virtues. For, while at your age you are still pliable, and your habits are still unformed, they are indiscriminately led in this direction or that. Therefore, let the practice of virtue grow apace with your bodily development, that custom may lighten what the weakness of human frailty finds abhorrent. So now let the small size of the intestines adapt itself to minimal amounts of food, so that while presently the stomach is led on by its very vigor, it will later be easily satisfied with a small measure of nourishment.

(11) Your tongue should be accustomed to restricting itself to a few words, and should learn from holding its peace what by speaking it may later find difficult to bear, so that if now it neglects to observe strict silence, it will later be unable to control the sensual urge to speak. May your knees grow numb from frequent genuflections, and in fact, let your other members be tamed by various penitential practices lest, like some, you may later be seen standing there rigid and unbending, and empty-handed, as they say, preparing to give worship to Ceres. Be careful of your duty to show courtesy, and always be prompt to refuse deference that is offered to you, but instead always be prepared to serve others. When something must be prepared or brought, immediately rise to the occasion, that it may appear that the voice of authority was directed especially toward you.

(12) Yet, of this I would particularly like to warn you to take careful note, not to be offended by the private fasts of some of your brothers. For I am aware of the vices of some people who are just like me. Indeed, some are so tormented by malice, and are so bitter with envy when others are fasting, that they convert the latter's well-being into their own destruction and, as I might put it, fall headlong from the ladder that was the means of progress for others. "One is only allowed to act," they say, "in accordance with the common rule of the monastery or in imitation of the example of our superiors."[19] To which one can easily reply, that since "rule" derives from "ruling,"[20] it would rather seem to apply to strict fasting than to dissolute living, or to the stomach's voracious appetite. And therefore, those should rightly be considered to be among our great predecessors whose example we should follow, who are known to have entered by the narrow gate, and to have lived according to the law of sobriety and the strict discipline of the cross of Christ. Wherefore, when disagreement arises over the word "rule," the

---

19. *Benedicti regula* 7: "Octavus humilitatis gradus est, si nihil agat monachus nisi quod communis monasterii regula vel maiorum cohortantur exempla." [The eighth step of humility is: let the monk do only what the common rule of the monastery or the example of the elders urge.]

20. Cf. Isidore, *Etymologies* 6.16.1.

latter should rather be challenged to practice fasting, than have the former restrained from the rigorous choice they have made. And do not resent corrections, but freely accept them, no matter how unpleasant or many they may be. For, as gold or silver is made to shine by polishing, so also our soul, when rubbed by correction, is purged of its sins as from a kind of rust or tarnish.

(13) Beware, moreover, lest by the example of others, when you refuse to obey, you fall into biting and complaining calumny, God forbid, against a negligent superior. And so, you should be reminded of Samuel who was so patient and humble in devoting himself to his lazy and slow-moving master, that he came running to him three times when he was called in the dead of the night, and did not complain that his sleep had been repeatedly interrupted. Surely, he could then have objected and found fault with him, and said, "Why are you not ashamed to use such authority on a stranger, while you neglect giving orders to your own sons?" But as Scripture relates, he did not get excited and reproach him with his complaints, but promptly complying with his command, simply said, "You called me: here I am."[21]

(14) Have you sinned now and then? There is, surely, no one who does not commit sin, and perhaps it has come to your attention that the first raft available after shipwreck is the straightforward confession of sin, for prompt confession produces easy forgiveness. But if one takes refuge in defending a false position, what was perhaps slightly punctured by a needle will be seen as broadly pierced through by a lance. Thus it happened that, when David was accused of committing a crime, as soon as he confessed his sin, saying, "I have sinned against the Lord,"[22] he at once heard these words from the lips of the prophet: "The Lord has laid on another the consequences of your sin: you shall not die."[23] And since this is the proper occasion, I should not like to have you deceived: there are some who have lived in a religious order since they were boys, and perish only because

---

21. 1 Kgs 3.5.
22. 2 Kgs 12.13.
23. 2 Kgs 12.13.

of disobedience, mixed with pride, while many living in the world, after committing horrible crimes, are deserving of forgiveness through the practice of humility. Note that David was guilty of adultery and murder,[24] while Saul, on the other hand, disobeyed Samuel.[25] But why is it that the one, without assistance from anyone, immediately found forgiveness, while neither his own admission of guilt, nor the sad, bitter, and lengthy appeal of the prophet could reconcile the other to God? Evidently, if we widely search the writings of Scripture, we find Saul speaking at greater length about his repentance than David. The latter used the words that I quoted above, "I have sinned against the Lord," while the former said, "I have sinned because I ignored the Lord's command and your orders: I was afraid of the people and deferred to them."[26] And later, repeating the same process, he said, "I have sinned."[27] And then followed the long-suffering prayer of Samuel, of whom Scripture plainly says, "And Samuel was grieved, and all night he cried aloud to the Lord."[28] But what did the divine voice say to him in reply? "How long will you mourn for Saul because I have rejected him as king over Israel?"[29]

(15) What is the meaning of this, that the repentance of one man is lovingly received, while the other's is rejected and severely punished, except that Saul by proudly making light of the sin of disobedience, never wholeheartedly repented, while David, on the other hand, used only a few words, but the bitterness of true sorrow filled his whole being, transfixed by the sword of the fear of God? Those, I say, who, when pretending to be obedient, impudently brag that they are immune to committing greater crimes, should not neglect to consider these matters. Indeed, we often see some of these frequently going to confession, devoutly prostrating themselves on the ground, facetiously rather than humbly accusing themselves in ringing and elaborate words, and thus never having their behavior profit from proper correction. Such, to be sure, like Saul repent in word but remain proud at heart.

24. Cf. 2 Kgs 11.26–27.
26. 1 Kgs 15.24.
28. 1 Kgs 15.11.
25. Cf. 1 Kgs 13.8–9.
27. 1 Kgs 15.30.
29. 1 Kgs 16.1.

(16) When you are in good health, do not of your own accord give in to fatigue. Are you listening to what I am saying? For this greatly disturbs me in many monasteries, that some monks who are physically sound and have no need of medical attention today submit themselves to the phlebotomist who will open their veins, tomorrow make use of leeches, and on the day after tomorrow prepare different kinds of medication. In the meantime the finest wheat is milled, and cakes are made under the most exact conditions and then baked only over cooling embers. Rivers and seas are thoroughly searched and the butcher's stalls are empty because the fish had stayed too deep and could not be put up for sale. It is even thought to be a happy misfortune if a district that abounded in fish is found to be unproductive, since necessity begets plenty, while plenty breeds poverty. Meanwhile, for whatever kind of animal that is brought in for slaughter, whether found on land or in the sea, a skilled cook must be sought. He must regulate the fire with such discretion that, with a skilled and masterful use of temperature, it reaches to the bone and still does not burn the surface of the meat. Like some sleight of hand, the heat seems to pass over the exterior without touching it, but in passing seems to penetrate to the innermost part. But why need I say more? At length, when sitting at table or even lying down, these monks take dainty food for their squeamish stomach, and with avid fastidiousness certainly do not require someone to prove that the maladies they invent are true.

(17) Never become ambitious, moreover, to be elected superior, so that when you come to die, you are unaware of your own vocation. In my time there was a certain monk in the same monastery of Classis where you now live, who was appointed assistant prior and eagerly sought to become the abbot there. But while doing everything he could, assembling committees, scheming, and tirelessly hammering out his deceptions, he became ill and was brought to death's door. In that state he suddenly became delirious, unable to say what rationally crossed his mind. "See," he said, "I shall soon have it, they are going to give me the monastery. There is the staff, I shall take it and I will have won." And so, with these words on his lips, he died,

and left the brothers with an unfavorable opinion of his future.

(18) Pay no heed to those who are negligent, but give close attention to monks who are zealous and careful about their soul. The former should be viewed, not with the intention of judging their evil deeds, but the latter, that you might learn to emulate their good example and practice it. And so, select for yourself some of the brothers, namely, the outstanding ones in the community, whose good life you can safely imitate. And that you may more easily reach the objective toward which I am leading you, I will relate the following story about the ancients. The inhabitants of Crotona at great cost hired Zeuxis of Heraclea to paint an outstanding portrait of Diana, and by using every skill of his art, produce an image of her that would surpass all others. He then requested them to gather all the girls of the city in one public showing, that he might derive the elegance of his future work from their beauty. But since it was improper for these good and modest girls to appear in public, their brothers were brought to the wrestling school, that the painter could learn from their handsome appearance how much more beautiful their sisters were. But since nature had not endowed all of them with the same good qualities, because what it had given to one part of the body it often denied to the other, and while one and the same body was outstanding for this feature, it suffered from some defect in another: the painter chose only five from the scrutiny of all these boys, and used them to form a composite of the ideal beauty he sought.[30]

(19) But why do I protract this long narrative? I do so only that you should choose just a few from the many who are available, and use them as a model as you strive to fashion the beauty of the spiritual man. For example, just as the painter borrowed from one the sparkling eyes, from another the less prominent ears, and from still another the milk-white cheeks diffused with a ruby glow, so you too should learn prompt obedience from one, and from another fervent charity; from this

---

30. Cf. Cicero, *De inventione rhetorica* 2.1.1–3. Damian's narrative differs significantly from the source, where Zeuxis is asked to paint the portrait of Helen and, after seeing the boys, asked to view their sisters.

one how to spend the night in prayer, and from that the practice of long periods of silence. Just as the artist transformed the qualities of various bodies into one beautiful image, so by using the differing virtues of holy men you too may renew in yourself the image of the one true God, that later you may happily return to recognize that very God himself.

(20) Carefully avoid duplicity. Be straightforward, so that your words reflect what you have in mind. Unleavened bread, to be sure, is long-lasting because of its firmness, while leavened bread is spoiled when it becomes filled with holes. In unleavened bread one finds sincerity and truth, but in leavened bread there is corruption and wickedness.[31] He who lives simply, is the unleavened bread and has put on a new nature, but he who practices double-dealing is leavened bread, and persists in the error of his former life, and hence does not arrive at the grace of a new beginning. For what good is it to profess in words that one is a Christian, when in reality he is an antichristian?

(21) Always be totally involved in the Prophets, totally imbued with the Gospels. At all times occupy your mind with various readings from Scripture, so that no part of it will allow the admission of fantasy and idle thoughts. But if perhaps the language distresses you, and the honeyed sweetness of God is tasteless on the lips of your heart, the prophet says, "How sweet are your words, O Lord, in my mouth, sweeter on my tongue than honey."[32] Pray, fast, and cut yourself off from all the pleasures of earthly delight, so that what appears insipid, not of itself but on your own account, may become sweet in your mouth. We are aware that those young men who decided not to touch the food assigned to them by the king were deemed worthy to receive in exchange knowledge and understanding of books of every kind. In addition, for being the leader in this decision Daniel was given the gift of interpreting all visions and dreams.[33] What a wonderful way God has of repaying us, that those who refrain from indulging in carnal pleasures find their mind free to enjoy the riches of spiritual understanding. There-

---

31. Cf. 1 Cor 5.8.
33. Cf. Dan 1.17.
32. Ps 118.103.

fore, let your flesh become dry, that your mind may feast on luxurious food.

(22) One should avoid delicacies in eating, so that he who judges in secret may observe the wars that are waged within us, and may set before us the rich fare of heavenly nourishment in exchange for food that will turn into excreta. Nor should you improperly attach the wrong meaning to what that man of God, Romuald, had to say to his disciples. "Brothers," he said, "whenever you are dining in a monastery, while others are intent on the food set before them, eat sparingly at the beginning of the meal, and when the others appear to have had their fill, you should then begin. In that way you can avoid playing the hypocrite, and without giving offense can observe the rule of sobriety." At Pomposa I further observed a monk, superbly trained in the law of God and in regular discipline, who, as the story has it, mutually agreed with the brother who sat next to him that when, according to custom, a personal carafe of wine was placed before each of them, both would be satisfied with the daily allotment that was meant for one of them, and thus the two used to satisfy themselves by practicing sobriety. But in the heat of summer, which was extreme in that area, when his companion was absent he allowed the wine in his own carafe to turn sour, to the point that worms were often found swimming about in the glass.

(23) And then there was Martin the Bald, for that was the name people gave him. When he was dying, and his whole body had grown to monstrous size caused by the humor of dropsy, he requested that all of us who had gathered round his bed should each in turn do him the favor of scourging him with the discipline. Once he had died in perfect faith after devoutly confessing his sins, he later appeared in a dream to one of the brothers. He was in a verdant and flower-filled grove in some most brilliant region, clothed in a white stole, his face suffused with light. But he was lying on a couch adorned with wondrously beautiful coverings. Let this part of my story about him be sufficient, however, else in completing my narrative, I will exceed the bounds of epistolary brevity.

(24) I had, indeed, here decided to call a halt to my writing,

but when I see someone who is dry after having thirsted so long, it would be a sign of excessive greed to give him only a small ladleful of wine to drink. Therefore, beware, my dear son, lest as you go on living in the monastic cloister, you take part in discussing secular affairs with your brothers; disdain both speaking about them as well as listening to them. In fact, holy anger should take over on the spot, and burning zeal should promptly silence those who give vent to such silly and improper speech. You should say, "What has an upright life to do with wickedness? Can light consort with darkness?"[34]

(25) In truth, what business has a monk involving himself with the trifling affairs of laymen? To what purpose should I carry within the confines of the monastery the noisy courts of justice, the tribunals of judges, or the courts of kings? What good is it to tell a dead man about battles, or to speak of dowries to those whose marriage has been broken up by divorce? To regale some with noble titles of their birth, or to defame others for being as recent as the shoemaker? What is this foolish preoccupation with these and other inane things, but to divert our mouths from the clear waters of divine praise and to soil our lips with filth and mud? And so the Lord deservedly complains in the words of Jeremiah, "Two sins have my people committed: they have forsaken me, a spring of living water, and they have hewn out for themselves cisterns, cracked cisterns that can hold no water."[35] In fact, look at the structure of our monastery, and note that it is four-sided, that the very shape of the house may clearly teach that it is to our benefit to be separated on all sides from the disturbances of a worldly life.

(26) It is most improper and unbecoming, moreover, and evidently totally absurd for what is generally spewed forth in the taverns where drinks are served, for what is daily discussed in the houses where women are spinning and weaving, to be the topic of conversation in the choir of holy monks. Surely, where I see the prophets and apostles eager to speak to me, where I behold Christ explaining his Gospel for me, should I

---

34. 2 Cor 6.14.
35. Jer 2.13.

abandon them to inquire whether ships recently crossing the Adriatic had yet landed, to ask about the price of salt, or whether the official had set a higher price for a measure of corn? Therefore, let all this foolish gossip be removed from the lips of the knight of Christ, and let the tongue that is reddened by the Blood of the immaculate Lamb, indeed, of the most high Word himself, disdain being contaminated by the dregs of idle speech.

(27) Do not speak ill of anyone, and consider it below your dignity even to listen to detractors. "Have nothing to do with detractors," Solomon says, "for suddenly disaster will overtake them, and who knows what the ruin of such men will be?"[36] This will be the case, both with him who calumniates another, and with him who listens to detraction. If occasion demands, you should rather reprove the offender for the sin he has committed, be rough with him, and do not be afraid to upbraid him severely to his face. But you must not attack someone who is absent, nor speak of him in biting terms in the presence of others. Yet it often happens, I know not why, that we patiently put up with one who savagely reproaches us, when we are unable to bear with one who accuses us even slightly. Make this demand on yourself that your disposition be always in accord with the mind of your abbot, and never follow your own decisions, but always humbly comply with his command. Therefore, beg God to make him an instrument of his truth for you, and discern what should be done with you according to the disposition of his will.

(28) Do not ever draw up a genealogy of your forebears, that you might boast of the empty nobility of someone else's name. Surely, he who is an heir of God and a coheir with Christ surpasses every family of earthly origin. Truly, it is a grand thing to be a Christian, not just to appear or be called such. And he who is displeasing to God more often pleases the world. In fact, some seem to use artful skill in exaggerating the fame of their evil ancestors by appearing to disparage them, and that they might seem to have been powerful and magnificent men, ac-

---

36. Prov 24.21–22.

cuse them of pride or even cruelty. Do you understand what I am saying? I accuse Achilles of being guilty of shedding much blood, that you may think that he was vigorous in the cause of war. I denounce Hannibal for invading Italy, that you may have no doubt that he was daring and strong.

(29) Remember frequently to engage in prayer, that with your body prostrate on the ground, your spirit may rise up to heaven. Often go to sleep with an empty stomach, and let sleep soothe the thirst you take with you to bed. Keeping vigil at night, practiced in moderation, is productive of perfect prayer, but indiscriminate idleness often becomes the occasion for talking, for he who is unable to read or pray because he cannot keep his eyes from shutting or his lips from yawning, will now and then find time to engage in idle chatting. Wherefore, put off going to bed till it is late, but rise in good time for night prayers. Drowsiness should anticipate your retiring, and retiring should not come before you are sleepy, so that the more difficult it is to give in to necessity postponed, the more eagerly will the tired body take to sleep.

(30) Meanwhile, avoid rumormongers, gloryseekers, and fawning flatterers as you would the bite of a venomous snake, and as antidotes for their poison they should at once hear the words, "Let them quickly be turned away in shame who cry 'Hurrah' at me."[37] I am not content that you be mediocre, my son, for I wish to see in you the very best, the most perfect. Therefore, put aside all idleness and sloth, consider yourself to be your own enemy, fight and battle with yourself and, armed with the sword of evangelical discipline, cut off the heads of all the vices that are at war with you. Always bearing hardships and adversities for the love of Christ, trust in the practice of virtue. Shudder at whatever appears pleasurable and soothing to the flesh, and count it as truly a snare of the devil. For whoever hopes to find allurements of the flesh in the monastic way of life is only trying to squeeze juice from a dry stick. Cut off from your lips every kind of scurrility, urbane wit, and the pleasantries of charming speech as you would the foreskin of the

37. Ps 69.4.

Gentiles. We are, you know, the disciples of fishermen and not orators, and one should hear from the mouth of a Christian, not the Latinity of Cicero, but the simplicity of Christ. Subduing all your own desires, like the Apostle gird yourself at all times with the sufferings of Christ, and always show that you bear the stigmata of the cross so that the more closely you now follow in the footsteps of him who was sentenced to death, the more eminently you may enjoy his company when he comes as your judge.

(31) Greet all the holy brothers of your monastery for me. But if you should find my dear brothers, Boninus and Peter, singing like angels, as at times they are wont to do, in my name give them this small poem:

> Like a nightingale's sweet serenade is the song you intone in the choir,
> Let the innermost voice of your heart be at tune to the chant you are singing.

LETTER 133

Peter Damian to all of his hermit communities. Fearing a loss of vocations to hermit living, Damian in this letter prescribed limits in the use of the discipline by his subjects. While admitting that "the bark of this practice was worse than its bite," that fear of it was greater than the pain inflicted, he nevertheless restrained his hermits from voluntary excesses, quoting Deuteronomy to sustain his new ruling. Instead, they should discipline the spirit and resolutely perform other good works.

(1065–1070)

TO THE HOLY BRETHREN living in the hermitage, the monk Peter the sinner sends his greetings.

(2) The rule of discretion is properly observed in a community of spiritual brothers, if the guidance the prior provides imitates the attention he gives a horse. It is obvious that he uses the spur to urge it on, the reins to hold it back. He goads on the horse that is moving too slowly, and curbs one that is prancing and proudly neighing. Similarly, the superior of the brothers must both urge on the sluggish by using words of exhortation to stimulate them, and to those who are moving more impetuously than they should, he will apply the reins of discretion.

(3) Did not Moses urge on the people of Israel with a kind of goad, if I may use the word, when he said, "Each of you set aside a contribution to the Lord. Let all who wish and have a ready heart offer it to the Lord: gold, silver, and brass; violet, purple, and scarlet twice-dyed, fine linen, goats' hair, and rams' skins dyed red, acacia wood, and oil for the lamps"?[1] And did he not curb that same people who were moving too fast, by using the bridle of moderation when he forbade them to offer

---

1. Exod 35.5–8.

their gifts? For it is written, "when they set to work, the people brought freewill offerings morning after morning, whereupon the workmen were compelled to come and said to Moses: 'The people are bringing much more than we need.'"[2] And then the text continued, "So Moses sent word round the camp that no man or woman should prepare anything more as a contribution for the sanctuary."[3]

(4) And now, to get to the matter for which all of this is a preamble. You holy and devout men are not unaware, my dear brothers, that this scourging with the discipline to which you are so fervently dedicated, when practiced in moderation could be beneficial to you, but admittedly when applied indiscreetly can be harmful. On this account, then, your bodies grow tired and weak, and occasionally, as some think, they succumb to sickness when subjected to so many blows, especially when some of you daily recite one continual psalter or even two, while taking the discipline. To this I might add, that when some brothers, wishing to come to the hermitage, hear these things, they are deterred and overwhelmed by fear. And since the discipline is thought to be more appalling than it actually is, and the fear of it is greater than the pain it inflicts, when certain weaker brothers hear that you use it for such long periods, they are completely overawed, and are promptly restrained from entering the hermitage.

(5) Wherefore, using a mitigating norm of discretion, I ordain that no one in the hermitage shall be forced to practice autoflagellation. But when holy fervor incites one to this method of penance, he is permitted to take the discipline during the recitation of forty psalms in any given day, to this extent that he does not exceed the total of forty psalms. Yet, during the two Lents that precede Christmas and the holy feast of Easter, it is permitted to go to sixty psalms, accompanied by the discipline, and let no one, God forbid, rashly presume to go beyond this rule of moderation that I have prescribed. In this way, therefore, I am not removing something that is good, but plac-

2. Exod 36.3–5.
3. Exod 36.6.

ing limits on what is superfluous. Nor am I denying the brothers something that contributes to their welfare, but setting discretionary bounds. If he wishes, each may take advantage of going as far as the law allows, but it will not be permitted to go beyond.

(6) By acting in this fashion, I am not, as it were, exceeding my authority, but am imitating the example found in God's law. For through Moses the Lord says in Deuteronomy, "If a guilty man is sentenced to be flogged, the judge shall cause him to lie down and be beaten in his presence."[4] And the text then continues, "The number of strokes shall correspond to the gravity of the offense. They may give him forty strokes, but not more lest from excessive beating your brother die before your eyes."[5] Note that the Lord commanded the sinner to be scourged, and still limited the number of blows, so that while punishing the guilty one, he used discretion in moderating the rigor of the punishment.

(7) And so, my dear brothers, observe this norm in taking the discipline, chastise your spirit instead, and dutifully perform other virtuous deeds, that the most high God, who will remunerate your passing exertions, may see fit to compensate you with rewards that will last forever.

4. Deut 25.2.
5. Deut 25.2–3.

LETTER 134

Peter Damian to the brothers in all his hermitages. With concern for the peace and harmony of his communities after his death, he commanded them under pain of excommunication to restore to its proper hermitage whatever in their house had not been given them as a gift in perpetuity.

(1065–1071)

O ALL THE BROTHERS living in each of the hermitages under the care of my administration, the monk Peter the sinner assures you of the bond of his love for all.

(2) You know, my dear brothers, that these houses that have been committed to me, are as one while I am alive, and that whatever things are needed pass indiscriminately to you from this house, and are also brought by you to this hermitage as fraternal harmony demands. And I beg the Holy Spirit that after I am dead, the same harmony flourish among you that now by the bond of charity unites you in one heart and one soul.

(3) But now I am constrained to counsel you with cautious provision, lest perhaps after your charity has grown cool, self-love provide a stumbling block among you over keeping any one thing in your possession. Wherefore, I adjure you and call you to witness before the bench of the terrible judge, that after my death, whatever belongs to another hermitage and you perhaps discover to be in your possession, you must restore immediately, and without any intrigue or crafty argument, purely and simply return whatever is not yours. Now, I say that whatever I did not confer on another in perpetuity should not be considered a gift but as the property of one house that I, because both were under my jurisdiction, allowed to remain in another.

(4) Whoever, therefore, shall violate this my decision, shall be subject to excommunication until he has done condign satisfaction.

LETTER 135

Peter Damian to Cencius, the prefect of Rome. This letter appears for the first time in Damian's letter collection, assembled from five fragments that survived in the *Liber testimoniorum veteris et novi testamenti (Collectanea)* of John of Lodi. While the fragments do not with certainty belong to one letter, they are sufficiently alike, and can be put together in the order of their appearance in the *Collectanea*. All the pieces contain interpretations of passages from the Old Testament, and illustrate the theme of purity in the spiritual life. This might seem to be heady stuff for the city manager of Rome, until one reads Damian's later *Letter* 145 (7 January 1067), where he commends Cencius for acting as a substitute homilist for him in St. Peter's Church on the feast of the Epiphany.

(1065–1071)

HEN A MAN HAS MARRIED a wife, and has had her, but she does not win his favor because he finds something shameful in her, he shall write a bill of divorce, give it to her, and dismiss her."[1] Therefore, would that this wife of ours, namely, the life of our body, never find favor with us, but as is proper, let its abhorrent filth always offend the sensibilities of our minds. Once she has accepted the bill of divorce according to the law of penance, may she be so finally dismissed from the confines of our marriage, that she may never again return to our embrace. And so, the wise man says, "Do not let your eyes linger on a woman's fine figure, or your thoughts dwell on beauty not yours to possess."[2] For since she is said to belong to another, she is rightly thought to be Hagar, who was not a wife, but a concubine.[3] Now Hagar may be said

1. Deut 24.1. 2. Sir 9.8.
3. Cf. Gen 16.2.

to mean "foreign woman" or a "neighbor."[4] And because, in the words of Solomon, this same shameless woman says, "I have sprinkled my bed with myrrh, aloes, and cassia,"[5] she can properly be compared with the second concubine of Abraham. Now Keturah[6] has the meaning "sweet smelling." Indeed, our bodily life smells of the perfume of falsehood. Hence, it is also said in Proverbs, "Be on your guard against a loose woman, and from the seductive tongue of a stranger. Do not desire her beauty in your heart."[7] For this seductive tongue, namely, that of the life of the body, prompts miserable men to say, "Come then, let us enjoy good things while we can, and make full use of creatures with all the eagerness of youth. Let us have costly wines and perfumes to our heart's content, and let no flower of spring escape us," and so forth.[8]

(2) But on the other hand, it is written of the woman who signifies the religious life, "A good wife makes a happy husband; she doubles the length of his life. A staunch wife is her husband's joy; he will live out his life in peace."[9] How is it that a man's years are twice as long, except that here he lives a holy life, and hereafter will be victorious in the glory of heaven? These two lives to be sure, the spiritual and the physical, are at variance with one another because of a kind of jealousy, and they entice the hearts of men to different goals. The former, indeed, restrains the urge to gluttony, so that one does not exceed the bounds of temperance in eating, while the latter rejoices in noisy and foolish amusement. The former lifts up one's spirit and holds it aloft with a longing for heaven, the latter burdens it with worldly affairs and the accumulation of wealth. The former patiently endures whatever begets injury or adversity, while the latter, on the other hand, is partial to useless violence, and occasions ordeals that must be borne.

(3) "So his servants searched all over Israel for a beautiful maiden for King David and found Abishag, a Shunammite, and brought her to the king. She slept with the king and took care of him, but he had no intercourse with her."[10] Who is this girl

4. Cf. Jerome, *Nom. Hebr.* 3.3 (CC 72.61).
5. Prov 7.17. 6. Cf. Gen 25.1.
7. Prov 6.24–25. 8. Wis 2.6–7.
9. Sir 26.1–2. 10. 1 Kgs 1.3–4.

who was especially selected from all the land of Israel, and presented to King David that she might sleep with him and warm him when he was cold? Inquire of Solomon, and he will explain to you the mystery of this girl: "Acquire wisdom," he says "and gain understanding."[11] Do you also wish to hear of this maiden's embrace? He says, "Do not forsake her, and she will keep you safe; love her, and she will lift you high; take hold of her, and she will bring you glory; honor her, and she will embrace you."[12]

(4) Let us, therefore, embrace wisdom, that is, a life of holiness, as our wife, that we might beget noble offspring, worthy of our inheritance. From such a wife the posterity that will succeed us will not die, but is destined to endure forever. Indeed, the issue bred of corruption must surely perish, but the child born of virginity cannot die. Nor is that which was begotten of incorruptibility subject to the defect of corruption. But let us examine the interpretation of these names that we may the better understand this mystery. Now, Abishag has the meaning "my overflowing father" or "the roar of my father." This overflowing father does not indicate a surplus that is not at all necessary, but the superabundant grace of God the Father. A roar, however, points to the powerful sound of sacred preaching, so that whoever lies in the embrace of Abishag, that is, the religious life, like the lion from the tribe of Judah,[13] may resound with the thunderous voice of holy preaching. But in our language the word Shunammite means "scarlet." Truly, a holy soul is reddened by the sacramental Blood of the Lord, and also burns with the fire of the Holy Spirit.

(5) So also in the handwriting [on the wall], Peres is said to mean scarlet,[14] which, by a mysterious separation, broke down the barrier between two nations, while Rahab the prostitute, typifying the Church, fastened a strand of scarlet cord to the house, that in the destruction of Jericho her family might be saved.[15] Thus also in another place Scripture says of holy men: "They are the people who were connected by marriage with the

11. Prov 4.5.
12. Prov 4.6–8.
13. Cf. Rev 5.5.
14. Cf. Dan 5.28.
15. Cf. Josh 2.18.

family of Rahab."[16] And Truth himself says in the Gospel, "I have come to set fire to the earth."[17] And this fire, as it burned in the hearts of the disciples, compelled them to say, "Did we not feel our hearts on fire as he talked with us on the road and explained the Scriptures to us?"[18] Therefore, his mystic and spiritual marriage begets the warmth of grace in the Shunammite, and in Abishag gives birth to the offspring of holy preaching, so that whoever bears this child in the innermost reaches of his heart, will not fail to manifest it in words. And what he bears in his heart as scarlet, he should bring forth in words with the mighty sound of holy preaching. And so, we conceive in the Shunammite the fire of divine love, that we might, as it were, give birth to this child of Abishag, the roaring sound of our preaching.

(6) "Prudence will keep watch over you, and rescue you from the adulteress, from the loose woman with her seductive words."[19] And a little farther on, "No one who resorts to her finds his way back or regains the path of life."[20] Who is this prostitute or loose woman whose access is forbidden to us, but the secular life, the physical and earthly life, into whose delights miserable men hurl themselves, in whose deceptive pleasures they dissipate their energy, and, if I might put it so, with adulterous embraces immerse themselves in her?

(7) But listen to what the same Solomon says of the good wife: "Let your fountain, the wife of your youth be blessed, rejoice in her."[21] Undoubtedly, the wife of our youth is the holy life, with which, to be sure, we were joined ever since by pledge and engagement when we promised in baptism that we would renounce the devil and all his display. And then the text goes on, "A lovely doe, a graceful hind, let her breasts inebriate you at all times, and may you continually delight in her love."[22] What is meant by the hind that climbs to the mountain top, if not the holy Church, which lifts itself up in the love of the heavenly fatherland? What is the significance of the hind's two

---

16. 1 Chr 2.55; cf. Sabatier 1.632. 17. Luke 12.49.
18. Luke 24.32. 19. Prov 2.11, 16.
20. Prov 2.19. 21. Prov 5.18.
22. Prov 5.19.

breasts, if not the two Testaments? We are inebriated at these two breasts when we bathe in the spring of sacred Scripture, and in our thirst drink of its spiritual wisdom. Therefore, we are commanded to delight in this wife, that we may be nourished by the food of heavenly eloquence.

(8) But then the text continues, "Why, my son, are you seduced by an adulteress and why do you embrace a loose woman?"[23] He, indeed, who takes pleasure in the delights of a carnal life is seduced by an adulteress. Not without cause is she called a loose woman, since she is forbidden us by command of God's law. And so, once again Solomon speaks of both women when he says, "Call Wisdom your sister, greet Understanding as your loved one, and protect yourself from the adulteress and from the loose woman with her seductive words."[24] And immediately he adds, "I glanced out of the windows of my house through the lattice, and there among the boys I noticed a foolish lad, passing along the street, at the corner, stepping out in the direction of her house."[25] Here we should note that the carnal life, which is called a prostitute, is described as being able to deceive only the young and foolish. Hence, elsewhere Solomon says, "The Lady Stupidity is a noisy creature; filled with allurements she knows nothing at all. She sits at the door of her house, on a seat in the highest part of the town, to invite passersby indoors as they hurry on their way. 'Come in, you simpletons,' she says. And she spoke to the fool."[26] Now he who is a mature man and has good sense, can never be deceived by the enticements of carnal pleasure, or overcome in the violent struggle with surging passions, no matter how frequent they may be. This woman is successful, and the earthly life of the flesh defeats only those whom a deliberately evil will and the foul smoke of earthly desire make blind. And so, the text rightly goes on, "At twilight, as the day faded, at dusk as the night grew dark, suddenly a woman came to meet him, dressed like a prostitute, prepared to deceive souls."[27]

(9) A life of the flesh inebriates the heart that dotes on lust,

23. Prov 5.20.
25. Prov 7.6–8.
27. Prov 7.9–10.
24. Prov 7.4.
26. Prov 9.13–16.

and makes it grow dark as on the blackest night, as it fails to lift the eyes of the soul toward heaven, but fixes them on the earth. And then the text continues, "A woman who is talkative and flighty, who cannot bear being quiet, never content to stay at home, lying in wait at every corner, now in the street, now in the public squares."[28] Here, moreover, he expresses the inconstancy of carnal men, subject to the vice of fickleness, and shamefully alienated from dignity. And to this he added, "I have woven my bed with cords, and covered it with colored linens brought from Egypt."[29] What else is meant here, but the pleasure of the flesh in which a lustful man throws himself as in a bed, and binds himself in the tangled chains of sin? And what else is meant by covering his bed with colored linens brought from Egypt, but the life of men living in luxury, never resting on the solid foundation of truth, but colored by the pretense and false likeness of deceit?

(10) Now when that prostitute says, "Come let us be inebriated with the breasts, and let us enjoy shared embraces, until the day appear. For my husband is not in his home; he has gone away on a long journey,"[30] this is what is meant: Christ is the faithful husband of every soul. He is not at his home, and goes on a long journey, when he sees the defilement of any man's conscience and therefore takes his leave. And then the text adds, "He has taken a bag of silver with him, until the moon is full he will not be home."[31] Now our Redeemer took with him a bag of silver, when at his ascension into heaven he carried with him the riches of our faith. He will return when the moon is full, that is, when the universal Church has run its course. For the Lord will come in judgment when the number of the elect has reached completion. But after having much to say of the pestilential cunning of this woman, with which she hunts the souls of the damned, which I do not choose to cite because of its length, he at length concludes, "Many has she pierced and laid low, and many brave men have been slain by her. Her house is the road to hell, which leads down to the halls of death."[32]

28. Prov 7.10–12.
29. Prov 7.16.
30. Prov 7.18–19.
31. Prov 7.20.
32. Prov 7.26.

(11) Again using the symbolic figure of woman, listen to what a difference there is between the spiritual and the carnal life. "A capable wife," he says, "is her husband's crown; one who disgraces him is like rot in his bones."[33] There is, then, rot in this woman's bones, for as anyone addicted to a carnal life tries to be superior to others, as he boasts of performing some great deed, which the bones here signify, his bad reputation spreads through the people and gives off a stench like that rising from rank decay. And of these women another wise man says, "If you have a wife after you own heart, do not divorce her; but do not trust yourself to one you cannot love."[34] A wife after one's own heart is a life of virtue, a holy life. But a wife you cannot love is a life according to the flesh, which you should surely hate. Indeed, if you do not trust yourself to her, it will be your fate, like Samson because of Delilah,[35] to fall into the hands of the enemy because of her. And in Deuteronomy it is written of this hateful woman, "When a man has married a wife and has lived with her, and she does not win his favor because he finds something shameful in her, he should write her a bill of divorce, give it to her, and dismiss her."[36]

33. Prov 12.4.
34. Sir 7.28.
35. Cf. Judg 16.20–21.
36. Deut 24.1.

LETTER 136

Peter Damian to the nun, Hermisindis. This letter is a reconstruction of a communication to a nun, found in the *Liber testimoniorum veteris et novi testamenti*. This work, entitled *Collectanea* by Gaetani, comes probably from the hand of Damian's biographer, John of Lodi, assembled before 1082. John omitted all personal references to the addressee, and used the selections to demonstrate Damian's style in scriptural exegesis. These excerpts illustrate the theme that the fabric of human pride soon falls apart.

(After 1065)

S MEN JOURNEYED IN THE EAST, they came upon a plain in the land of Shinar and settled there. They said one to another: 'Come, let us make bricks and bake them hard'; they used bricks for stone and bitumen for mortar."[1] Indeed, since Christ is truly the East,[2] as the prophet attests when he says, "Here is a man whose name is the East,"[3] those come from the east who by an evil life or by abusing their neighbors leave the company of Christ. Now Shinar may be said to mean "tearing out the teeth" or "their offensive odor."[4] And so, those settle in the plain of Shinar who are not living in the stronghold of virtue, but rather in the valley of vice; and they grow teeth, that by their detractions they may, as it were, gnaw and bite at their neighbors. And they give off an offensive odor as they begin to rot in the filth of their foul way of life. But almighty God tears out their teeth when he destroys the words and deeds of evil men. Hence, in the same chapter he also says, "That is why it is called Babel, because the Lord there made a

---

1. Gen 11.2–3. 2. Cf. Luke 1.78.
3. Zech 6.12.
4. Cf. Jerome, *Nom. Hebr.* 10.16 (CC 72.71).

babble of the language of all the world; from that place the Lord scattered men all over the face of the earth."[5]

(2) Therefore, it was rightly said that these proud men, who were also striving for empty fame as they said to one another, "Come, let us build ourselves a city and a tower with its top in the heavens, and make a name for ourselves before we are dispersed all over the earth,"[6] were living in the plain of Shinar, which in our language, as I said above, has the meaning "tearing out the teeth" or "their offensive odor." This interpretation is correct, because all evil men, as they take pride in opposing the commands of God's law, and in their heart arrogantly give themselves airs before God, often damnably disparage their neighbors while they themselves wallow more deeply in the cesspool of an obscene life. And indeed David said of the striking out of teeth, "You have struck all who oppose me without cause: you have broken the teeth of sinners."[7] And elsewhere he says, "God will break the teeth in their mouths: the Lord will break the jaws of the lions."[8] And yet another prophet speaks of their offensive odor, "The beasts have rotted in their dung."[9] And Isaiah: "Instead of perfume," he said, "you shall have the stench of decay."[10]

(3) Consequently, whoever wishes to build a structure that is not subject to quick collapse, must not use bricks and bitumen, which readily break apart, but rather stones and rock to form the walls, and cement of lime and gravel that will bind the walls together so that they will not fall. That these Babylonians we spoke of used bricks for stones and bitumen for cement is a symbol of the building that is the life of the flesh, that will be quickly destroyed by the force of the wind or the violence of the waves.

(4) The storecities that Pharaoh built of clay and straw,[11] namely, of clay that makes one dirty, and of straw that is destined for the fire, are called Pithom and Rameses, and are not without mystic significance. For Pithom may be said to mean

---

5. Gen 11.9.
6. Gen 11.4.
7. Ps 3.8.
8. Ps 57.7.
9. Joel 1.17.
10. Isa 3.24.
11. Cf. Exod 1.11.

"the mouth of the deep" or "suddenly."[12] And according to Paul's statement,[13] whoever now builds on the foundation that is Christ Jesus, using wood, hay, and straw, whatever the worth of each man's work might be, fire will test it. And the higher this structure of the carnal life rises, the deeper and more suddenly it will fall, to be swallowed by the whirling waters of the deep. Hence it was written, "They spend their lives in prosperity, and in a moment they go down to hell."[14] Therefore, both expressions, "the mouth of the deep" and "suddenly" are well employed, because one does not fall slowly from the heights of a carnal life, but rather suddenly, which this latter term implies, and that which seemed to be an ascent to the summit is actually the mouth of the deep, as the prophet asserts when he says, "When they were lifted up, you drove them headlong into ruin."[15] But Rameses is said to mean "food" or "moth."[16] For, all the damned are the food of the devil on whom he feasts as a wolf devouring the sheep, and he grows fat on their wickedness as if he were enjoying a banquet. Of them David also says, "Like sheep they run headlong into hell, and death shall feed upon them."[17]

(5) "The Lord said to Moses: 'Throw the staff you carry in your hand on the ground.' He threw it down and it turned into a snake. Moses was suddenly afraid, and ran away from it. And the Lord said to him: 'Seize it by the tail.' He took hold of it, and it again turned back into a staff."[18] We are all aware that the serpent brought about man's death. Therefore, death is derived from the serpent. But who is the staff if not Christ, of whom the prophet says, "a staff shall grow from the root of Jesse."[19] And so, the staff turned into a serpent, and Christ was brought to his death. Moses was afraid, and fled, which means that when the Lord hung on the cross and died, all the apostles

---

12. Cf. Jerome, *Nom. Hebr.* 13.6 (CC 72.75).
13. Cf. 1 Cor 3.13.   14. Job 21.13.
15. Ps 72.18.
16. Cf. Jerome, *Nom. Hebr.* 9.30 (CC 72.71).
17. Ps 48.15.
18. Cf. Exod 4.3–4 and Sabatier 1.142. Damian adapted this citation from Augustine, *Sermo* 6.6, where he is quoting from memory.
19. Isa 11.1.

were shaken with fear and abandoned the foundation of certain hope and steadfast faith. And since the tail is the extremity of the body, what else can it here signify but the end of the Lord's passion? Moses then seized it by the tail, and nothing more of the serpent was seen in the staff, which means that at the end of the mystery of the Lord's passion on the cross, every faithful soul then returned to the faith, and Christ, after death had been destroyed, by his glorious resurrection restored their faith in him as it was before.

(6) So Aaron took the censer, ran into the midst of the assembly, which the fire was now destroying, and standing between the dead and the living he offered the incense: and thus the furious plague stopped.[20] Whom does Aaron typify if not our Redeemer? For when rejoicing like a strong man to run his race,[21] he took the censer of his passion and stood between the dead and the living, and by interposing his cross, on which the incense of his sacred body was burned, and the heavenly lamb was roasted, he separated the living from the dead and kept the destructive fire from them like a wall that stood between them. This was done, that the devouring flames might overwhelm the infidels, of whom it was written, "And now a fire consumes God's enemies,"[22] and the just who live by faith[23] escape the fire of damnation. Now, we know that the thieves between whom the Lord was crucified were the first of these dead and living, one of whom was chosen, while the other, because of his unbelief, was rejected. Therefore, this mountain of strength carried among the dead and the living the incense of the unique sacrifice that was offered to God the Father on the altar of the cross, when he poured out the fragrance of his knowledge among the believers and unbelievers. Thus we have the statement in Canticles, "Your name like perfume is poured out."[24] And the Apostle says, "But thanks be to God, who continually leads us on in Christ's triumphal train, and everywhere uses us to diffuse the fragrance of his knowledge. We are indeed the incense offered by Christ to God, both for those who are on the way to salva-

20. Cf. Num 16.47–48.
22. Heb 10.27.
24. Cant 1.2.

21. Cf. Ps 18.6.
23. Cf. Heb 10.38.

tion, and for those who are on the way to perdition: to the latter it is a deadly fume that kills, to the former a vital fragrance that brings life."[25]

(7) Saul agreed to give his elder daughter Merob to David in marriage. When the time came to hand her over, however, she was not given to him, but was married to another man. But David fell in love with Saul's other daughter, Michal, and he married her.[26] Now Merob has the meaning "of the crowd," and Michal "all the water" or "from all."[27] And what does Merob signify but only the crowd of unbelievers that belongs to the multitude that is rejected? "For many are invited, but few are chosen."[28] And what does Michal typify but the holy Church, from which all the elect have their origin, or which consists of all the elect? And even though she did not bear a son, her sterility is not an obstacle to this interpretation.

(8) There is one mystery here, that she was joined to King David in marriage, and another that she remained childless. The first meant that she was chosen to be joined in marriage with Christ the Lord, the other that she was not found worthy of the gift of fertility, but brought upon Israel the shame of sterility. David, indeed, married the daughter of the proud King Saul, while Jesus, vigorous and truly desirable, rescued the Church from menial service to the proud prince of this world, and joined her to himself by the bond of intimate union. Now, the proud Saul, that is, the evil spirit, was unable to deprive him of Michal, who is the holy Church of the elect, as he did Merob, because her faithful defender unalterably took her into the protecting arms of his love, as he exclaimed in the Gospel, "My own sheep shall never perish; no one shall snatch them from my care."[29]

(9) Those who despise the fabric of lust and of an earthy way of life, and build a spiritual edifice, turn bricks into stones, as it were, and construct their house that will never fall, not on the

---

25. 2 Cor 2.14–16.
26. Cf. 1 Sam 18.20, 27.
27. Cf. Jerome, *Nom. Hebr.* 36.8–9 (CC 72.104).
28. Matt 20.16 in the Vulgate, but not in the Greek text. But see Matt 22.14.
29. John 10.27–28.

sand of worldly hope, but on the rock of faith, which is Christ.[30] And so, in Isaiah it is said, "The bricks are fallen, but we build in hewn stone; the sycamores are hacked down, but we will use cedars instead."[31] Surely, he will build with hewn stone instead of bricks that fall to the ground, if he chastises his wanton passions and vices with a rigorous life of penance, if he overcomes the law of the flesh by the law of the Spirit, and exchanges the strength of the body for the power of the soul. Hence Isaiah says again: "Those who look to the Lord will renew their strength."[32] For by saying that they will not receive but will renew, he clearly indicates that the strength he replaces is different from that which begins anew. Therefore, the psalmist says to those who are chosen, "Be strong and take courage, all you whose hope is in the Lord."[33] And Solomon says, "Look, sixty of Israel's chosen warriors escort the litter of Solomon."[34] Now, brave men escort the litter of Solomon when with untiring yearning all the saints guard the intimate repose of our peace-loving Redeemer.

(10) "He made me drunk with wormwood."[35] Like a delirious man, or like one out of his mind, the drunkard is barely aware of what he endures. And every perverted man, as he madly yearns for the riches of the world, as he is weighed down by all his effort, does not perceive as evil that which he is forced to bear, because he enjoys the attraction to all that wears him down, for which he must pay the price.

(11) "Like sheep they run headlong into hell, and death shall feed upon them."[36] Christ has sheep that he leads through the gates of heaven to pleasant pasture; and the roaring lion also has sheep that he cruelly stuffs into his greedy mouth. We do well in calling the devil Death, for since he is the author of death, he brutally attacks us and leads us to destruction. And so, John says, "And there was a horse, sickly pale; and its rider's name was Death."[37]

30. Cf. 1 Cor 10.4.
31. Isa 9.10.
32. Isa 40.31.
33. Ps 30.25.
34. Cant 3.7.
35. Lam 3.15.
36. Ps 48.15.
37. Rev 6.8.

LETTER 137

Peter Damian to the hermit community of Gamugno. He exhorts his brothers to fast on Saturday in honor of the burial of Christ on that day. They should fast gladly, as they do on three other days of the week, and not be distracted by the thought of food and drink, not using bodily infirmity as an excuse to weaken their resolve. He told them of a wondrous apparition an old hermit had experienced, and how in his vision he had visited Jerusalem as a reward for his Saturday fast.

(After 1065)

O THE HOLY BRETHREN living in the hermitage of Gamugno, the monk Peter the sinner sends the kiss of peace in the Holy Spirit.

(2) Managers of rentbearing estates or stewards of lands, while making every effort to please their lords, do not permit the fixed rates to be reduced during the period of their tenure. I too, to whom the guardianship, not just of sundry physical things, but of your souls was committed, would be very much afraid if the return on your crops that should be brought to the Lord's barns were lessened while I was in charge, if through my connivance, God forbid, the full measure of your holy service were not fulfilled. For whatever is done in this world, redounds to the benefit of man, but the fruit of souls belongs only to the service of the Creator.

(3) Therefore, we must the more fearfully await the judgment of God, by which we must give an account, not of the food soon to be evacuated into the latrine through the intestines, but rather of souls that bear the image of their Creator. Clearly, we are not called upon to answer for the fields that are broken up and plowed, but for rational lands that must be cultivated to receive the seed of heavenly wisdom. And thus, as I

must be fearful in my task of caring for your welfare, so you too must with great joy strive by your holy efforts for the crown held out to you. Nor must you lessen what you have begun, but lighten the burden by looking forward to your goal.

(4) Among the other flowers of your holy mode of living and your practices of devotion, I suggest to your charity that you observe the accustomed norm of fasting on four days of the week, and especially on Saturday, about which there is already vacillation in the mind of some, except that it is not carried out by the weak. I know, to be sure, that fasting is practiced on three days without opposition or debate, but on Saturday the weak and tepid spirit begins gradually to waver between fasting and eating, and like one standing at a fork in the road, doubts which way he should go, and is soon cut loose from his firm resolve and occupies himself with thoughts of tables, dishes, cups, and whatever belongs to feasting. He pretends to be physically weak, is constantly thinking about the delights of eating, and despairs being able to get to sleep during the coming night. Meanwhile, that inveterate inciter to wanton gluttony comes on the scene, stirs up a lust for food, and infuses the poison of pernicious delight. He recommends the golden path of discretion, and argues that one should especially avoid the ruinous results of indiscretion. It is better to eat with moderation, than to nourish a ravenous appetite by doubling one's hunger.

(5) This ancient seducer neatly plants the hook of his trickery in their descendants, just as of old he baited it to ensnare the parents of the human race. He had led on our parents by piercing them with the arrow of gluttony, and this clever spy still uses the avenue of gluttony to get us in his toils. Even today he employs certain flatterers and buffoons, and incites them to express outwardly what he plants in their mind, so that the miserable man easily falls when assailed by so many catapults and engines of war, amid such a storm of arrows and missiles, against whom both besieging tongue and uproarious thoughts conspire in their attack.

(6) Nor should I omit, moreover, that in those of weak spirit the same conflict arises over Tuesdays during both Lenten seasons when we fast five days a week, as that over Saturdays dur-

ing the rest of the year when the total number of fast days is four. For since the evil spirit is not satisfied to have the servants of God desecrate Saturdays in Lent, he tries at least to have them to violate the fast on Tuesday. But when the rigorous observance of this day is lost, he at once turns his attention to opposing Saturday, so that the ancient adversary never ceases to engage in battle, and the servant of God never loses the opportunity for victory.

(7) Now, my dear brothers, without good reason do not set aside the rule handed down by the Fathers,[1] which you also observed for many years, and with the salutary practice of honoring the life-giving cross also associate fasting on the day the Lord was in the tomb. For these three days, Friday, Saturday, and Sunday, mysteriously contain three different periods of time. And so, we must observe these days in a special way, two by mortifying the flesh, and the third with spiritual rejoicing. For on Friday the Lord hung on the cross, on Saturday he rested in the tomb, and on Sunday he rose from the dead. Friday, as it were, represents this whole life in which we now live like dying men, and during which we are exhorted to take up the cross each day and follow Jesus. But Saturday, which, as we know, is said to mean "rest,"[2] typifies that interval between the day of our death and the day of resurrection, on which, after again assuming our bodies, we are brought before the bench of the eternal judge. But Sunday will be that span of eternity after the judgment, which will have no end of light and glory.

(8) Therefore, on this Saturday of transient time each of us should chastise his body, that he might pleasantly take his rest in the period that follows. In this life the ardent soul should mortify the allurements of his flesh, that in the life to come he may rejoice in happy feasting. Here with the holy women let him lament at the burial place of the Lord, that he may then

---

1. Cf. E. Vacandard, "Careme," *DTC* 2.2, 1731, citing Innocent I (401–417) in his letter to Decentius of Gubbio (PL 56.516), where he states that fasting on Friday and Saturday was customary. See also the two quotations from Pope Sylvester, cited by Damian in his *Letter* 118.11 (*Vita s. Silvestri* [Mombritius, *Sanctuarium* II:510]); Ryan, *Sources* no. 207.

2. Cf. Jerome, *Nom. Hebr.* 75.29 (CC 72.154).

behold the glory of him who rose from the dead. Sorrowful eyes, pallid lips, neglected appearance, and unkempt hair are signs that we are disciples of the crucified, even as he lies in the tomb, so that as we now suffer with the apostles in tears and fasting, we may later be in their company at the banquet of honey and broiled fish. But that the profit and utility of fasting on Saturday may be evident not only in words but also in deeds, I think it will not be out of place to promote your edification by borrowing a short passage from my writings.

(9) For I recall having written what I am about to say when I once discussed the eight fasts. "Shortly after having written these lines," I said, "the following happened to me by chance, or rather, by divine providence, and I must tell you about it. A certain older brother who for almost thirty years now had lived in his hermit's cell, came to me, and in private told me about a vision he had had. 'Master,' he said, 'I often experienced animosity and anger toward you because you always insisted that we fast on Saturdays. In the mean time, I longed to travel to Jerusalem.

"'As this desire grew daily stronger, while I was asleep one Sunday night a certain cleric, brilliantly clad, appeared to me in a vision, and said, "Brother John," for that was his name, "do you wish to go to Jerusalem?" When I replied that this was what I wanted, in my dream he promptly took me there, and as we visited many graves, he especially pointed out whose graves they were. With him leading the way, I came at length to the sepulcher of the Lord. And there, near the sepulcher, stood a handsome cleric whose appearance was most peaceful, properly wearing a white stole about his neck. And he said to me, "The day before yesterday as you were fasting, you truly venerated the life-giving cross, and yesterday you also paid your respects to the Lord's tomb. And now, without the slightest doubt, you should recognize that you verily celebrate and venerate the cross on Friday and the tomb of Christ on Saturday if you fast on those days while you chant and pray."

"'After being thus instructed by what he said, I lost the ill feelings I had had toward you, father, and from then on, when I had the strength, I fasted on Saturday with no less devotion than on Friday.' This holy brother told me these things while totally unaware that I was writing about them, and to this day does not know about it."[3]

I have not hesitated, therefore, to recopy this passage, so that if my other work does not happen to be available to you, this letter at least will not escape the attention of your community.

(10) And so, my dear brothers, we must be on our guard lest this holy life grow lukewarm, and by gradually being subverted, God forbid, it should totally collapse. For I am well aware that of the great and arduous deeds that were formerly achieved, hardly more than trifling evidence now survives. And just as what our predecessors neglected to do, is not revived by us, so what in our time fell by the wayside, those who come after us will never restore. And thus, those lines of Horace ring true:

> Our parents' age, worse than our grandsires',
> Has brought forth us less worthy and destined
> Soon to yield an offspring still more wicked.[4]

Consequently, we shall be guilty, not only of our own negligence, but also of the kind of life that others live; and while we ourselves fail by becoming lax, we also produce the cause of defection in those who come after us. For when their indolent life is pointed out to them, they at once come back to us, use us as a shield in their defense, in that while we were their predecessors in this way of life, we should therefore be considered the source of their guilt.

(11) "We are no better than our fathers," they will say; "we carry on with what we find, and hold fast to what we have learned." And so, we shall become the apostles of other people's listlessness, and teachers not of erudition but of forgetfulness; not leaders in winning the battle, but the first who take to flight. Remember what was written, "Woe to those who have given up the struggle!"[5] "And now I," he said, "vest in you the king-

---

3. Cf. Peter Damian, *Letter* 118.15.
4. Horace, *Carmina* 3.6.46 (*The Odes and Epodes,* trans. C. E. Bennett [Cambridge, MA: Loeb Classical Library, 1952]. The MSS here invert the last two words, and thus alter the Latin meter.
5. Sir 2.16.

ship that my Father vested in me."⁶ Why? Not, surely, because you seized it, but, as he said, "because you are the men who have stood firmly by me in my times of trial."⁷

(12) Wherefore, my dear brothers, let us cut away this reproach from our times, and faithfully pass on to our descendants the untarnished and undiminished badge of virtue that we received from our fathers. If the eremitic life is to be reduced in its effectiveness, let others diminish it, so that we might not be considered the leaders in this fraudulent sacrilege. Nor may our fathers who are the founders of this plan of life, by their accusations and sharp insistence when they come to their reward, compel us to undergo the sentence of condemnation. For while they made every effort to imitate the combat of the holy martyrs, we only debate the feastdays of the martyrs. And even though we did not engage in battle, we are only too eager to rejoice over past victories.

(13) This whole life of ours is like the sabbath of that last resurrection, and we are now celebrating, as it were, the eve or the vigil of the eternal feast for which we yearn. But he who is going to a marriage, or is awaiting the banquet of some great feastday, does not eagerly take breakfast the hour before the event. By living soft and luxurious lives, should we anticipate, as it were, the established hour for eating, since as invited guests we have already begun to make our way to the marriage banquet of eternal celebration? What does eating have to do with the grave, or banqueting with the tomb? If we are guarding the burial place of the Lord with the disciples, and not with the soldiers, let us bring a mixture of myrrh and aloes,⁸ and not cooking pots and kettles. The former represent bitterness of spirit, while the latter typify voluptuous pleasure. At the grave we should surely beat our breast, and not inflate our stomachs with food. We should weep bitter tears, and not engage in draining our cups. We should not gorge ourselves on neat wine, but mix our drink with tears.⁹

(14) Nor have I inconsiderately prescribed these things and

6. Luke 22.29.
7. Luke 22.28.
8. Cf. John 19.39.
9. Cf. Ps 101.10.

thus acted without discretion, as if I were refusing to be humane toward the weak and those who are ill. For, he who is sick should be so discreet in allowing himself liberties, that he does not fail to observe this salutary and customary rule when he recovers. He should be indulgent in his manner of living, but in such a way that one who is healthy may nevertheless remain steadfast in his practice of penance. My dear brothers, let us therefore not consider it a burden to observe the fast on Saturday, so that by now chastising our bodies as we are buried with our Redeemer in death, we may also rise with him[10] and later feast in the splendor of heavenly glory.

10. Cf. Rom 6.4.

LETTER 138

Peter Damian to his brother, Damianus. Conscious of his advancing years, and confronted with the observation that in whatever group he finds himself, he is always the oldest person present, he is compelled to think of death. But the thought frightens him, as he accuses himself of every imaginable sin. His greatest failing, he confesses, is scurrility, a jocose tendency to lightheartedness in speech, always a problem for him that was never overcome, even after he had entered the religious life. After this written confession, he begs Damianus to exorcise his brother's demon by his prayers.

(After 1065)

TO HIS DEAR BROTHER, sir Damianus, the monk Peter the sinner, his unworthy servant and son.

(2) I want you to know, my dear father and lord in Christ, that my spirit is constantly afflicted with sorrow as I carefully watch the day of my death coming ever closer, and appearing before my eyes as if it were present. For while I count the long years, and notice that my hair is turning white, and become aware that in whatever group of people I find myself, almost all are younger than I am, I put aside all my concerns and think only of death, meditate on the grave, and do not avert my eyes from my last resting place. Nor is my unhappy spirit satisfied with this dread sight alone, fixing the limits of its attention on the death of the body, but is soon hauled before the judge, there to muse, and not without great trepidation, over what can be held against it, and how it can plead in its defense.

(3) But how miserable I am, deserving to be mourned with an inexhaustible supply of tears, since I have committed every evil deed, and through the long years of my life have observed hardly any single command of God's law! Wretched man that I am, what evil things have I not done, and in what vices and

crimes have I not been involved? I confess that "my life has fallen into the pit of misery, my soul has been destroyed in my wickedness."[1] Pride, passion, anger, impatience, malice, envy, gluttony, drunkenness, concupiscence, robbery, lying, perjury, silly talk, scurrility, ignorance, negligence, and other maladies have laid me low, and all the vices like raging beasts have devoured my soul. My heart and my lips are defiled; I am stained with guilt in sight, hearing, taste, smell, and touch. I am dissipated in every way in thought, word, and deed. In fact, I have committed all these evil things, and alas, have never achieved worthy fruits of repentance.

(4) One of these faults I lament more bitterly, in which, as my conscience affirms, I admit that I am especially guilty. Scurrility, indeed, has always been habitual with me, that even after my conversion to the religious life has never completely left me. Now, even though I have often fought against this wild monster, and frequently used the hammer of penance to smash the teeth of this wicked beast, I was able to check it for a time, but could never achieve total victory over it. For the entrenched and habitual practice of any vice, even though every effort is made to uproot it from the innermost recesses of the soul, often stands insolently at our door, as it were, and tries at least to lick our hand if it is barred from attacking us with its teeth. Under the guise of spiritual joy, when I try to appear in a pleasant mood in the company of my brothers, I stoop to lighthearted speech, and when for the sake of fraternal charity I purposely plan to abandon my normally stern attitude, I carelessly allow my unbridled tongue to indulge in useless talk. But since the Lord says, "Blessed are the sorrowful, for they shall find consolation,"[2] what sort of judgment will await those who not only do not weep, but what is worse, like people on the stage engage in howls of merriment and inane laughter? And since consolation, indeed, is not meant for those who rejoice but for those who grieve, what comfort can they expect from the future judge if they now abandon themselves to the evilly seductive pleasure of empty revelry? Again, since Truth itself

---

1. Cf. Lam 3.53 (not found in Sabatier).
2. Matt 5.5.

says, "Alas for you who laugh now; you shall weep,"[3] at the dreadful judgment what shall be the reply of those who not only engage in laughter themselves, but by their jocose speech give rise to raucous merriment in those who hear them?

(5) Here I should note, that while laughter is the enemy of the soul, it is much more destructive to utter scurrilities. By being devoted to scurrilous language, leading to unnecessary festivity, one ruins others along with himself, and in addition, is guilty of uselessly uttering idle words, since it is written, "There is not a thoughtless word that comes from men's lips but they will have to account for it on the day of Judgment."[4] Now when I think of these words of the Gospel, what else comes to mind but that a kind of business transaction is here proposed to us? For by momentary laughter we buy perpetual weeping, and by temporal weeping we acquire everlasting happiness. And so it is that holy men now exert every effort to plant tears and sorrow, that they may reap the harvest of eternal joy, as the prophet attests when he says, "A man may go out weeping carrying his bag of seed; but he will come back with songs of joy, carrying home his sheaves."[5]

(6) In the field of our heart we must set out the young plants of virtue that they may grow, and properly water them with frequent drenching rain. It is necessary that we fervently devote ourselves to performing shining deeds, and yet always have at hand the salutary water of tears to extinguish everything that is superfluous. To this point we read that Moses made seven lamps for the tabernacle, along with their tongs, and firepans in which the burning remnants might be extinguished, all of the purest gold.[6] What should we understand by the seven lamps, if not the seven gifts of the Holy Spirit? Truly, we make seven lamps for the tabernacle, if we collect in our soul the gifts of the Holy Spirit, received from God's bounty.

(7) But since in these very deeds of holiness that we ardently perform under the inspiration of the Holy Spirit, certain things intrude that are superfluous and smack of earthly corruption,

---

3. Luke 6.25.
5. Ps 125.6.
4. Matt 12.36.
6. Cf. Exod 25.37; 37.23.

so that along with the lamps we must also have tongs. What is meant by the tongs, if not the application of severe penance? For, whatever is unnecessary for the lamp is plucked out by the tongs, just as by severe penance the guilt of human depravity is wiped away. And so, Peter said to those who were performing unnecessary deeds, "Repent then so that your sins may be wiped out,"[7] as if he were clearly saying: Apply the tongs and cut off the aberrations of evil deeds. It is therefore proper that tongs accompany the lamps, since even though we strive through the grace of the Holy Spirit to shine with the light of good deeds, and human corruption gives rise to superfluous things, we need the remedy of penance. And because it is necessary that tears of a contrite heart extinguish these very superfluities that penitential discipline cuts away, we are reminded that after preparing lamps and tongs, Moses also made vessels in which the smoldering remnants might be extinguished. Now these vessels are our hearts, which must always be filled with a flood of tears and lamenting. These vessels should also contain the oil of which it is said in the Gospel, "the prudent girls took flasks of oil with their lamps."[8]

(8) If it is true, therefore, that those who are illustrious because of their shining deeds are still in need of tears, what should be thought of a miserable person like me and of others who act in a similar way, who commit many dark deeds, and cannot boast of any apparent good works? How necessary it is for us to abound in tears, how much we need constantly to experience grief! How proper it is that we not make others laugh by some witty remark of a sharp-tongued buffoon, but rather appear to them to be sober men with eyes always cast down. By so acting, our very deportment will reflect that perfect penance which should primarily glow in the hidden sadness of our heart. And thus, we not only provide ourselves with the remedy for the cure we seek, but can give others an example of fruitful penance.

(9) Wherefore, my dear brother, prostrate at your feet, I beg your holiness to protect me with the shield of your prayers

---

7. Acts 3.19.
8. Matt 25.4.

against this wild monster, and by exorcising me, in your wisdom expel the poison of this virulent serpent. And I implore you to offer constant prayers to God, not only for this fault, but also for all the others that I confessed to you above, and earnestly seek a hearing for me at the throne of God's mercy.

LETTER 139

Peter Damian to the hermit Tebaldus and his brethren. This fragmentary letter, edited for the first time in 1914,[1] in conformity with his known attitude in the matter, recommends restraint in the use of bodily penance. The norms set by the ancient fathers must not be exceeded.

(Before 1066)

O MY DEAR BROTHER, sir Tebaldus, and to the other brothers, the monk Peter the sinner offers the ministry of his proper service.

(2) My dear brothers, in the austere mode of life you are leading, you are, no doubt, influenced by the fervor of the Holy Spirit. But it is necessary that by the good offices of the same Spirit discretion curb the headlong course that in all goodwill you propose to follow. For almighty God, who rides and directs the rational soul, uses both reins and whips; by reins, indeed, he restrains those who are excessively nimble lest they run too quickly, by goads and spurs he stimulates them, lest through lethargy and laziness they fail to reach the goal of holiness toward which they strive. It is clearly written, "If you sacrifice correctly, but do not properly apportion the offering, you have sinned."[2] He sacrifices correctly, if, as he offers his life to God in sacrifice, he takes the road to holiness; but he does not properly apportion it, if he exceeds the bounds set down by the holy Fathers. . . .

---

1. D. De Bruyne, *Revue bénédictine* 31 (1914) 92; reprinted in Lucchesi, *Clavis* 129–130.
2. Gen 4.7 (Sabatier 1.21).

LETTER 140

Peter Damian to Pope Alexander II. The occasion for this letter, in which Damian fortifies his position with many citations from the sacred canons, was the assertion made in his presence by the chaplains of Duke Godfrey of Tuscany—Tudethchinus and John—that those who had bought the office of bishop from kings or princes were not guilty of the heresy of simony.[1] They argued that by this purchase, bishops received from princes only the possession of ecclesiastical estates, while by reason of the imposition of hands they acquired their episcopal rights and dignity. Here, perhaps, Damian comes closer to condemning lay investiture than in any of his writings, but asks the pope to take action, not against the lay powers, but only against bishops involved in the transaction.

(Beginning of 1066)

O SIR ALEXANDER, the bishop of the highest See, the monk Peter the sinner offers his service.

(2) Just as the loss of any household property is

---

1. For the year 1066, an entry in the *Chronicle* of Bertholds of Reichenau indicates that Damian had clearly acquired a reputation as a polemicist against simony and clerical marriage or incontinence from letters from this period, although it adds that some thought he treated clerical offenders too kindly. This may be illustrated as well by *Letter* 146, in which Damian defends himself against charges that he is too tolerant of simoniac priests and bishops, since he was unwilling to repudiate the effectiveness of the sacraments they performed. For the *Chronicle*, see *Die Chroniken Bertholds von Reichenau und Bernolds von Konstanz 1054–1100*, MGH, Scriptores rerum Germanicarum, n.s. 14, ed. Ian S. Robinson (Hanover: Hahnsche Buchhandlung, 2003), p. 203. Damian's call for restraint to those who threatened to throw the Church into disorder because of their excessive demands to punish simoniacs—including the case of John Gualbertus and the Vallombrosans who had broken with the bishop of Florence and plunged the See into confusion (see *Letter* 146)—is also treated by Phyllis Jestice, "Peter Damian Against the Reformers," in *The Joy of Learning and the Love of God. Studies in Honor of Jean Leclercq*, ed. E. Rozanne Elder, 67–94. Cistercian Studies Series 160 (Kalamazoo, MI: Cistercian Publications, 1995).

brought to the attention of the head of the family, it is also proper that harm suffered by the Church be referred to the supreme pontiff. For, as the former, with all the force available to him, is prepared to resist the evils attacking his home, so too will the latter restore the foundations of a tottering faith, or even of the religious state that has begun to crumble.

(3) Unfortunately, in our day a new heresy has appeared,[2] and unless the force of your authority oppose it as soon as possible, we must fear that, like cancer, it will wildly spread to spell destruction for the Christian religion and danger to souls. Indeed, some clerics who purport to be such by their external appearance, who are utterly cold in their separation from God, but are aflame with the fires of ecclesiastical ambition, obstinately pontificate on this theme: one is not guilty of simoniacal heresy if he acquires a bishopric by purchase from a king or other earthly prince, so long as he was consecrated without payment.

(4) And so, as I was recently conversing with his excellency, Duke Godfrey, two of his chaplains were present, one of whom, since he was a foreigner, bore the strange name Tudethchinus, while the other was a Venetian, named John. Now these two, like Hymenaeus and Philetus in the preaching of Paul,[3] or certainly like Jannes and Mambres in the time of Moses,[4] men who defied the truth, never ceased spreading this doctrine, and claimed that this idea was Catholic and contained in the canons, namely, that by law one should not be called a simonist who was proven to have acquired a diocese without the imposition of hands. They said, in fact, that when this took place, it is not the Church that is alienated, but its property, nor does one buy the episcopal office, but the title to lands. For, by this payment of money, one purchases only the goods and the proprietary wealth, and not the office or the sacrament of the Church.

---

2. For simony as a heresy see J. Leclercq, "Simoniaca heresis," *Studi Gregoriani* 1 (1947) 523–530; J. Gilchrist, "*Simoniaca heresis* and the Problem of Orders from Leo IX to Gratian," *Proceedings of the Second International Conference of Medieval Canon Law at Boston, 1963* (Vatican City 1964) 209–235.

3. Cf. 2 Tim 2.17–18.

4. Cf. 2 Tim 3.8, Exod 7.11, referring to the magicians of the Pharaoh. The Vulg. has Mambres, not Jambres.

LETTER 140   105

They have paid, they say, for that by which they become wealthy; they receive freely that which they require to be bishops.

(5) Here we have a new type of schismatic, sacrilegious lips that should be condemned to everlasting silence. In one and the same man they construe two persons, so that one is a bishop who is sinfully put on the auction block, but the other is a rich man paid for by an assigned sum of money. The former, like another Sardanapalus,[5] belches amid the delicacies served at the banquet, the latter presides like an apostle over the care of souls. By so acting, he who buys a field, must be said to have acquired only the dusty ground and not the harvest it produced. Also, when a slaver sells a man, he must not be considered to have sold his soul, but his body.

(6) Moreover, when we read that the body of man is fashioned with completely distinct members on the forty-sixth day after the mother has conceived,[6] and is shortly thereafter animated by God, since only the body and not the soul proceeds from the seed of the father; therefore, the father must be considered to have begotten only the body and not the child, which consists of soul and body. But since this is wholly absurd, and he is rightly called the father from whose loins only the body and not the soul has emerged; so undoubtedly one must be called a vendor of the Church if he rises to the dignity of the episcopal office through the earthly property that he buys, and by dealing in corporal gain, he thereby becomes a purchaser of the sacrament.

---

5. The last king of the Assyrians, on whom see RE 2/1: 2436–2475. He is also identified as Assurbanipal.
6. Cf. Augustine, *De diversis quaestionibus LXXXIII* 56 (CC 44A.95; Eng. trans. in FOTC 70 [1982] 98); idem, *De natura et origine animae* 4.4 (CSEL 60.384–385); idem, *Quaestionum in Heptateuchum libri septem* 21.80 (CC 33.111); Jerome, *Epistola* 121.4 (CSEL 56.16). Damian's contemporary, Odorannus de Sens, also preserves Augustine's explanation of the number forty-six. See his *Ad Everardum monachum, de tribus quaestionibus* 4, in *Opera omnia*, ed. Robert-Henri Bautier, Monique Gilles, Marie-Elisabeth Duchez, and Michel Hugo (Paris: Editions du Centre National de la Recherche scientifique, 1972) 146. J. T. Noonan, *The Morality of Abortion* (Cambridge, MA: Harvard University Press, 1970) 5, 12–13, 15, 20–21, where he discusses older theories of ensoulment based on Aristotle, *History of Animals* 7.3 (583b). But Aristotle required forty days for males and ninety days for females before animation.

(7) Tell us, therefore, whoever you might be, you who boast that you are only the buyer of earthly goods by which, however, you aspire to rise to the dignity of episcopal excellence; and while you say that you have received from the prince only the earthly benefits of the Church, claim that you are some sort of steward, and are not installed to function in the episcopal office. Tell us, I say, of what type was this investiture, and indeed what was the symbol that the prince handed you? If it was a bough of a tree, or a simple rod, you might rightly congratulate yourself, because as you assert, you were inducted as a steward in charge of lands, and not into the office of bishop; and therefore it is not required that you be subject to the bishop who is to be preferred to you. But if after the receipt or the promise of money, the secular prince handed you the pastoral staff, how can you brazenly offer an excuse for putting the episcopal office up for sale? Surely, unless by this investiture the prince had first endowed you with the title to the episcopal dignity that would follow, the future consecrator would never have granted you the episcopal sacrament by the imposition of hands. Now, because of that which you received for a price, you were later promoted to the episcopacy, and therefore, even though the imposition of hands is not purchased but freely given, nevertheless, as far as you are concerned, it is not free from the stain of venality. For, if this trafficking is known to him, it contaminates the consecrator, and consecration freely imparted is unable to purge the buyer. The foul obscenity of tainted exchange defiles one who is clean, but the imposition of hands, freely granted, cannot remove the stain from one who is unclean.

(8) Perhaps I might be accused of lying if I did not back up what I say with evidence from sacred Scripture. Now this is what the prophet Haggai said, "These are the words of the Lord God of Hosts: Ask the priests to give their ruling: If a man is carrying consecrated flesh in a fold of his robe, and he lets the fold touch bread or pottage or wine or oil or any kind of food, will that also become consecrated? And the priests answered, 'No.' Haggai went on: But if a person defiled in soul touches any of these things, will that also become defiled? 'It will,' answered the priests. Haggai replied: So it is with this people, and so is

this nation in my sight and all that they do, says the Lord; whatever offering they make here will be unclean."[7] And thus, in these prophetic, or rather, divine utterances it is clearly shown that the man who buys, and is therefore defiled in soul, pollutes the dignity of the orders that he receives. For this dignity, even though it is freely received by the imposition of hands, in no way cleanses the buyer.

(9) Again I return to investiture, and inquire of you who boast that you did not receive the church, but the estates of the church. In fact, when the prince handed you the staff, did he say, "Receive the lands and the wealth of this church," or rather, which is certain, "Receive the church"? But if you received the goods of the church without the church, you are schismatic and sacrilegious, you who separate the goods of the church from the church, and violently turn to your own personal use that which belongs to another. But if you received the church, which you can in no way deny, without doubt you have become a simonist, and venality made you a heretic before the imposition of hands rendered you consecrate. For then you most evidently bought consecration when you received for money that, on account of which you were to be advanced to consecration. Thus, the one depends on the other, so that he who accepts the earthly goods of the Church aspires to the grace of consecration, and he who achieves consecration retains for himself the property of the Church that should be used for the needy and for dispensing other works of charity. In this way, even though there was no mention of ecclesiastical property in the imposition of hands itself, still he who is consecrated becomes the steward of the Church's property; and when he accepts the Church, even though nothing is said of consecration, he is chosen, however, in view of his later consecration.

(10) It is clear, that from the very beginning of the infant Church this salutary custom had its origin among the faithful, that everyone sold his property and laid the money at the feet of the apostles and of apostolic men, with which they provided for the needs of the poor.[8] Later, however, it seemed proper to

---

7. Hag 2.12–15.
8. Cf. Acts 4.34–35. See also Damian, *Letter* 74.2. Cf. Burchard of Worms,

the holy Fathers, namely, to those who were their successors in the ranks of governing the Church, that those who were converted to the Lord should not sell their lands, but should hand them over to holy churches, not in temporary fashion, but by perpetual right to serve the needs of the poor.

(11) And indeed, in Moses' words it is commanded in the Law: "Nothing," he said, "that a man devotes to the Lord, whether man or beast or field, may be sold or redeemed. Everything so devoted once will be most holy to the Lord."[9] Note here, that it is most clearly forbidden to sell or redeem whatever is devoted to the Lord, but it is commanded that such things remain forever most holy. Why, therefore, do you boast of having paid a price for things most holy, and, contrary to God's law, of having received for payment God's property, which should be freely received and freely given? And that, as if it were not a sin, because such dealing had taken place without consecration? But perhaps you have no fear, because while this ancient law forbids the crime, it does not assess a penalty. Therefore, take note of what Boniface, the bishop of the Roman Church, wrote in his decretal letter: "No one," he said, "is permitted to ignore the fact that everything that is devoted to the Lord, whether man or beast or field, or whatever has once been consecrated, shall be most holy to the Lord, and belongs by right to the priests. Wherefore, because he shall be inexcusable, everyone who diverts, destroys, invades, or takes these things from the Lord and from the Church to whom they belong, shall be judged sacrilegious until he mends his ways and makes satisfaction to the Church, and if he is unwilling to correct his fault, he shall be excommunicated."[10] But many years previously, among other things, Pope Anaclete remarked, "Whoever sequesters the property of the Church, commits a sacrilege and shall be considered guilty of sacrilege."[11]

Decretorum libri XX, III, 2 (PL 140.673); Jaffé 172 (p. 28); Hinschius 247; Ryan, *Sources* no. 131.

9. Lev 27.28.

10. Burchard, XI, 17 (PL 140.863): Pseudo-Bonifatius papa = Benedictus Levita 2.405 (MGH.LL 2.2.96); CJC I, 687, C 12, q. 2, c. 3; Jaffé 357.

11. Burchard, XI, 18 (PL 140.863); Regino II, 283 (PL 132.338); Jaffé 2.

(12) Also, Pope Lucius had this to say in his decretal, "Those who plunder the goods and properties of the Church we anathematize and expel from the Church, and by apostolic authority banish and condemn and judge them guilty of sacrilege."[12] I could put together many other texts of the Catholic Fathers, unless I were clearly aware that this did not commend itself to epistolary brevity.

(13) And so, you should be obviously convinced by these and other pronouncements of the holy pontiffs, that either you received the property of the Church without the Church, and therefore should be anathematized as a plunderer or as one sacrilegious, and ought to be expelled from the Church; or certainly, which is clear and which you cannot deny, you paid for the Church together with the Church's property, and therefore it is proper that by vigorous canonical judgment you be condemned as a true simonist and heretic. This sentence also is surely canonical, which says, "If any bishop or priest or abbot shall have received his office through money, he and his consecrator shall be deposed and in all ways be cut off from the holy community of the Church, and let him be anathematized as Simon the Magician was by Peter."[13]

(14) Here we should note that the text does not say, "He shall have received this consecration or imposition of hands," but rather, "If anyone shall have received this office." This is also a canonical decree that one finds promulgated in council by the holy Fathers: "One must beware and especially avoid, and by virtue of the Blood of Christ prohibit bishops and kings and all higher powers, all their associates and electors of whatever kind, and those who give their assent, or those in ecclesiastical orders who grant ordination, so that no one receives a position of authority through the heresy of simony, by means of

---

12. Burchard, XI, 19 (PL 140.863–64); Regino II, 285 (PL 132.339); Jaffé 123; CJC I, 816, C 17, q. 4, c. 5.
13. *Canones apostolorum* 30 [Turner I, 1, 20]; *Collectio Dionysio-Hadriana* (PL 67.144); also in Pseudo-Isidore *Collectio Decretalium* (PL 130.17); Regino I.236 (PL 132.235B); Variant readings: MS Vat. lat. 1355; MS Cas. 45: Franz Pelster, "Der Dekret Bischof Burkhards von Worms in Vatikanischen Hss.," in *Miscellanea Giovanni Mercati* 2, Studi e Testi 122 (1946) 140, n. 69; Ryan, *Sources* no. 234.

any faction, artfulness, promise, or provision, or by any grant given by himself or by a person commissioned by him."[14]

(15) At this point we should also note, that while first speaking of bishops, the text at once includes kings and all higher powers, so that this heresy is to be avoided not only by bishops who impose hands upon those to be consecrated, but also by secular princes who, although unjustly, nevertheless in the same way hand over the churches to future rectors.[15] For when a thing is obtained through payment, that too undoubtedly is received which follows of necessity. In fact, an episcopal church is granted to someone so that he be confirmed by consecration to exercise authority over it, and without doubt money was exchanged with a view to the objective toward which the candidate for orders aspires. Hence it is clear, that not only they who are preferred to the greater churches, but also those who perniciously receive rural communities or canonical benefices by paying the price, do not escape the heretical snares of simony. For by that which they acquire through purchase they aspire to sacred orders, and they are already destined for ordination when they receive those things that serve them in reaping the profits of sacred orders. Indeed, he is already initiated into episcopal orders when he is appointed to receive the dignity of that rank.

(16) Let this suffice, which I have briefly written against those who acquired a church through payment without the imposition of hands, and who claim theologically that they are not simonists. Those, to be sure, who express this idea ingenuously, and support it as their own opinion, should rightly be called foolish or stupid; but since some of these people insolently affirm this position, and obstinately strive to promote it by certain subtle sophistries and arguments, they rightly incur the charge of being heretics, a thing that I am not happy to say. It is not error that makes one a heretic, but stubbornness and inflexibility. Nor are all those who hold erroneous opinions to

---

14. Burchard, I, 21 (PL 140. 555), citing the Council of Milan, c. 43 (MGH.Capit. 2.408f).
15. Cf. Blum, *St. Peter Damian* 22, n. 87.

be called heretics, but only those who obstinately and brazenly preach what is false.[16]

(17) And so, venerable father, armed with the sword of heavenly wisdom, confront these preachers of Satan and apostles of Antichrist, and like another Joshua,[17] use the unsheathed blade of canonical power to overthrow the Amalekites fighting against Israel. Let this bitter and hellish plant be swiftly removed from our midst lest, God forbid, its deadly poison enter the mouths of children. From your hands, moreover, may those who are ill drink an antidote of such aromatic herbs, that it may remove the filth of poisonous error and restore the purity of sound and sincere faith.

(18) At the conclusion of this letter let me suggest one more thing to your Grace, that as far as possible, no one be permitted to become or remain a bishop who had contrived to rise to the episcopal office by payment, or even, which is more damnable, by courting curial favor. God forbid that he should obtain the spiritual dignity of ecclesiastical preeminence, who has fostered the favor of a secular prince in striving for a prelacy.[18]

---

16. For his definition of a heretic, Damian depends on Augustine, *De utilitate credendi* 1 (CSEL 25, 1, 6ff.); idem, *De civitate Dei* 18.51.1 (CC 48.649.7ff.); Isidore, *Liber de haeresibus* 25.
17. Cf. Exod 17.10.
18. Cf. Blum, *St. Peter Damian* 24–25 n. 94.

LETTER 141

Peter Damian to the chaplains of Duke Godfrey of Tuscany. Noting his usual modus operandi of going to his copious library for references to the sources, he deplores his absence from Fonte Avellana and the noise of the building operation at Gamugno. In a vein similar to that in *Letter* 140, he takes up and refutes the chaplains' three assertions: 1) that clerics should be permitted to marry; 2) that those who bought their way to the priesthood or the episcopate are not to be charged with simony, so long as they received the imposition of hands gratis; and 3) that he himself is motivated by avarice.

(Beginning of 1066)

 O THE DEAR BROTHERS in Christ, the chaplains of Duke Godfrey, the monk Peter the sinner sends his greetings.

(2) When I am writing something that I especially wish to preserve, surrounded by an extensive library of various volumes, I call to mind the opinions of the masters, and always resort, when necessary, to their works. But now that I find myself high amid the snowy crags of this mountain, and am eager to erect the structure of this monastic building, I am not only unable to pore over the pages of books that are not at hand, but am also disturbed by the resounding noise of stonecutters and masons. I can hardly concentrate on my own thoughts, and so, I fear writing to you, lest while unassailable evidence as is appropriate for such matters from sacred Scripture does not secure the rustic style of my writing, as soon as you read it with supercilious air and furrowed brow, you will disdain it as the crazy nonsense of a dreamer, or the trifling ditty of some little old woman.

(3) And still, like David dribbling down his beard in the presence of Achish King of Gath,[1] I would prefer being called a

---

1. Cf. 1 Sam 21.10.

lunatic, and like Jesus, as Mark asserts,[2] to be thought a lunatic by the Jews, rather than fearing the stigma of ignorance, to be condemned for remaining silent at the judgment of a majestic God, saying with Isaiah, "Woe is me for having held my peace, for I am a man of unclean lips."[3] And again, "Divine folly is wiser than the wisdom of men."[4] And as the same Apostle says, "Since the world failed to know God by its own wisdom, God chose to save by the folly of the Gospel those who have faith."[5] For this is what Samson typified when he marvelously slew a thousand Philistines with the jawbone of an ass.[6] Now Samson, whose name means "their sun,"[7] is Christ, who by using the jawbone of an ass, namely, a dumb and unassuming animal, slew many when by the lips of fishermen and simple folk he destroyed the stubborn pride of the human race, so that he who had come to fight against the spiritual powers of the air,[8] would win his triumph, not with orators and philosophers, but with the help of meek and inexperienced men.

(4) To be explicit, there are three points that you make, to which, with all due respect, I must reply. Indeed, you promote the notion that ministers at the holy altar can legally have relations with women. This also you assert, and attempt to prove by certain specious arguments, that he is not to be called a simonist, who as a result of a money payment receives command over a church, but only he who through venality insinuates himself into obtaining the imposition of hands an consecration. And lastly, which is less important, you brand me with the charge of avarice. Why you should presume so to attack me, since this causes me only minor distress, I will take up only briefly, and consequently I shall address the other two objections that concern the common good of the Church, omitting all reference to myself. "For my part, it does not matter to me in the least, if I am called to account by you or by any human court of judgment."[9]

2. Cf. Mark 3.22.
3. Isa 6.5.
4. 1 Cor 1.25.
5. 1 Cor 1.21.
6. Cf. Judg 15.15–17.
7. Cf. Jerome, *Nom. Hebr.* 33.23 (CC 72.101).
8. Cf. Eph 2.2.
9. 1 Cor 4.3.

(5) And so, getting to the point,[10] while I was celebrating Mass, the wives of the vassals, namely, of the duke and marquis, made an offering of Byzantine solidi. Now, after the Mass was finished, one of my monks named Paul left them on the altar as I was leaving the church. But one of your people stole them, unbeknown to you, and in fact, while you were absent and through no fault of yours; but since he was one of your associates, in some way he involved you in the guilty action. But he was soon caught in the act, and violently threatened by dread of Beatrice, the most excellent duchess, a spirited woman, he secretly brought the gold to my brother and begged him to intercede on his behalf. As soon as I learned of the affair, I ordered that the money be returned to the cleric, and exhorted him to restore it to his lady and trust in her forgiveness. But since he vehemently refused, and despite my pleas could not be induced to do so, on the next day he at length secretly gave the money to my brother, and thus freed himself of this burden on his smitten conscience.

(6) Why, therefore, do you accuse me of avarice, since you know that I am so contemptuous of the quest for money? Why do you sharpen your tongues against me, and do not hasten to direct your biting condemnation toward someone to whom making money is not repugnant? For Solomon says, "Like a dart or a sword or a sharp arrow is a false witness who denounces his friend,"[11] and the psalmist states, "The sons of men, whose teeth are spears and arrows and whose tongues are sharp swords."[12] Am I to be charged with cupidity if I refuse to accept what was stolen, forgive the crime, and, returning good for evil, restore the guilty man to the favor of his mistress? Am I, let me ask, to bear the mark of avarice because I calmly endured this accusation, or should it not be he who by stealing a sacred object from a sacred place, desecrated the office of the priesthood in which he served? By so speaking, I am not attack-

---

10. An excellent example of Damian, the rhetorician, using paraleipsis, as he frequently does, thereby proving that the chaplains had stung him by their accusation of covetousness.
11. Prov 25.18.
12. Ps 56.5.

ing such a brother, but under the provocation of your base charge, I am merely compelled to clear myself. I am only a disciple of fishermen, and therefore do not excite the sea of Demosthenes or the torrent of Cicero. And because I must show compassion for my offending brother, I am not eager to see him suffer the retribution that is his due. I should at least be allowed to say this, that since, as the orators and rhetoricians relate, evidence should be gathered from his associates and from those who are his friends, I should not rightly be accused of the sin of avarice if my brother, with little regard for the money and despising it, left it in the church. But if I may say so, you should rather be so charged, since it was your colleague who cleverly contrived to take what belonged to another.

(7) But now, coming to your shameless assertion that ministers of the altar should be allowed to marry, I consider it superfluous to unsheathe the sword of my own words against you, since we see the armed forces of the whole Church and the massed array of all the holy Fathers ready to resist you. And where so great a host of heavenly troops opposes you, one can only wonder that your novel and rash attempt at doctrine does not submit when confronted by such authority. But even though the body of canons is presently not at my disposal,[13] I will still not hesitate to cite certain statements of the Fathers, either those that were oft repeated from memory, or that can be found in some odd sheets of parchment that are at hand. In fact, in his letter blessed Clement wrote the following: "Ministers of the altar," he said, "whether priests or deacons, should be selected for service of the Lord, if they have left their wife before ordination. But if after ordination the minister should go naked to his wife's bed, he shall not enter the sanctuary, carry the Blessed Sacrament, approach the altar, receive the bread and wine for the Mass from those who offer it. Nor shall he come forward to receive communion of the Body of the Lord, pour water for washing the hands of the priest, close the outer doors of the church, perform minor duties, nor even present

---

13. Cf. Ryan, *Sources* no. 237 and pp. 158–160, where he attempts to identify Damian's *corpus canonum* as the *Collectio Hadriana aucta*.

the cruet for the sacred chalice."[14] And a little further on, "A cleric shall not enter a woman's dwelling unattended, nor shall he do so without the assent of his superior of mature age. A priest shall not converse alone with a woman, nor an archdeacon or deacon visit the homes of married women under the pretext of humility or service, or even confide a secret to a woman either through clerics or servants. If this should become known, he shall be relieved of his office, and the woman shall be forbidden entrance into the church."[15]

(8) It is also said in the Council of Nicea, "We ordain that unmarried men who are promoted to the clerical state may take wives if they so wish, but lectors and chanters only."[16] Citing also from the Council of Carthage, "Moreover, when reference was made to certain clerics who were only lectors, living incontinently with their wives, it was resolved that bishops, priests, and deacons, in accord with the statutes pertaining to them, should abstain from intercourse even with their wives. Unless they so lived, they should be removed from ecclesiastical office."[17] Again, in another council of Carthage, among other things bishop Aurelius had this to say, "It was resolved that venerable bishops and priests of God, and also deacons or those who administer God's sacraments, be continent at all times, that they might simply obtain what they ask for from God; so that what the apostles taught, and antiquity has preserved, we too may closely guard."[18] To this, Faustinus, the bishop of the church of Pontia, of the province of Picenum, legate of the Roman Church, added, "Be it resolved that a bishop, priest, or deacon, or those who handle the sacraments, safeguarding chastity should abstain from living with their wives." And all the

---

14. *Epistola praeceptorum Sancti Clementis papae* . . . 46 (Hinschius 48); cf. Ryan, *Sources* nos. 239 and 183, explaining Damian's *Letter* 112, where this text is also cited, but with important variants.

15. *Epistola praeceptorum Sancti Clementis papae* . . . 46 (Hinschius 48); cf. Ryan, *Sources* no. 239.

16. *Collectio Dionysio-Hadriana, Can. apost.*, c. 27 (PL 67.144); cf. Damian, *Letter* 112; Ryan, *Sources* nos. 191, 240.

17. *Collectio Dionysio-Hadriana, Conc. Carthag.*, c. 70 (PL 67.205); cf. Damian, *Letter* 112; Ryan, *Sources* no. 186.

18. *Collectio Dionysio-Hadriana, Conc. Carthag.*, c. 3 (PL 67.186f.); cf. Damian, *Letter* 112; Ryan, *Sources* no. 184.

bishops responded, "Be it resolved that at all times chastity be safeguarded by all those who serve at the altar."[19]

(9) But that there be no further doubt that subdeacons must refrain from living incontinently with their wives, the same Aurelius much later added, "It was resolved according to the decree of various councils, that subdeacons who handle the sacred mysteries, that deacons, priests, and bishops according to statutes proper to them, should also abstain from living with their wives, so that it would appear that they had no wives. Unless they do so, they shall be removed from ecclesiastical office."[20]

(10) Also Pope Gregory, among other things, wrote the following to Peter the subdeacon, "Three years ago, subdeacons in all the dioceses of Sicily were forbidden, according to the custom of the Roman Church, ever to live with their wives. This seemed to me to be difficult and out of place, so that he who was not used to such continence, and had not previously promised to observe chastity, should be forced to separate from his wife, and because of this, God forbid, would fall yet more deeply. Hence it seemed proper to me that from this day forward, all bishops should be told that they may not presume to ordain any subdeacon unless he has promised to live chastely, so that they may not forcibly be provoked to seek past things that by vow they had promised to avoid, and carefully guard against future circumstances. But those who after the same prohibition, enunciated three years ago, have lived chastely with their wives, should be praised and rewarded, and exhorted to persist in their good performance. But we shall not allow those to advance to sacred orders who, after the above prohibition, are unwilling to live chastely with their wives. Wherefore, no one shall be permitted to enter the service of the altar unless his chastity has been demonstrated before he is admitted to the ministry."[21]

19. *Collectio Dionysio-Hadriana, Conc. Carthag.*, c. 4 (PL 67.187); cf. Damian, *Letter* 112; Ryan, *Sources* no. 185.

20. *Collectio Dionysio-Hadriana, Conc. Carthag.*, c. 25 (PL 67.191); cf. Damian, *Letter* 112; Ryan, *Sources* no. 188.

21. Gregory I, *Registrum* 1.42 (MGH.Epp. 1.67); John the Deacon, *Vita Gregorii* 2.58 (PL 75.122C); Damian, *Letter* 112; Ryan, *Sources* no. 192.

(11) Next, the decree of Pope Leo, "Now since living in marriage and begetting children is a matter of choice for those who do not have clerical orders, yet to demonstrate the purity of perfect continence, not even subdeacons are allowed to marry, so that those who have wives should live as though they did not have them, and those who are without wives should remain single.[22] And if it be proper that such a regulation be safeguarded in this order, which is the fourth from the top, how much more should it be observed in the first, second, or third, so that no one be judged fit for the honors of the diaconate, the priesthood, or for the episcopal dignity if he is detected not yet refraining from the pleasures of marriage?"[23] And also Pope Sylvester, "While not permitting a subdeacon to enter the married state, we command that he not presume to do so by recourse to subterfuge."[24]

(12) But if you should insist that the decretals of so many apostolic men be disregarded, and should despise the laws that proceed from their lips like so many channels of the Holy Spirit speaking to us, it behooves you to listen to the judgment that blessed Pope Damasus passes concerning you: "Those who willfully violate the canons are judged severely by the holy Fathers, and are condemned by the Holy Spirit, by whose inspiration and gift they were written. For it is not improper to say that they blaspheme against the Holy Spirit, who freely and not through force, as was previously stated, wantonly act contrary to these sacred canons, or who dare to speak against them, or of their own accord agree with those who wish to oppose them. For such presumption is clearly in accord with those who blaspheme the Holy Spirit since, as was already said, it opposes him by whose command and favor these same holy canons were published."[25]

---

22. Cf. 1 Cor 7.1–16.
23. Leo I, *Epistola* 14.4 (PL 54.672f.); Burchard, II, 148 (PL 140.650A–B); *Collectio Dionysio-Hadriana* (PL 67.293C); Damian, *Letter* 112; cf. Ryan, *Sources* no. 189.
24. *Constitutiones Silvestri*, c. 8 (Mansi 2.625); Jaffé ante 174; Damian, *Letter* 112; cf. Ryan, *Sources* no. 190.
25. *Rescriptus Beati papae Damasi* (Hinschius 21); Jaffé 241; Damian, *Letter* 112; cf. Ryan, *Sources* no. 194, where this text is ascribed to Pope Anaclete.

(13) Let those, therefore, who oppose me, those who are at variance with me over this issue, take heed, for in being my adversaries they are clearly blasphemous rebels against the Holy Spirit, and by their blasphemy outrage him, against whom an indignity is forgiven neither now nor in the future.[26] But at this point I omit further sanctions of the holy pontiffs, lest I be thought to exceed the limits of epistolary brevity. For annoying long-windedness begets disgust, and certainly he for whom the evidence of the saints is not sufficient, wherever it was gleaned, will not be satisfied by further arguments.

(14) Your additional objection, which you say is provided for in the canons, that whoever despises the service of a married priest shall be deprived of communion,[27] speaking with your permission, while you heedlessly attend to the superficial meaning of the text, you do not grasp the wisdom of the Church's interpretation. He, to be sure, is called a married priest, not if he now has a wife, but rather if he had a wife before receiving the dignity of the priestly office. If, indeed, we disdain such a priest, it follows that we must also despise the blessed apostle Peter, which would be an impious thing to say.[28]

(15) Moreover, you also take in hand that mighty and celebrated sword of Goliath from the epistle of blessed Paul to the Corinthians, and unsheathing it, you attempt to attack the forces of the people of Israel: "Because of immorality," he said, "let each man have his own wife; the husband must give the wife what is due to her, and the wife must give the husband his due."[29] Now, since in this text the word "each" is used, you contend that ministers of the altar are also included along with laymen; and while in reference to this apostolic statement you are like cattle chewing up literary fodder, you fail to taste with the mouth of human devotion the essentials of spiritual interpreta-

---

26. Cf. Luke 12.10.
27. See Burchard, III, 75 (PL 140.689D), citing *Concilio Agathen.* c. 8 = *Interpretatio q.d. Isidori vulgata* of *Conc. Gangren.*, c. 4 (ed. Turner II, 2, 188); *Concilium Gangrense*, 4 (PL 84.113); Ps.-Isid., *Concilium Gangrense* (PL 130.270). See also the *Hadriana* (ed. Turner II, 2, 189); *Regulae Gangrenses* (PL 67.157); and *Canones Concilii Gangrensis, ex interpretatione Dionysii exigiui* (Mansi 2, 1106).
28. St. Peter was previously married.
29. 1 Cor 7.2–3.

tion. And what is more, you do not at all distinguish the chaff from the kernels, and disregarding the norms of selection, you mix everything together. Now the Apostle used the phrase, "Let each man have his own wife," in reference to his audience. But at the very beginning of this letter he makes it abundantly clear that in this epistle he was not speaking to priests and preachers, but rather to the people. "My brothers," he said, "I have been told by Chloe's people that there are quarrels among you. What I mean is this: each of you is saying, 'I am Paul's man,' or 'I am for Apollos'; 'I follow Cephas,' or 'I am Christ's.' Surely Christ has not been divided among you! Was it Paul who was crucified for you? Was it in the name of Paul that you were baptized?"[30] From these words it is obvious that the Apostle was rebuking, not priests, but the people, who were forming factions in asserting that they were disciples of various teachers. Therefore, when he said, "let each man have his own wife," he thereby allowed marriage for those to whom he was speaking.

(16) Here I may add, that the words *each* or *all* do not always include a whole multitude, but are often restricted within certain limits as reason might dictate. Such an example is had when the Lord says, "When I am lifted up from the earth, I shall draw all men to myself."[31] For he did not draw the traitor Judas to himself, nor did he associate himself with the bad thief, but lifted up all men to the heights of his friendship, that is, all the elect only. And the Apostle states that it is God's will that all men find salvation,[32] and wishes no one to perish. But when the prophet says, "Whatever the Lord pleases, that he does,"[33] why does he allow the reprobate to be lost? Surely, since he wishes no one to be lost, without doubt he is able to do everything that he wishes. Hence, when one says that God wishes all to be saved, it must be understood that this refers only to the elect. According to this rule, when the Apostle says, "let each man have his own wife," he does not include all men, but only those, in keeping with the norms of legitimate authority, who are allowed to have wives. Otherwise, how could those en-

30. 1 Cor 1.11–13.
32. Cf. 1 Tim 2.4.
31. John 12.32.
33. Ps 134.6.

ter marriage who defile the bed of their father, or, what a monstrous thing to say, sleep incestuously with their sisters?

(17) And so, let monks, too, publicly announce their engagement, contract marriage, and according to the judgment of your law, never blush at fondling their squalling babies in their tender embrace. And, in fact, since canonical authority frequently equates monks and deacons in sinning or repenting, how can you forbid marriage for monks, while indeed allowing it for deacons? For how is it that they are unequal only in their relations with women, since in all other sins they are considered equal? You must therefore decide, either that monks may marry, something that is sacrilegious to say, or that deacons must totally refrain from this obscene and ignominiously vile practice. And the same must be required of subdeacons, as confirmed by various decrees of the holy Fathers, which was demonstrated above. Some think that subdeacons actually hold the office of Nathinites or temple servants,[34] which is not the case. For as Jerome asserts in his *Hebrew Questions*, Nathinites may be understood to mean "those who are presented."[35] They are the Gabonites, because they were appointed by Joshua to serve the tabernacle of the Lord.[36] So, there is a great difference between Nathinites and subdeacons, since the former serve the tabernacle or the temple of the Lord as slaves, while the latter function in the fourth place in their duty to the altar, nearly equal to deacons as their ministers. And therefore, just as they are directed to take part in the sacred mysteries of the Mass together with priests and deacons, so they must also participate in observing perpetual chastity.

(18) Finally, when you say that it in no way pertains to the crime of simoniacal heresy if one receives the administration of a church by paying a subsidy for it, so long as he freely acquires the imposition of hands, what a great scandal is caused in the Church, and how far, in fact, your contention differs from the course of ecclesiastical discipline, needs no lengthy discussion,

---

34. Cf. 1 Chr 9.2, 2 Esd 10.28.
35. Cf. Jerome, *Nom. Hebr.* 47.4 (CC 72.117).
36. Cf. Josh 9.22.

since it is clear to all. For, whoever pays for a church, is also considered to have acquired consecration to which, certainly, he is promoted by accepting that church. By engaging to purchase the church, he undoubtedly also pays for consecration, without which he could not hope to preside over that church. On the other hand, you argue that since he receives investiture in ecclesiastical property, he by no means receives spiritual grace. He acquires the estate of the Church, but not the sacrament of the Church's charism. Certainly, whoever divides the Church by the brackishness of such hellish wisdom, such poisonous trickery, since he is a heretic because of this trafficking, by dividing the Church he also incurs the crime of schism.

(19) There have been some, to be sure, people of sincere faith and faulty instruction in Catholic belief, who distinguished between the human and divine nature in such a way that they maintained that the mediator between God and men possessed two persons. But those who were endowed with such mental acumen that they could penetrate the mystery of the incarnate Word, have truly affirmed that both natures were united in such an inseparable bond that not even in death could the divinity of Christ be dissociated from his body, otherwise he would not be true God if even at the point of death he ceased being God. Consequently, blessed Ambrose said, "The body of Christ indeed tasted death, but the power of God that is impassible did not leave his body."[37] In his sermon, also Pope Leo the Great did not hold a different opinion in this matter: "Unless the Word," he said, "had become flesh, and such a solid bond of unity had existed between both natures, so that not even the short period of death could separate the assumed human nature from the divine nature assuming it, mortality would never have been able to return to eternity."[38] And the same pope said elsewhere, "What the divine nature, which did not depart from the other nature of man it had assumed, had separated by its power, by its power it brought together."[39]

(20) But while you do not divide Christ, you have no fear of

---

37. Ambrose, *De incarnationis Dominicae sacramento* 5.40 (PL 16.828D).
38. Leo I, *Sermo* 70 (SC 74/3.118).
39. Leo I, *Sermo* 71 (SC 74/3.125).

dividing the Church, which is his body. For the Apostle says, "I now complete in my flesh those things that are wanting in the sufferings of Christ, for the sake of his body, which is the Church."[40] The soldiers, indeed, were afraid to rend the garment of the Lord, but you have no fear of tearing the Church to pieces. You, in fact, do not seek to gain the wealth of churches, so that you may aspire to the grace of consecration, but you are compelled by necessity. Therefore, you allow yourselves to be consecrated, so that you do not lose the property of the Church. You do not yearn to be made bishops in the Church, but your only objective is to come into possession of the church as if it were yours by some hereditary right. By so doing, you imitate those who used the prophetic words of David: "Let us possess the sanctuary of God as our inheritance."[41] And of such men the same psalm says to God, "With one mind they have agreed together to make a league against you."[42] For this statement strikingly applies to you, who with one mind are in accord, since in speaking against the sacred canons, you are unanimous in that you use similar means; and you form a league against God, as you publish a law that is novel and contrary to the norms of the Church.

(21) The prophet discloses those who are fighting against the Lord when he enumerates them in the verses that follow: "The tents of Edom," he said, "and the Ishmaelites, Moabites and Hagarenes, Gebal, Ammon, and Amalek, and foreigners together with the citizens of Tyre, Asshur too comes with them. They lend aid to the descendants of Lot. Deal with them as with Midian and Sisera, as with Jabin by the torrent of Kishon. They perished at Endor,"[43] and so forth. Now, if I explain the meaning of their names, we shall find that they agree with your way of thinking and acting. For the Edomites are said to be "bloody" or "earthly."[44] This fits you nicely, for as you promote these ideas of yours, you obviously demonstrate that you are of flesh and blood, and totally earthbound. You are also the Ishmaelites, that is, "men who obey"[45] the world and not God, the

---

40. Col 1.24.
41. Ps 82.13.
42. Ps 82.6.
43. Ps 82.7–11.
44. Cf. Jerome. *Nom. Hebr.* 63.22 (CC 72.139).
45. Cf. Ibid. 7.15 (CC 72.67).

flesh and not the divine law. Moab, however, has the meaning "from the father,"[46] by which words, since paternal incest is here understood, your lust too is condemned. Then here are the Hagarenes, that is, "alien residents" or "strangers,"[47] by which names we indicate those who by outward association pretend to be fellow citizens of the Christian people, but by opposing the law of Christ, live among them in the spirit of strangers and foreigners. Gebal is said to mean "a deceptive valley,"[48] by which are meant those who are insincerely meek and falsely humble. Ammon may be interpreted as a "confused people" or "a people of sorrow,"[49] by which we should understand those who by disturbing the people with their novel teaching, beget grief and sadness for the Church of God. Amalek means "a people who lick,"[50] by whom surely we may understand the enemies of Christ, of whom it is said in the psalm, "And his enemies shall lick the ground."[51]

(22) Although the word "foreigners," as used in Latin, has the meaning "aliens," and consequently "enemies," still in Hebrew they are called Philistines, which signifies "those who fall because of their drinking."[52] By such are meant those who are intoxicated by lust of the flesh, and who are thrown down headlong, falling, as it were, because of excessive drinking. Also Tyre, which in Hebrew means "lot," also has the meaning "distress" or "trouble."[53] By this word we clearly have in mind those who are deemed subject to perpetual trouble and distress because of their evil deeds. Midian is said to mean "turning aside judgment."[54] They, to be sure, turn aside judgment, who violate the justice of God's law by teaching false doctrine. Sisera means "the exclusion of joy."[55] For whoever wantonly immerse themselves in licentiousness and carnal pleasures, exclude themselves from the joy of heavenly delight. Jabin is said to mean "a wise man,"[56] which in its opposite meaning is applied to those

---

46. Cf. Ibid. 8.17 (CC 72.69).   47. Cf. Ibid. 3.3 (CC 72.61).
48. Cf. Ibid. 7.1 (CC 72.67).   49. Cf. Ibid. 3.4 (CC 72.61).
50. Cf. Ibid. 3.2 (CC 72.61).   51. Ps 71.9.
52. Cf. Jerome, *Nom. Hebr.* 13.11 (CC 72.75).
53. Cf. Ibid. 30.20 (CC 72.97). 54. Cf. Ibid. 70.4 (CC 72.147).
55. Cf. Ibid. 33.18 (CC 72.101). 56. Cf. Ibid. 32.25 (CC 72.100).

of whom the Apostle says, "Where is your wise man now, your man of learning, or your subtle debater in this passing age? Has God not made the wisdom of this world look foolish?"[57]

(23) Oreb may be interpreted to mean "dryness,"[58] for he who burns with the passion of carnal desire, is not worthy of being drenched with the pouring rain of the Holy Spirit. Zeeb means "wolf,"[59] and Zebah "victim."[60] And so, the reprobate, who are the plunderers of this world, are the wolves; and they are victims, because as they attempt to devour the weak, they are themselves exposed to the teeth of the devil, that is, the allegorical wolf. But that the explanation of these names not be at variance with the course of this disputation, I may say that false teachers in the Church are like wolves in the forest. In fact, they are at once wolves and victims, for as they kill the innocent who are like sheep, with the cruel teeth of their depraved teaching, they themselves become the prey, thrown into the maw of the devouring devil to satisfy his insatiable appetite. Of such also the psalmist says, "Like sheep they run headlong into hell, and death shall feed upon them."[61] Now the devil is known as Death, as it is written in the Apocalypse, "And there was a horse, sickly pale; and its rider's name was Death."[62]

(24) You must therefore beware lest, as you satisfy your hunger by the killing of little ones, you yourselves become victims of the hidden plunderer, to be turned into food by this voracious and insatiable murderer. Zalmunna is said to mean "the moving shade,"[63] for as every carnal man seeks for shaded happiness, by despising truth he is carried away by the varied desires of the world. But Kishon, the torrent where all these peoples were defeated, means "their obstinacy."[64] Surely, those who teach perverse doctrine, stoutly and obstinately resisting the truth, will perish in their hardheartedness. Endor, moreover, where they fell, has the meaning "the fountain of begetting,"[65]

---

57. 1 Cor 1.20.
58. Cf. Jerome, *Nom. Hebr.* 14.18 (CC 72.77).
59. Cf. Ibid. 34.1 (CC 72.101).   60. Cf. Ibid. 49.9 (CC 72.120).
61. Ps 48.15.   62. Rev 6.8.
63. Cf. Jerome, *Nom. Hebr.* 33.20 (CC 72.101).
64. Cf. Ibid. 31.28 (CC 72.99).
65. Cf. Ibid. 27.18 (CC 72.93).

in the flesh no doubt, for they who delight in this practice deserve to be victims of deadly slaughter, since they do not aspire to flourish in the place where they shall neither be married, nor take wives, a place where they can die no more.[66] They prefer rather to live in the place where whatever is begotten, must necessarily end in death. Therefore, you have fallen at Endor, in the spiritual slaughter wrought by God's sword, since you teach that ministers at the sacred altar should decide to enter incestuous marriage and beget illegitimate children.

(25) And finally, you who assert that the Church of God should not be administered with spiritual moderation and foresight, but be owned by some quasi-hereditary right, are clearly liable according to all the interpretations of the names that I briefly explained above. But while there are still more than enough arguments that I might use in refuting these themes to which I have briefly and quickly responded, I shall nevertheless call a halt to my writing, so that in the leisure to catch my breath, I may recover my strength to dictate at greater length, if that should yet be necessary. My dear friends, forgive my bold language, and if you find that my salty remarks were too sharp as they gushed forth in my attack on you, do not blame me, but rather yourselves for having forced me to write to you.

66. Cf. Luke 20.35.

LETTER 142

Peter Damian to the community in the hermitage of Gamugno. In one of his most widely known letters, Damian takes the hermits of Saint Barnabas of Gamugno to task for their scandalous living. Not only have they neglected his instructions, but they have deterred young men—in this case, Erlembald Cotta of Milan, who reported to him on their way of life—from joining the community. He especially makes two points: they must avoid gluttony and avarice. The first, the overindulgence in food and drink—mulled wine at Christmas—to deter consequent temptations of the flesh; the second, as destructive of the poverty they profess, because it incites them to quarrels with seculars and excessive interest in temporal affairs. In the course of his discussion of the use of alms, he proposed the revolutionary doctrine that "he who takes from the rich to help the poor is not to be labeled as avaricious, but rather as the distributor of common goods."[1] Instead of undue concern for temporalities, they should foster devotion to the Mother of God, who will protect them from attack and devastation. As usual, he illustrates his advice with *exempla*, and in conclusion begs pardon of his brothers for his harsh words.

(May 1066)

 O THE BRETHREN in the hermitage of Gamugna, Peter, sinner and monk, greetings.

(2) "A wise son," says Solomon, "makes his father glad. But a foolish son is a grief to his mother."[2] Again he says, "A son who fills the granaries in summer is a credit; a son who

---

1. On Damian's understanding of his role as a distributor of goods to the poor, see Irven M. Resnick, "Odo of Tournai and Peter Damian. Poverty and Crisis in the Eleventh Century," *Revue Bénédictine* 98.1/2 (1988) 114–140; see also Peter Černik, "Per la storia del lessico economico medievale: le 'epistolae' di Pier Damiani (1043–1069)," *Studi medievali* 40/2 (1999) 633–680.
2. Prov 10.1.

slumbers during harvest, a disgrace."³ Why I say these things, I will explain in what follows. A man, traveling from Milan on his way to visit me, passed your monastery. As he himself told me, he sought in my name to obtain lodging with you. Worn out by his travels, he stayed on somewhat longer to rest but made it a point to keep an eye on your behavior, noting carefully that some of you—without mentioning names—chattered away like old women about trifles and idle nonsense, saw others consorting with laymen, telling unseemly jokes, and engaging in elegant wantonness. Whence it happened that, besides despising you and because of you our entire congregation, he completely abandoned the very purpose of becoming a monk, in so far as that purpose can be impeded.

(3) It is, indeed, proper that our life bear fruit, not only by avoiding detours and trackless deviations from the path of justice, but also by not depriving others by bad example of access to the service of God. In truth, we should persistently heed the reproachful words of penance that we hear from the prophet, "Through you the name of God is blasphemed among the Gentiles."⁴ Note also what Scripture states about the sons of Heli: "The sin of the young men was very great before the Lord, because they withdrew men from the sacrifice of God."⁵

(4) There are many, moreover, who are buffeted by a violent world as by the storms and waves of an angry sea, and who so despair of avoiding the shipwreck of their own soul they put to port in the calm waters of this hallowed order. How much blood is on the conscience of him who, in the guise of the monastic life, lives so negligently in his chosen profession that by his wayward life he perverts those who seek to enter? Surely, the judgment of the Gospel fits such a man: "Whoever causes one of these little ones to sin, it were better for him to have a great millstone hung around his neck, and to be drowned in the depths of the sea."⁶ It was truly more tolerable for him as an individual to be whirled about in the reeling world that he had forsaken, than that he should now prevent many from entering this saving estate.

3. Prov 10.5.
5. 1 Sam 2.17.
4. Rom 2.24, Isa 52.5.
6. Matt 18.6.

(5) Hence, if our life seems so deformed and wretched as to be offensive even to men of flesh and blood, how, do you think, is it judged by the angels who always surpass us in spiritual dignity; or by God, who exceeds the very purity of the angels? This fearful fact must consequently be pondered, unless we should wish our life's ill fame to offend the angels assigned to guard us, causing them to bring charges against us before God rather than defend us by their testimony.

(6) This also has recently come to our attention regarding your gloriously holy life, that several points pertaining to the regulation of chastity that we established as a norm for you have now been so widely forgotten as though they had been commanded by some demented shepherd: namely, that during the twofold Lenten season wine should not be drunk nor fish eaten; that except on solemn feast days legumes should not be brayed; that no hot dish be prepared for the evening meal; that foods fried in oil be served only rarely. We further imposed many similar rules, whose observance one might rather deplore than write about. No wonder that, now that I am gone, this matter should be taken for granted, since when I was with you at Christmas this year, mead mixed with various spices was prepared without my knowledge. Which, as I declared, I abhorred all the more, struck by the novelty of the deed, as until then I had not even heard of such a thing happening among hermits.

(7) But let no one judge that, in saying these things, I hold the opinion of those who forbid God's creatures to take food;[7] nor that I oppose the Apostle's decision commanding us to eat whatever was served,[8] and to refuse nothing that had been gratefully received.[9] For it is one thing for me to assert that God's creatures are indiscriminately good; another that I provide bodily chastisement for the observance of chastity and sobriety. The tree in paradise, produced by a good Artisan, was indeed good; yet, by the same Creator's command it was good not to eat of it.[10] But while one good is not easily related to the

---

7. Cf. 1 Tim 4.3.
9. 1 Tim 4.4.
8. Cf. 1 Cor 10.27.
10. Cf. Gen 2.16–17.

other, death is immediately begotten of the poisonous seed of pride. That which was good by nature became evil by the sin of disobedience; and what had been forbidden for our profit by the Author of life, became deadly for man through the unwarranted use of his freedom.

(8) This sin of the first man, my brothers—if I may speak with your leave—you have not failed to repeat down to this very day if from desire of sensual allurements you taste of that which was forbidden you. For as often as the hand disobediently reaches for food such as we have described, the fall of the first parent is doubtlessly so many times repeated, and the shoot bursts forth from the stem in conforming branches. As the waters flow, the stream will correspond to its source, the current to its origins.

(9) This also not a little disturbs me that, in exceeding the limits of obedience despite my commands, you indiscriminately accept alms from laymen, eagerly enlarge your holdings, and, in a word, both publicly and in private scurry to become rich. By so doing, you torture yourselves with the bitter pangs of worldly desire, deprive both yourselves and your posterity of the sweetness of an unencumbered life, implicate yourselves in the snares of lay concerns, and what is worse, become the occasion of endless quarreling with laymen, or rather of serving them—not bearing in mind the words of the illustrious preacher, addressed to those who have truly forsaken the world: "Having food and sufficient clothing, with these let us be content. But those who seek to become rich fall into the snares of the devil and into temptation and into many useless and harmful desires, which plunge men into destruction and damnation."[11] And he continues, "For covetousness is the root of all evils, and some in their eagerness to get rich have strayed from the faith and have involved themselves in many troubles."[12]

(10) What distinction, indeed, can be found between accepting gifts or offerings from an enemy and soiling one's own soul with the filth of the giver? Thus it was written, "Tainted his

11. 1 Tim 6.8–9.
12. 1 Tim 6.10.

gifts who offers in sacrifice ill-gotten goods! Mock presents from the lawless win not God's favor."[13] And again, "The Most High approves not the gifts of the wicked—nor for the offerings of the godless or their many sacrifices does he forgive their sins."[14] Truly, what does it profit a just man to build up by his prayers what the wicked man by his evil life quickly destroys? To this point the same wise man says, "If one man builds up and another tears down, what do they gain but trouble? If one man prays and another curses, whose voice will the Lord hear?"[15]

(11) Again, why do we amass riches? Is it because, like spendthrifts who are adept in their pursuit, we always anxiously seek to spend them for our own use, a thing that we are forbidden by a nature that is satisfied with the minimum? Meanwhile, however, in dreaming about riches we feast only our unhappy eyes since we are forbidden to divert them to the relief of our necessity. Thus, when Solomon remarked that "the covetous man is never satisfied with money, and the lover of wealth reaps no fruit from it,"[16] he immediately concluded, "Where there are great riches, there are also many to devour them. Of what use are they to the owner except to feast his eyes upon?"[17] That wealth induces anxiety in its owners and does not allow them to relax in security, should be noted by monks whose profession clearly aims not at distraction but at disengagement from worldly cares. Again Solomon says, "Sleep is sweet to the laboring man, whether he eats little or much, but the rich man's abundance allows him no sleep."[18]

(12) Moreover, even if one does not rob or steal, or never cheats through deception or craftiness, he nevertheless sins grievously if only by simply coveting another man's possessions. Consequently, it is stated in the Decalogue, "You shall not covet your neighbor's property."[19] The sort of guilt involved in desiring another man's goods—if I may purposely omit much other evidence—may be learned from one example of blessed Peter. "Let none of you," he says, "suffer as a murderer, or a thief, or a

13. Sir 34.21.
14. Sir 34.23.
15. Sir 34.28–29.
16. Eccl 5.9.
17. Eccl 5.10.
18. Eccl 5.11.
19. Deut 5.21.

slanderer, or as one coveting what belongs to others."[20] By associating the covetous man with murderers, thieves, and slanderers, who, to be sure, do not possess the kingdom of God, Peter clearly shows, by grouping them so, how damnable and serious is this crime.

(13) And his meaning becomes all the more evident if one notes carefully the sequel to his words. For he immediately added, "But if he suffer as a Christian, let him not be ashamed; but let him glorify God under this name. For the time has come for the judgment to begin with the household of God."[21] If I may speak of those who seek other men's goods, he indeed suffers not as a Christian but as an anti-Christian if he yearns for another's substance while enduring the care of adversity. Christ came to offer himself and to bring heavenly glory; but when the Antichrist comes, he attempts to steal a truly precious treasure, namely, the souls of men. Consequently, if one who covets another's goods is not a Christian, on what grounds can he be called a monk?

(14) It should be noted that he who takes from the wealthy rather than from the unfortunate to provide for his brothers who are in need, or who supports some pious work, or, more importantly, who relieves the poor in their necessity, should not be counted an avaricious man, but as one who justly moves common goods from one group of brethren to another. One man is richer than others, not for the reason that he alone should possess the things he holds in trust, but that he disburse them to the poor. He should distribute the goods of others, not as their owner but as an agent, and not merely through motives of charity, but of justice. Thus, when the prophet said, "Lavishly he gives to the poor," he did not add that "his mercy," but that "his justice shall endure forever."[22] Also, when the Lord spoke of giving alms, he said, "Take heed not to practice your justice before men, in order to be seen by them."[23] He explained that he wished almsgiving to be reckoned especially as justice, by immediately adding, "Therefore, when you give alms, do not

20. 1 Pet 4.15.
22. Ps 111.9.
21. 1 Pet 4.16.
23. Matt 6.1.

sound a trumpet before you, as the hypocrites do."²⁴ Since giving of one's own bespeaks mercy, it is in the province of justice to distribute what belongs to others. Wherefore, he who takes from the rich to give to the poor is not to be thought a thief, but a dispenser of common property. We have briefly discussed these points to distinguish those who prey on the possessions of others from faithful stewards, so that vice might not conceal itself under the appearance of virtue, or, on the other hand, that a false notion of vice be permitted to obscure the quality of true virtue.

(15) If, after accepting the talents of silver, Gehazi, the servant of Elisha, had provided for the sons of the prophets, as he deceitfully claimed, he should never have had to endure the sufferings of leprosy. He contracted the infection, however, of which the donor was freed, because he accepted the goods of another, not to promote a work of mercy, but to satisfy his greed to possess them as his very own. Hence the man of God said, after properly correcting him, "Was not my heart present when the man turned back from his chariot to meet you?"²⁵ And he added, "So now you have received money and garments to buy oliveyards, and vineyards, and sheep, and oxen, and menservants, and maid-servants. But the leprosy of Naaman shall also stick to you and to your seed forever."²⁶

(16) They are indeed of the seed of Gehazi, who hoard against the day of contingent ill fortune what they had accepted to promote works of mercy. By seeking to appropriate wealth acquired through charity, posterity will reflect its mean and degenerate ancestry and will doubtless bear the leprosy of another's crime. Nor should we overlook what was said here, "And Gehazi went out from him a leper as white as snow."²⁷ Snow is white, but it is also cold. Now the hypocrite, who by feigning hidden sanctity disguises himself as an angel of light, hardly glows with the fires of love. Like snow, he is both white and frozen because he pretends to apply himself to works of mercy, but has never penetrated the depths of genuine love.

---

24. Matt 6.2.
25. 2 Kgs 5.26.
26. 2 Kgs 5.26–27.
27. 2 Kgs 5.27.

(17) But why should I go on? I have said it in your presence, and I say it now that I am absent, with as much fervor then as now: Despise riches lest you go begging forever; choose to be poor that you may reign unendingly. "Blessed are the poor in spirit," Christ said, "for theirs is the kingdom of heaven."[28] And Solomon remarked, "He who hates ill-gotten gain prolongs his days."[29] Again he wrote, "Wealth is useless on the day of wrath, but virtue saves from death."[30] And he continued, "Better a poor man who walks in his integrity than he who is crooked in his ways and rich."[31] And in another place, "He who is in haste to grow rich will not go unpunished."[32] Finally, "The avaricious man is perturbed about his wealth, and he knows not when want will come upon him."[33]

(18) The restraint of [monastic] discipline should likewise curb the desires of gluttony. Indeed, he strives in vain to erect a tower who sets the foundation in shifting sand. Whoever seeks to build a house with stones of virtue, must first root out the bristling thickets of carnal desires. To this point Solomon said, "Diligently work your field so that afterward you may establish your house."[34] He, to be sure, builds a proper house of the Spirit who first clears the field of his body of the thorns of vice. On the other hand, if the briers of carnal passions and desires are allowed to spread through the field of the flesh, the complete structure of virtue, starving for goodness, will collapse from within. Hence Solomon also said, "I passed by the field of the sluggard, by the vineyard of the man without sense; and behold! it was all overgrown with thistles; its surface was covered with nettles, and its stone wall broken down."[35]

(19) How shall we interpret the field or the vineyard of the sluggard except in terms of the flesh of any idle man who is unwilling to exert himself in the tasks of spiritual husbandry? What further is meant by the thistles but the incitements of gluttony and carnal allurements? And again, how shall we interpret the nettles except as carnal desires? And how, finally, shall we un-

---

28. Matt 5.3; cf. Luke 6.20. 29. Prov 28.16.
30. Prov 11.4. 31. Prov 28.6.
32. Prov 28.20. 33. Prov 28.22.
34. Prov 24.27. 35. Prov 24.30.

derstand the stone wall, unless by it is meant the structure of virtues held together, as it were, by the mortar of charity. Therefore, the field of the foolish and indolent man is overrun by thorns and thistles when the body, indulged by idleness, is not exercised by the discipline of incessant work, but is sensuously pampered in its pursuit of lust and wantonness. The crumbling wall is consequently demolished, because the whole fabric of virtue is destroyed as by the ramming blows of incontinence.

(20) The prince of cooks, to be sure, destroyed the walls of Jerusalem.[36] The stomach is rightly called the prince of cooks, because its needs are served by the elaborate effort of cooks. Whoever, therefore, wishes to harvest a rich spiritual crop must constantly put his back to the plow of discipline and chastity in furrowing the field of his body. Just as he would break up the soil of his fallow lands with a weeding hoe, he should crush with the blows of continual penance whatever he discovers in himself to be unyielding and unproductive. Nor should he hesitate to root out the thistles of insistent gluttony and the sharp briers of carnal desires, by which the fair fields of his heart are conditioned to produce an abundant spiritual harvest. Hence Solomon also said, "He who tills his own land will have food in plenty, but from idle pursuits a man has his fill of poverty."[37]

(21) To this type of agriculture, surely Joshua figuratively exhorted the descendants of Joseph, "If you are too many," he said, "go up to the forest and clear out a place for yourselves there in the land of the Perezzites and Raphaim, since the mountain regions of Ephraim are so narrow."[38] But they complained and said to him, "We cannot go up to the mountains, since the Canaanites living in the valley region all have iron chariots." Joshua replied, "You are a numerous people and very strong. You will have not merely one lot but you will pass to the mountain and cut down the wood and clear it to make room to dwell in, and you may be able to proceed further when you

---

36. Cf. 2 Kgs 25.10. The *prince of cooks* was Nabuzardan, the general in charge of the destruction of Jerusalem. He had previously been the *buticularius* (butler) of King Nebuchadnezzar. See RE 16.2: 1495, s.v., "Nabuzardan."
37. Prov 28.19.
38. Josh 17.15.

have destroyed the Canaanites whom you say have iron chariots and are very strong."[39]

(22) All of which I might possibly explain—and in many words—if the bounds of epistolary brevity did not forbid. It will suffice to say only this by way of summary: When Joshua commended the people to clear the forest, he meant precisely what, in our time, Jesus, who bore the same name, had in mind when he bade his followers root out the wild-growing thorns of vice. He advised them to wage implacable war against the Canaanites and to ascend the mountains, in that they should eagerly combat the barbarous hoard of vices and reach the heights of lofty virtue.

(23) In saying, too, that like cowards they protested their inability to oppose those who fought in iron chariots, he meant our weak and brittle selves, who often despair of sustaining the attack of evil spirits that charge like iron chariots. For when the wantonness of gluttony, the whirlpool of lust, and the plague of all vices are massed against us like the roaring charge of the Canaanites, what is this but the Canaanites attacking us in iron chariots, and blocking our access from the plains of carnal living to the saving heights of virtue? But the divine commander of our forces inspires our weakness to fight with constant bravery against the assault of the enemy and urges us to scale the heights.

(24) Yet how can we triumph over our enemies if we forever gorge ourselves in feasting and wallow in our cups? Indeed Solomon said of these excesses, "He who loves pleasure will suffer want; he who loves wine and perfume will not be rich."[40] And again, "Wine is arrogant, strong drink is riotous; none who goes astray for it is wise."[41] What is meant by accustoming the stomach to wine and exquisite food except to open the door to the enemy of the soul? Hence Solomon further said, "If a man pampers his servant from childhood, he will turn out to be stubborn."[42] He, indeed, properly restrained this servant with the scourge of abstinence, he who said, "I chastise my body and

---

39. Josh 17.16–18.
40. Prov 21.17.
41. Prov 20.1.
42. Prov 29.21.

bring it into subjection."[43] He argued against this servant when he said, "Food for the belly and the belly for food, but God will destroy both it and them."[44] This servant should be crushed underfoot, he indicated, when he said, "For many walk, of whom I have told you often and now tell you even weeping, that they are enemies of the cross of Christ. Their end is ruin, their god is the belly, their glory is in their shame."[45] Note that two terrible things are mentioned here: they are enemies of the cross of Christ, and that their god is the belly. The same Apostle projects a fearful sentence when he says, "If any man does not love the Lord Jesus Christ, let him be anathema. Maranatha."[46] He, moreover, who makes of his stomach a god, in a sense is guilty of denying God. In consequence, these two terror-filled ideas appear as one, namely, being an enemy of Christ, God forbid, and worshiping another besides the one God.

(25) Two of the brethren, one a young man, the other old, were engaged as custodians of an estate known as Ravenniana, belonging to the monastery of Classis. On the eighth day before Christmas, a Friday preceding a Saturday on which twelve lessons were customarily read, the young monk said to the elder, "Brother Laetus," for that was his name, "what shall we do today?" The old man said, "Do what you please. For my part, I shall have some wine and shall not be satisfied, as it is written, to live on bread alone."[47] Incidentally, he was a jolly man, stout, sound, and hardy. When the table was set, both sat down to eat. The former, however, was satisfied with bread and water, and disciplined himself by observing the fast prescribed by the *Rule*. But the latter indulged himself with wine and with whatever else was there. If he, indeed, had known what was in store for him, he would not have reduced the rigors of abstinence and pandered his wanton gluttony. For just eight days later, when the world was rejoicing in the glory of the Lord's birth, he died; and while others were invited to table to celebrate the joyous feast, he was borne to his grave, accompanied by a gathering of weeping relatives.

43. 1 Cor 9.27.
45. Phil 3.18.
47. Cf. Deut 8.3, Matt 4.4.
44. 1 Cor 6.13.
46. 1 Cor 16.21.

(26) A certain monk reported to me, that while carrying a dish of fried food into the refectory, a sudden urge to gluttony affected him. Directly, he popped a piece into his mouth and secretly ate it. Suddenly, such a fierce wave of passion assailed him that, acting as he had never done before, he could no longer contain himself until with his own hands he had discharged a defiling flow of semen. This monk indeed rightly judged his servant to be insolent, as the wise man said, as a result of having pampered him.[48] Of this monk certainly it can be said that "after the morsel, Satan entered into him."[49] Without doubt, the stomach and the genital parts are in close proximity to one another; when the former is heedlessly nourished, the latter are incited to reproachful acts. Therefore, we must destroy avarice if we would live at peace and be independent of laymen. We must curb gluttony if we are to be distinguished by the true splendor of chastity. Let idle words be foreign to our lips and may the severe judgment of an angry God constantly restrain us from everything superfluous. We should therefore consider it a disgrace to surrender meekly to the attacking forces in this battle within us; but let us rather strive to return to the author of our manhood, flying the banners of glorious victory.

(27) Moreover, I am much distressed, and the guilt of serious sin is on your conscience, because certain rules that I established for your community, as I said above, have now been forgotten and willfully abandoned. That which I once saw fit to prescribe must not be violated without my consent. For whatever has been commanded for the community by public law, must either be observed by all without exception, or rescinded by common consent. On the other hand, if it is violated at will by anyone, the offense is deserving of severe punishment.

(28) To be sure, because Achan, son of Carmi, contrary to general command did not resist taking what was under the ban of Jericho, he did not escape fiery destruction even after he had been stoned.[50] He who had been incited by the fires of avarice, fed the flames with his own flesh in a holocaust of

---

48. Cf. Prov 29.21. 49. John 13.27.
50. Cf. Josh 7.

vengeance. Jonathan, moreover, deserved to die because, by anticipating the hour set for eating, he changed the law promulgated for all.[51] Also, because only the man who dared to gather wood in the desert on the Sabbath had broken the common law, he alone paid the penalty and was stoned to death[52]—not because it is criminal to gather wood when urged by necessity, but for the reason that it is no ordinary crime to disobey an accepted rule of law.

(29) But now let me also cite an example close at hand. In the monastery of St. Vincent, located a short distance from Mount Petra Pertusa,[53] I had established as a strict regulation that the beginning of Lent be observed with special rigor: that for three days all the brethren fast on only a little bread and water; that no word pass their lips except when reading or praying; that they walk barefoot in grief and mourning; that after chanting the office in common they chastise one another with switches. While the brethren cooperated willingly and with spiritual joy in these practices, and had more than demonstrated their goodwill, even exceeding what had been commanded, there was one among them who secretly broke the rule of fasting. This brother was skilled in many arts and crafts, in writing and secretarial work, in pottery making and in building, so that somehow this line of verse seemed to fit him:

> Augur, rope-dancer, doctor, or astrologer, all sciences he knew.[54]

And as is usual in such cases, because he felt proud of his ability in many necessary skills, he was often allowed to act just as he pleased.

(30) About the middle of Lent he appeared to be generally in good spirit, a stout man, active and healthy—when suddenly he came down with a mild cold. When I met him on the occasion of visitation, I at once had a mind to tell him what I had heard and to forbid him to say Mass because of certain infractions. But fearing to irritate him, I was somewhat at a loss, I admit, and deliberated for some time. In short, I finally took the

---

51. Cf. 1 Sam 14.24–30.
53. At the Furlo Pass.
52. Cf. Num 15.32–36.
54. Juvenal, *Saturae* 3.77.

hard approach, reaching the conclusion that it was more prudent to offend man than the majesty of the omnipotent God. I therefore said to him, "Dear brother Maurus, confess your sins and do penance, and if there is something on your conscience that hinders you from the wondrous celebration of the Mass, do not think it beneath your dignity, venerable brother, to obey the sacred canons." At that he answered, "I have confessed all my sins to numerous holy men, but was never commended to refrain from celebrating Mass."

(31) On the second day of his illness, just before dawn, as he sat up in bed—he was not lying down—he anxiously demanded to receive the sacrament of the Body of the Lord. While the abbot and I and the rest of the brethren stood about the sick man's bed, the abbot began to reprimand him, asking why one who showed no signs of death should beg for viaticum with such vehemence. But despite this reproach the sick man persisted in his request and, as the priest was approaching with the Blessed Sacrament, he turned to one of the brethren and whispered into his ear, confessing some grave sin. As the astonished confrere later told me, all happened so quickly that he was unable to determine the exact amount of penance. Still undecided, and speaking softly to the penitent in an undertone, he imposed fifteen years of penance. But just as the sick monk received the Sacred Mystery from the hand of the priest—my God! I am again unnerved as I tell you—he suddenly breathed his last, vomiting a flow of bile. This poisonous substance continued to flow from his mouth until the burial, so that as long as the corpse lay on its bier, the bloody matter constantly ran along the floor of the church.

(32) I have taken pains to report this event accurately, not only that they may hear and be shaken who, through their eagerness for personal pleasure, violate the established order of discipline, but also to benefit those who carry on their conscience a crime that they expect to confess on their deathbed. The latter, indeed, are guilty because they postpone those things that should be done; and the former, in the life to come, will undoubtedly pay at greater interest the debt of penance that they had neglected to perform.

(33) Let me tell you about another event that happened in the same monastery. It had been ordered, and for almost three years now it was the custom that each day the office of the ever-blessed Virgin be said in addition to the canonical hours. There was in the community a certain Gozo who was a monk by profession, an unworthy character, but a man of keen and brilliant talent. He began to argue that what St. Benedict had commended was more than enough and that recently contrived burdens should not be imposed on the brethren. Nor, said he, are we holier than the ancient Fathers, who had evidently judged these things unprofitable and superstitious and had set limits to our chanting and to all other regular observance. With the latter we should be content, so that they who carelessly turn from this norm may not be led into error by impassable detours.

(34) In a word, he insisted on opposing the Queen of the World, and achieved his purpose. By his adroit scheming he persuaded the brethren to abandon the customary veneration of the Blessed Mary. But the judgment of God is not unconcerned at our perverseness. Immediately such a hail of adversity, such a storm of wars and afflictions struck their monastery that menacing swords daily threatened the monks with death and destruction. On all sides there were raids and devastation; rural holdings with buildings and cottages went up in flames; dependents and serfs of that holy place were brutally killed. Not only the phantom of death, but death itself stalked its prey, so that the monks were overcome by the nausea of living, since in the crash of war they found it impossible to maintain the monastic office, so profitable to their peace. At no little cost the Emperor was reached in Germany and pragmatic sanctions bearing imperial seals were procured.[55] But no further help appeared. In all our endeavors, to be sure, it is not the effort but the result that counts.

(35) Hence, when the brethren continued to urge me to in-

---

55. This account probably refers to the events of 1052–1055, when Duke Godfrey of Lorraine, who was married to Beatrice of Tuscany, revolted at the death of Duke Boniface. This occasioned Emperor Henry III's coming to Italy a second time. Cf. Herbert Grundmann, ed., *Gebhardt Handbuch der Deutschen Geschichte*, 9th ed. (Stuttgart: Union Verlag Stuttgart, 1970), I, 318–19.

tervene as a mediator and, if possible, to arrange peace treaties between the combatants, I replied to their request, "Christ is our peace, of whom the angels proclaimed shortly after his birth of the Virgin: 'Glory to God in the highest and peace on earth.'"[56] Consequently, because they cast from their monastery the Mother of Peace itself, they deserved to be engulfed by the winds and the waves of tribulation and disaster.

(36) But lest I unduly weary the reader—these monks were satisfied by no uncertain evidence that the words I spoke were true. Finding themselves in great need, they returned at last to their senses, humbly prostrated themselves on the ground, and after receiving a penance, unanimously promised henceforth never to neglect the customary praises of the Mother of God. Soon, indeed, if I may be excused the figure, after the storm such fair weather prevailed from that day until now, that the brethren enjoyed the calm of blessed peace and congratulated themselves at their rescue from the Scyllaean whirlpool, guided to port by the Virgin's Son. The saying of the prophet was truly fulfilled, "Return to me, and I will return to you, says the Lord."[57] Therefore, they who lightly tear up the statutes of their elders should bear these events in mind, and should fear with good reason lest the sword of God's anger come upon them.

(37) Forgive my words, dearly beloved brothers, and if perhaps I have exceeded to some extent the bounds of calm correction, attribute it rather to zeal for fraternal charity than to malice. Remember the words of Solomon, "Better is an open rebuke than a love that remains hidden. Wounds from a friend are better than the deceitful greetings of an enemy."[58] And again, "The man who remains stiff-necked and hates rebuke will be crushed suddenly beyond cure."[59]

(38) May Almighty God, the physician of souls, my dearly beloved, turn the absinthe of my speech into sweetness for you; and may the wondrous Enlightener enkindle at the flame of his Spirit whatever is cold or dark within you.

56. Luke 2.14.
57. Mal 3.7.
58. Prov 27.5.
59. Prov 29.1.

LETTER 143

Peter Damian to the Countess Guilla, the wife of Rainerius II, the marquis of Monte S. Maria. He advises the young countess, recently married, to reform the malpractices of the estate to which she has come: oppression of the poor and unjust legislation against the interests of the serfs. She should take the initiative, and her husband will follow suit. Restitution for past plundering is also in order. In this letter Damian reveals himself as normally heterosexual, providing a riposte to those who would suggest that, as the author of the *Book of Gomorrah* (*Letter* 31), he was a homosexual.

(Shortly before 1067)

TO THE EMINENT COUNTESS GUILLA, the monk Peter the sinner promises his earnest prayers.

(2) Since it is better to be undisputedly ignorant of a matter over which conflict might arise, than always struggling to forget it, it is safer for me to converse in writing with young women in whose presence I am apprehensive. Certainly, I who am already an old man can licitly and securely look at the face of an old woman lined with wrinkles, whose features are moist with the rheum from her watering eyes; but like boys from the fire I guard my eyes at the sight of more beautiful and attractive faces. My heart is indeed unhappy, for a hundred readings of the Gospel mysteries do not suffice to retain them; whereas the recollection of beauty, seen but once, does not leave my memory. And forgetfulness is unable to impede the image of vanity, if the law written by the finger of God does not endure.

(3) But of such items elsewhere. Nor should I here write of things that are harmful for me, but rather of that which can profit you.

(4) By right of marriage, my daughter, you have indeed come to a most distinguished house, but one, I must say, that is

morally deficient; a house outstanding for wealth and dignity, but one that is disfigured by a depraved manner of living. Therefore, break the pattern of customary evil that you have found, abolish the practice of confiscating the property of the poor, prevent unjust taxes and impositions on the serfs, and following the example of King Josiah, establish a new order of affairs. He, in fact, discovered that the kingdom of Judah had been devoted to the worship of idols and contaminated by age-old sacrilege, not only in the days of his father but even of his grandfather. But as Scripture attests,[1] in the gorge of Kidron he promptly burned all the vessels that had been made for Baal, and destroyed the soothsayers and the altars on which they sacrificed in the high places. He broke the sacred statues and cut down the groves. He defiled the altars and pulled down the houses of the male prostitutes. And since it would take too long to recount everything that he did, it will suffice to say that he abolished all these abominable things, magnificently rebuilt the temple of the Lord, and restored the ceremonies of the Law.

(5) In imitation of this holy king, you too must destroy the practices of long-standing disorder, and introduce a new regime of wholesome and blameless deeds. For even though you will not find idols there that you should overthrow, you have discovered avarice that is equally deserving of punishment, which, as the Apostle states, "is the service of idols."[2] You should not delight in savoring the small holdings of orphans or the fattened birds of widows, as the Lord proclaims in the terrifying words of Moses, "You shall not maltreat any widow or orphan," he says. "If you hurt them they will cry out to me and I will hear their cry; my anger will be roused and I will kill you with the sword; your own wives shall become widows and your children fatherless."[3] In other words, if you harm women deprived of the comfort of their husband, and children who have lost their parents, your wives and children too, struck down in my wrath with condign punishment, will soon be left widows

---

1. Cf. 2 Kgs 23.4–14.   2. Eph 5.5.
3. Exod 22.22–24.

and orphans, so that anyone may injure them with impunity, just as you too were securely confident that the former could be mistreated without retribution.

(6) But now let me demonstrate this decree of the Lord, not from the past, but rather by an example from your own family. The brother of your father-in-law, namely, the Marquis Uguzo, was formerly Count Hubert. While his wife was living in the castle that was known as Suffena, she took a pig from a certain widow, and after it had been prepared for the banquet by her talented cooks, she sat down to eat. And as the widow had frequently begged that the pig be returned to her but was unable to receive even a tolerant hearing, with tears in her eyes she formally presented herself to the lady at her table, and requested that she at least be given a small portion for her sustenance. "Since I do not deserve," she said, "to enjoy in normal fashion, as I had hoped, the pig that I had nurtured, I should at least be allowed to taste it, if ever so slightly." In many words the proud countess turned down her request, and with angry and abusive language declared that the widow would never get a bite of it.

(7) But see how God in his justice is ever prepared to use his avenging sword to punish wickedness and pride. For after dinner on that same day, as the countess was sitting securely under a protruding part of the castle wall, digesting her meal at the widow's expense, without the slightest premonition of danger, suddenly leftover rubble from the ramparts fell away, and an immense pile of the broken overhang buried the unfortunate woman. Noisy bands of retainers came on the run from all sides, diggers appeared, and searched through the piles of earth. And as they burrowed haphazardly into the fallen mass, scarcely a scrap of the shattered body could be found. Parts of bones and limbs that only with the greatest effort they were able to scrape out, I might say, they eventually buried. And so, the countess who had denied the request of the widow for a small bit of pork, was rewarded by having her body torn to pieces.

(8) Therefore, noble daughter, do not live by plundering the poor, but recoil from food acquired through violence as you would from the poisonous bite of serpent. And since the

Apostle commands everyone to work with his own hands, "so that he may have something to share with the needy,"[4] you should intensify your farming, and thus your barns will be filled with abundant crops to be used in assisting the poor. For, as we read in the book *On Illustrious Men*,[5] Bishop Hilary of Arles helped the needy in times of necessity, not only because of his great compassion, but also by his own hard work, personally plowing the fields, and nobleman that he was, and far better educated than others, disciplining himself by working as a farmer.

(9) Yet it does not suffice to warn you against seizing the property of others, but I must further add that you should make restitution upon discovering things that have been stolen before your coming here. In this connection, in ancient times after the Roman commander, Scipio, was victorious in the war with Carthage, he returned to the cities of Italy, Africa, and Sicily all the spoils that had formerly been taken from them by the Carthaginians.[6] And what today the Gospel can hardly wring from those who profess to follow it, this pagan fulfilled before ever the Gospel had appeared.

(10) But perhaps you will reply to all this, that unless your husband take the lead in these matters, a weak instrument such as you can hardly hope to succeed. Nor will I disagree with what you say, for since by God's will a wife's dedication is to her husband, the weaker sex usually needs the authority of a man. But when a wife's opinion is more correct, it is proper that a husband not stand in her way by using his authority. The priest Ozias, in fact, set a deadline of five days for the Lord to come to their aid, and the high-spirited Judith reproached him for this decision: "These are not words that will produce mercy, but will rather stir up wrath and enkindle [God's] indignation."[7] When Abigail, moreover, changed the decision of the foolish Nabal,

---

4. Eph 4.28.
5. Cf. Gennadius, *De scriptoribus ecclesiasticis* 69 (PL 58.1100).
6. Livy (30.37.1–6) reports Scipio's peace terms, but makes no mention of the restitution of *spolia*. Nor does Polybius or Appianus refer to this event. Damian, however, used Eutropius, *Breviarium* 4.12.1–3 (MGH Auct.ant. 2.72).
7. Jdt 8.12.

she saved her household from slaughter at the swords of David.[8] And this she did for Nabal's benefit, by refusing to follow his bad judgment. When Manoah saw the angel, he began to lose hope, but his wife overcame his lack of courage and resolution: "We are doomed to die," he said, "for we have seen God. But she replied: If the Lord had wanted to kill us, he would not have accepted a whole-offering and a grain-offering at our hands."[9] Besides, if a husband were never to follow the advice of his wife, the Lord would not have said to Abraham, "Pay heed to everything that Sarah has to say to you."[10]

(11) Therefore, as far as possible, you should not delay returning whatever was acquired through injustice, or taken from others by violence—property, as you are aware, that adjoins the lands over which you now preside, lest these words that were written down appear to apply to you: "If you have proved untrustworthy with what belongs to another, who will give you what is your own?"[11] And thus, venerable daughter, reform the manners of your house, suppress violence and violations of the peace, and through discipline curb the administration of your estate that has gone unchecked. According to the will of God, dispose all that has been committed to you in such a way that, after your brief stewardship has run its course, you may be worthy to pass to the reward of your eternal inheritance.

8. Cf. 1 Sam 25.
9. Judg 13.22–23.
10. Gen 21.12.
11. Luke 16.12

LETTER 144

Peter Damian to the Empress Agnes. Fearing the advance of the Normans on Rome, the archdeacon Hildebrand persuaded Agnes to travel to the German court to engage her son, King Henry IV, in an expedition into Italy on behalf of the Holy See. In return, he was to receive the Imperial crown. Damian reluctantly consented to this plan, but now, in Rome, he changed his mind and begged the empress to return. He sends greetings to her companion on the trip, Lopertus, cardinal bishop of Palestrina, and papal legate, requesting also his quick return.

(January 1067)

O HIS LADY, THE EMPRESS AGNES, the monk Peter the sinner offers his service.

(2) I can hardly tell you how distressed I am, as in dreadful suspense I daily await the joy of your return. What a fool I was, and why in my stupidity and lack of wit did I ever agree to your journey? And what is more, why did I not use force to oppose your departure? Why, in fact, did I not snatch the horses' reins, and so far as that was permissible, prevent your leaving even with my bare hands? Indeed, after you were gone, your absence caused Rome to mourn, brought sadness to the church of blessed Peter, and sorrow to holy men and women in all of Italy. For like a golden star you appeared to illumine the darkness of those who pursued earthly goals, and by inciting them to God, by your shining example you restored light to those who followed you.

(3) And in a few short words, while I too deplore your long absence, I dread to see the walls of Rome. Therefore, return, my lady, return and bring festive joy for those who grieve over you, reduced to tears at the sparkling gem in the heavens somehow torn from its setting in Rome, the capital of the world. May the regal splendor of the imperial court cause you disgust, and

only the fisherman's boat pleasantly satisfy your sense of smell. Along with Petronilla,[1] may you too find your burial place in Rome, and may your illustrious father rejoice at his two daughters, one of the flesh, the other of the spirit, resting finally at his side. I also send greetings to my lord, Bishop Lopertus, and beg that he soon return.

1. According to legend, she was the daughter of St. Peter; see Gisela Muschiol, "Petronella," *LThK* 8.89.

LETTER 145

Peter Damian to Cencius (Cimtius), the prefect of Rome. He praises the prefect for discharging his office with justice, and for protecting the poor, and recommends to him the interests of the Church. But more startling is his commendation of Cencius's acting as a substitute homilist for Damian in St. Peter's church on the feast of the Epiphany when Damian's voice failed him, and he finished the sermon. He then took occasion to enunciate the doctrine of the priesthood of all the faithful, for whom preaching should not be an extraordinary function. Damian thus anticipated the emphasis on this idea that found its place in the decrees of Vatican Council II, but which at the first edition of his works (1606) was thought to be astounding, if not quasi-heretical.

(7 January 1067)

O SIR CENCIUS, prefect of the city of Rome, the monk Peter the sinner sends greetings.

(2) Just as praise for one's own achievements causes vain men to glow with pride, it incites in the good and sensible the grace of deeper humility. In fact, the latter are more properly challenged to increase their good works as they hear applause for the virtuous gifts that have been granted them. Only yesterday, at the prompting of God's goodness as I was preaching to the people in the church of blessed Peter, the prince of the apostles, on the feast of the Epiphany we were then celebrating, you spoke, not as befitting the prefect of the city, but rather as a priest of the Church. Indeed, one heard not the speech of a layman, but the blessed words of apostolic preaching. By so doing, can there be any doubt that you were following the example of him who, as king and priest, rules the world by virtue of his divine power, and offered himself for us to the Father as the mystery of life-giving sacrifice? By the grace of the

same Redeemer, whose members we are,[1] we too have received the gift of becoming exactly what he is. Consequently, John says in the Apocalypse, "Who loved us, and washed us from our sins in his own blood, and made us a kingdom, and priests to God and his Father."[2] And Peter says, "You are a chosen race, a royal priesthood, a dedicated nation, and a people claimed by God as his own, to proclaim the triumph of him who has called you out of darkness into his marvelous light."[3]

(3) It follows, therefore, that by the grace of Christ every Christian is a priest, and hence has a perfect right to proclaim his wondrous deeds. You, especially, obviously imitate the example of this priest and king, when on the bench you hand down legitimate decisions at law and by holy and zealous exhortation, in the church lift up the minds of the people assembled there. I, on the other hand, to whom the office of preaching was committed by sacerdotal ordination, suffer from difficulty with my voice, and thus am unable to be heard when many people are present. But when I recall such priests of apostolic caliber as Gregory and Ambrose overcoming a weak stomach and a feeble voice, I refuse to despair and take heart at being deprived of this consolation. Nor do I consider myself the object of a stern judge's anger, when I think that this same defect served to keep these eminent men humble. But this rather disturbs me and painfully pierces me to the quick, that when I grow hoarse, besides being unable to teach, I find it impossible to put forth even the tiniest spark of bright conversation.

(4) Now there are two things most necessary for the proficient preacher: first, that he abound in spiritual thought; and second, that he be preeminent for his virtuous life. But if any priest is deficient in either quality, namely, outstanding for his way of living, and eloquent in his teaching, one's life is undoubtedly more important than one's teaching. The fruit of good works is sweeter than the bare leaves of one's words, and renown for virtue is a more powerful example than eloquence or urbane and elegant speech. Wherefore, at the moment the Lord was born, as the Gospel history tells us,[4] an angel ap-

1. Cf. 1 Cor 6.15.
2. Rev 1.5.
3. 1 Pet 2.9.
4. Cf. Luke 2.9.

peared to the shepherds, and the splendor of God shone round them. And at once the text continues, "And the angel said to them: 'Do not be afraid; I have good news of great joy that will be to all the people. Today in the city of David a Savior has been born to you, who is Christ the Lord.'"[5]

(5) But at the Epiphany in which he was revealed to the Magi who were seeking him, the star that directed them to our Redeemer radiated light, but said not a word. But what is the significance of the angel who shone with splendor and also announced the Lord, if not the preacher's twofold grace, at once endowed with words of wisdom, and distinguished by the light of a religious life? And what should we understand by the star, if not every simple priest of upright life, who even though deficient in the richness of speech, by his outstanding deeds still shines, as it were, with the brilliance of his exemplary life, and those whom he fails to teach by his words, he inspires by the example of his intense spirituality? Therefore, since the Church's priests are "the heavens that tell out the glory of God,"[6] it is required that the priest who functions in the office of preacher shower his audience with the rains of spiritual doctrine, and glow with the radiance of a virtuous life, like the angel announcing the birth of the Lord to the shepherds, the angel who appeared in brilliant splendor and expressed in words the good news he came to announce. And to this point Malachi said, "The lips of the priest guard knowledge and they seek the law from his mouth, because he is the angel of the Lord of Hosts."[7]

(6) But if he who serves diligently as a preacher is unable by his speech to be a messenger of the Lord, let him at least be a star that gives forth the light of his holy life. By its brightness, surely, the star made known to the Magi the same message that the angel announced to the shepherds by using his voice. Thus, through Daniel it is said, "They that are learned shall shine like the bright vault of heaven, and they that instruct the multitude to justice shall be like the stars for ever and ever."[8] Still, it is

5. Luke 2.10–11.
6. Ps 18.2.
7. Mal 2.7.
8. Dan 12.3.

necessary for him who is wanting in eloquent speech to shine more brightly by reason of his meritorious life. And so it was that Moses said of himself as he spoke to the Lord, "I beseech you, O Lord, I am not eloquent from yesterday and the day before, and since you have spoken to your servant, I have a greater impediment and am slow of speech,"[9] and afterwards his face shone with such brightness that it obstructed the vision of the Israelites,[10] and because of its brilliance they were unable to look at him. But Aaron, of whom God said to Moses, "I know that your brother, Aaron the Levite, is eloquent,"[11] never enjoyed heavenly illumination.

(7) As I carefully meditate on what God said to these two men, I note that by imitating this event you have carried out, as it were, the duties imposed on both of them. "I will be in your mouth and in his mouth, and I will show you what you have to do. He will speak to the people for you, and he will be your mouthpiece; you, however, will be for him in those things that pertain to God."[12] For as you control the people by virtue of your jurisdiction as prefect of the city, and by reason of your judicial power, what else are you doing but fulfilling the office that Aaron held? And when by holy exhortation you call upon the same people to heed the things that pertain to God, what is that but loyally carrying out the spiritual design of Moses? So, well done, my energetic man; continue functioning like two men in the field of the Lord! May you progress and contend with everything that is in you, and persevere with honor in the things you have begun so well. At times by composing a case at court by justly weighing the evidence, at others mindful of your rank, using words of saving exhortation in the church, follow in the footsteps of Moses in matters that pertain to God, and again over issues that are of secular concern, act in the role of Aaron or of a priest.

(8) Therefore, be another Benjamin,[13] using both hands as you would your right, to repress with disciplinary measures the

9. Exod 4.10.
10. Cf. Exod 34.29–35.
11. Exod 4.14.
12. Exod 4.15–16.
13. Cf. Judg 3.15.

disputes of a disorderly people, acting in such a way that, so far as your status allows, you are able to preserve the rights of the Church as well. May people see in you the two-edged sword that came from the mouth of Jesus,[14] that with the weapon you carry you may strike terror in the seething hearts of rebels and be the first to defend the poor and the orphan and the rights of the Church from the attack of evil men. May those who break the law know that you are the avenger of outraged justice, and may the leaders of churches rejoice that as a vigorous and careful guardian you watch over their interests. Be a disciple of David[15] in the art of holy discretion, generously pardoning those who sought to do him harm, while being severe in punishing those who took part in killing others. Follow also in the footsteps of Judas Maccabaeus,[16] who never hesitated to attack his foes with lightning blows, and cut off the proud heads of tyrants with his avenging sword, to protect his fellow countrymen from the slaughter of the savage barbarians that threatened them. And so, fight implacably to defend the holdings of the churches, punish the violent oppressors of the poor, hold the line of justice and equity, and constantly dedicate your whole being, not to family affairs, but to the welfare of the city, so that as long as you live, Rome may honor you as the father of your country, and the holy Church may be glad to have you as its worthy defender. And after your death, may both always heap praise upon your memory, and may your name be held in benediction.

14. Cf. Rev 1.16.
15. Cf. 2 Sam 16.5ff., 4.5–12.
16. Cf. 1 Macc 5.65–68.

LETTER 146

Peter Damian to the citizens of Florence. Writing from Gamugno, he begs the Florentines to compose their differences with their bishop, Peter, whom they had accused of purchasing his office, and to await a decision upon investigation by the approaching synod in Rome. He repeats many ideas already proposed in his earlier *Liber gratissimus* (*Letter* 40), defending the validity of acts performed by a simonist bishop. Assuring his readers that he agrees with their opposition to simony, which for him was heresy, he refuses to condemn the bishop before his day in court. "It is more tolerable to excuse a sinner, than to prejudge an innocent man." He then takes on the monks of John Gualbertus in the city, who, seemingly in support of Cardinal Humbert's position, had degenerated into revolutionary action by logically nullifying all the acts of simonist bishops and priests, thereby proscribing all sacramental functions in Florence. He cautions these puritans against excessive righteousness and wisdom, and likens them to the Cathari in their anarchical denial of authority to pope, king, archbishop, or priest.

(Lent 1067)

O THE BELOVED IN CHRIST, the citizens of Florence, the monk Peter the sinner sends his service of fraternal charity.

(2) Recently, my dear friends, if you recall, I visited you and with great effort tried to compose the differences between you and your bishop, and restoring the bonds of friendship that had been broken, to promote harmony among you as a mediator of peace. But as I put forward many ideas, helpful to you in respect to the aforesaid bishop, but which were thwarted by unfavorable interpretation, and fared badly at the hands of unruly crowds, lest my reputation be unjustly impugned, and they, God forbid, be guilty of lying, let me put in writing what I often told you in your presence, so that what you heard me say, you may

now see in written form. May no deceitful person, moreover, dare to falsify my words or alter their meaning, since what I write and what I say coincide without the slightest discrepancy.

(3) Wherefore, ruling out the slightest possibility of rehabilitation, I anathematize and condemn the heresy of simony, the first of all heresies to spring from the bowels of the devil, which perversely raised its head against the practices of the early Church, and which still proceeds from the very bile of the devil, and like the plague passes into men worthy of damnation. And indeed Peter said to its author, "I see that you are doomed to taste the gall of bitterness and wear the fetters of sin."[1] But since a dove has no bitterness, and the Holy Spirit appeared over the Lord in the form of a dove,[2] he who is filled with the bitterness of gall, is incapable of possessing the spirit of a dove. Therefore, I do not hesitate to assert that all those who are corrupted by this damnable heresy are undoubtedly heretics, and according to the decrees of the sacred canons, judge them worthy of condemnation and deprived of their high office.

(4) And still, I am confident that the Church possesses such fullness of grace, that through her good things can come from evil men, purity can derive from those who are unclean, and I believe without the slightest doubt that sacraments can be conferred by detestable ministers. For she is truly the body of Christ, and according to the Apostle, "the pillar and bulwark of the truth."[3] This contention is not something novel that derives from my unfounded opinion, but is based on the sacred authority of the Catholic Fathers, established long ago. And what I wrote in the little work I entitled the *Liber gratissimus*,[4] is bolstered by many citations from the Old and the New Testament. But after totally condemning simonists, and unhesitatingly listing them as heretics, as I explained in the aforementioned book, even though the sacraments administered by them can be defended by decision of the canons, still, that conciliar censure might yet more thoroughly overwhelm them, it was decid-

---

1. Acts 8.23.   2. Cf. Matt 3.16.
3. 1 Tim 3.15.
4. Peter Damian, *Letter* 40. This title might be translated, "The Most Gratuitous Book."

ed in the Roman synod, held under the presidency of Nicholas of blessed memory, that those who up to that time had been promoted to the honors of any ecclesiastical rank, should remain ministers in the dignity they had received. But from then on, and forever, whoever allowed himself to be ordained by a simonist, would not be permitted to profit in any way from such promotion, and would thus waive all rights to function in his office as if he had never received them. And so, for this reason not only do I now disapprove of simonists, but disdain the sacraments confected by them.[5]

(5) If you have not forgotten, you often heard these things from my own lips. Nor do I now put in writing anything but what I have said. Therefore, if both you and I are in agreement over simonists, and concur in condemning their ordinations in the future, why are we still contending with one another? Obviously, it is the matter concerning your bishop, whom some of you accuse of having stolen into office by paying for it, while others freely and in good faith state that he entered gratuitously, and indeed by the door.[6] The former loudly promote their opinion with much wrangling, while the latter, saying that they are knowledgeable on this subject, refute the charge brought against him. And who am I to commit myself to standing between these bands of fiery combatants, and to impute such a deadly crime to a man before it is canonically proven? For even though error is always with us, and should everywhere be avoided, it is still more tolerable to find an excuse for a sinner than to prejudge an innocent man. The synod held each year is at hand, and the Apostolic See is approachable to all who would consult her. So, let everyone who thinks he has a just complaint against the bishop, knock at the door of the Roman Church. Nor can we little men on the corners of our alleys render invalid what was doubtless established at the highest level of world affairs.

(6) Therefore, take note that I am simply writing only of

5. Cf. *Conc. Rom* (1060, April) cc. 2–3 (MGH Const. 1.550); Anton Michel, *Papstwahl und Königsrecht, oder, Das Papstwahl-konkordat von 1059* (Munich: M. Hueber, 1936) 59, n. 54.
6. Cf. John 10.2.

those things that you heard me say when I was with you. And so, everyone guilty of lying should be ashamed, who, as he sees me hesitant to judge in a case involving such shaky controversy, still impudently shout that I am a defender of simonist heresy. Hence, let these few words suffice to explain my position to you, lest my extended remarks tire you with excessive verbosity.

(7) And now, I turn my attention to my fellow monks with whom, I am sure, this whole dispute originates. For they are saying that bishops such as these are unable to bless chrism, dedicate churches, confer clerical orders, or celebrate Masses at any time. And they are so shameless in their allegations, that this year in three parishes catechumens had to be baptized without anointing with chrism. But since Christ undoubtedly takes his name from the word "chrism," those who take away sacramental chrism are actually removing Christ from baptism. And surely, if I am not mistaken, no other heresy has emerged with such audacity, that it dared to separate chrism from the rites of baptism, that is, to take Christ from the word "Christian." But if we may believe that out of contempt for their own bishop, they secretly brought chrism from another diocese, as one of their partisans has contended, in so far as they were concerned, they committed adultery in spiritual matters and changed a sacrament into a sacrilege. This they achieved by rejecting chrism prepared in their own diocese, and in secret fraudulently substituted chrism from elsewhere.

(8) Consequently, in the last verse of his final homily, blessed Pope Gregory had this to say, "But may almighty God, who is speaking to you through me, on his own account speak to your hearts in these matters."[7] Hence, as he concluded composing his book, he clearly showed that almighty God had himself said all that was there written down. And so, in the homily he had prepared on bishops, he through whom this indwelling God was speaking most certainly admitted that the Holy Spirit was divinely given through the imposition of hands performed by a simonist: "For who are they," he asked, "who today sell doves in the temple of God, if not those who are paid for the

---

7. Gregory I, *Homiliae xl in Evangelia* 40.12 (PL 76.1312C).

imposition of hands, by which act the Holy Spirit is divinely given?"[8] And then he repeats this same statement, again making the point, as it were, for those who are slow to understand and are still in doubt. For he says, "Therefore, a dove is sold, because the imposition of hands by which the Holy Spirit is received, is put up for sale."[9] But since I have had much to say in my book about these matters, I shall not dwell any longer on them. For only he who reads will understand.

(9) The Church, moreover, is greater than Ramah, and Christ is greater than Samuel. Therefore, upon reaching Ramah where Samuel and David had fallen into a prophetic rapture, if the Holy Spirit came upon Saul, who at times was seized by an evil spirit so that he stripped off his clothes and, like the rest, fell into a rapture and lay down naked all that day and all that night,[10] why should we marvel that the Holy Spirit should come down upon any reprobate in the Church and should shower his charismatic gifts on others, not because of any merit of his, but because of his ministry? If the Spirit of God, I say, suddenly seized Saul, and for such a long period of time did not leave him, who was so thoroughly an instrument of the devil, and whom the wicked spirit obviously possessed, body and soul, what is so novel if the Holy Spirit with his heavenly splendor should illumine the cesspool of some wicked man, and yet itself remain untouched by the contagion of his abominable filth?

(10) But why do I now continue discussing this topic when, as I said above, the consecration of a simonist was recently forbidden? Obviously, because these very same people who teach that baptism can be administered without holy chrism, still become enraged over those who before the council were ordained freely by simonists, and dogmatically assert that they are just as heretical as the ministers of their ordination. They also blaspheme, anathematize, despise, reject, and hoot at their Masses and all the sacraments dispensed by them, and frightful-

---

8. Gregory I, *Homiliae xl in Evangelia* 17.13 (PL 76.1145B).
9. Ibid.
10. Cf. 1 Sam 16.15, 19.22–24.

ly curse all their blessings, even though the Apostle says that "slanderers will not possess the kingdom of God."[11] And by these curses of theirs they apply the evidence of the prophet Malachi, in which he says, "I will curse your blessings,"[12] not aware of what the Lord says of bishops in the book of Numbers, "They shall pronounce my name over the Israelites, and I will bless them."[13]

(11) It is the bishop who by his words calls down the Lord upon a man, but it is the Lord himself who makes that blessing efficacious for him. And so, the effect of this blessing does not follow from the merit of the bishop, but is brought about by calling upon God's name, so that the power of the Creator may fill the sound that proceeds from the mouth of man, and frequently through the ministry of an unworthy person God's might may truly produce its mystery. But fools and ignorant men of all sorts, blind to the meaning of the prophet's words, find themselves in error, not knowing what they are saying and to what they give assent.

(12) In fact, in sacred Scripture a curse is at times used to express sterility, just as a blessing is understood to mean an abundance of temporal things. Of such a blessing it is said in the book of Kings, "The Lord blessed Obededom and all his family. And when they told David that the Lord had blessed Obededom and all that was his because of the Ark of the Lord, he said: 'I will go and bring up the Ark with blessing into my house.'"[14] And so, when the psalmist began by saying, "Blessing I will bless her widow," to show what kind of blessing he had in mind, he then added, "I will satisfy her poor with bread."[15] And elsewhere he said, "He blessed them and their numbers increased."[16] Here it is clear that he gave them a blessing, that is,

---

11. 1 Cor 6.10.   12. Mal 2.2.
13. Num 6.27.
14. 2 Sam 6.11–12. The concluding part of this sentence is found only in Sabatier 1.529, citing MS St.-Germain-des-Pres 7, MS Corbie 3, and MS St.-Germaindes-Pres 9. The frequency of Damian's citations from the *versio antiqua*, registered in Sabatier as depending on a MS of St.-Germain-des-Pres, would suggest that his Bible derived from this monastic library.
15. Ps 131.15.
16. Ps 106.38.

he made them increase. Similarly, the sons of Joseph said to Joshua, "Why have you given us only one lot and one share as our patrimony? We are a numerous people; so far the Lord has blessed us."[17] Hence, at times a blessing means a great number, at others an abundance.

(13) On the other hand, in the words of Moses God says to every evil man who despises the Law, "A curse upon your barn and your stores. A curse upon the fruit of your body and the fruit of your land."[18] And somewhat farther on, "May the Lord send you famine and hunger."[19] Consequently, so that we do not interpret this text of Malachi to mean hurling curses and anathemas, but the threat of famine and hunger, he prefaced his statement by saying, "If you will not take my words to heart by honoring my name, then I will send poverty upon you." And then he added, "I will curse your blessings."[20] And so, by first mentioning poverty, he made it clear how we should understand "cursing your blessings," as if he were saying: If you shall despise my laws and fail to take them to heart, I shall cause you to groan in hunger and poverty, something you especially fear, so that the very sterility of your lands may be your death, as the blight of sterility threatens you in bearing the fruit of good works. And poverty will afflict your bodies, since you have neglected to provide food for our souls. And that I might establish this point still more clearly from the words of the same prophet, much farther along in his work he said, "Let the whole nation bring all the tithes into my storehouse; let there be food in my house. Put me to the proof, says the Lord, and see if I do not open the floodgates of heaven for you and pour a blessing on you as long as there is need."[21] Moreover, if here the Lord had wished a curse to be understood as an anathema, he would not have said, "I will curse your blessings," but rather: I will curse you who dare to bless those who do not deserve it.

(14) And to provide from the words of the Gospel further obvious proof of my contention, we read that the Lord had

17. Josh 17.14.
19. Deut 28.20.
21. Mal 3.9–10.

18. Deut 28.17–18.
20. Mal 2.2.

only this to say to the fig tree, "May no one ever again eat fruit from you."[22] It was these words that Peter called a curse, when afterwards he said to him "Rabbi, look, the fig tree that you cursed has withered."[23] Such a curse was also put on the first man, when it was said to him, "Accursed shall be the earth on your account; it shall grow thorns and thistles for you."[24] Thus, too, the curse of sterility excluded the blessing of abundance, as was the case in Pharaoh's dream, where cows devoured cows, and ears of corn swallowed up the other ears.[25]

(15) Therefore, just as on the one hand God promised observers of his commands no other blessing but that of abundance, on the other he threatened those who refused with the curse of poverty. Otherwise why would almighty God curse the blessing of a priest, which the power of his name makes holy? For since, as was said before, he undoubtedly is blessed by the Lord, on whose account the name of the Lord is invoked, how does it follow that the Lord would curse that blessing by which a person is blessed by calling on his name?

(16) And so it is, that canonical authority forbids rebaptism, even in the case of those baptized by the worst of heretics, so that God's name that had been invoked over him should not be made null and void.[26] Besides, when anyone attacks and disparages priests, he thereby also condemns their sacraments, something also that blessed Jude the apostle observes in his epistle when speaking of blasphemers. For in first referring to those who flout authority and insult celestial beings, he then remarked, "When the archangel Michael was in debate with the devil, disputing the possession of Moses' body, he did not presume to condemn him in insulting words, but said: 'May the Lord rebuke you.'"[27] Therefore, if the highest angel did not presume to pass judgment and condemn the devil, how is it that man is not afraid to ridicule the sacraments that are filled

22. Mark 11.14.   23. Mark 11.21.
24. Gen 3.17–18.   25. Cf. Gen 41.1–7.
26. Cf. Burchard, IV, 39 (PL 149.734B), citing *Conc. Rothomag.* 3, citing Gennadius, *Liber de ecclesiasticis dogmatibus veteris* 52 (PL 58.993C; Mansi 10.1200). See also Ryan, *Sources* nos. 49, 228.
27. Jude 1.9.

with the power of the Holy Spirit? For since Truth itself says, "If anyone sins against the Holy Spirit, for him there is no forgiveness either in this age or in the age to come,"[28] we must gravely fear that such people surely offend him, without whom the outrage of sin can never be remitted.

(17) But why do I complain of the disparagement of priests and of the sacraments, when almost everything is torn to pieces by them, spat upon in contempt, and put up to public ridicule? "There is no pope," they say, "no king, and lastly, no bishop or priest." And so it happened, according to report, that nearly a thousand people were deceived by this trumpery and nonsense, and left this world without receiving the sacrament of the Body and Blood of the Lord. In fact, they are convinced that no true sacraments can be administered by contemporary priests. There are many churches, moreover, where they consider it not only improper for them to enter, but where they judge them unworthy of even paying them their respect. For they disdain to pay honor to churches that they suspect were dedicated by bishops who for some reason they considered unworthy. Indeed, as Luke relates, "Paul said, 'I appeal to Caesar!' To whom Festus replied, 'You have appealed to Caesar: to Caesar you shall go.'"[29] Is the pope a greater criminal than Nero? Are we to believe that these monks are holier than Paul? But since Paul, who had previously been caught up to the third heaven,[30] did not refuse to appear before Nero, what monk can be so proud of his holiness that he dare condemn the decision of the Apostolic See, where, to be sure, attention is paid, not to a man's deserts, but to the regulations governing ecclesiastical office? These monks reach their decision on street corners, and defame the jurisdiction of synods. They pass judgment on monks, disparage everything that smacks of clerics, and are careful not to offend laymen who, indeed, deserve to be more sharply and bitterly censured. Should they see a monk approaching, they will say, "Look, here comes one of those scapulars." When they see a bishop or a priest passing by, they call

28. Matt 12.32.   29. Acts 25.11–12.
30. Cf. 2 Cor 12.2.

them beardless wonders. And when someone asks a blessing from these monks, they never answer, but promptly look the other way, claiming that he is unworthy of a reply.

(18) And if I, moreover, should speak to my fellow sinners and take a meal with them, I am at once subjected to abuse, ripped to pieces, and like them, made to suffer the same condemnation. What is more, we monks, we, I say, are the very ones who are thought unworthy of talking with them. This is hardly conduct befitting a monk, but is rather one of the irrational practices of the Pharisees. "The Pharisees and the doctors of the Law," said the evangelist, "began grumbling among themselves: 'This fellow welcomes sinners and eats with them.'"[31] And this is the root, the sum total of the matter over which the wild fury and ill will of the Jews flared up against the Lord, the source of the malice and venomous bitterness with which they conspired to kill him. Because they considered themselves the guardians of legal ceremonies, they accused the Lord of being a friend of publicans and the violator of the Sabbath.

(19) I delight in enduring this calumny with my Lord, and prefer to live sensually with him in the home of Levi, than "in the dwellings of the wicked,"[32] that is, with sanctimonious men who are repugnant to God. These people, in fact, turn up their noses at Christian morality and follow the doctrines of the Stoics, as they claim that all sins are completely alike.[33] I would prefer to follow a middle course with Jonathan, between the holy David and the reprobate Saul, Jonathan who, even though he surpassed Saul by the sincerity of his faith and truthfulness, did not come up to the spiritual quality and piety of David. My brothers should therefore be warned against being too just, against being too wise. Of the first of these Solomon says, "Do not be over-righteous."[34] And of the second the Apostle says, "Do not be more wise than you ought to be, but think your way to a sober estimate."[35] Wisdom that is clouded over by the dark-

---

31. Luke 15.2. 32. Ps 83.11.
33. Cf. Cicero, *Paradoxa Stoicorum* 3.21.
34. Eccl 7.17. 35. Rom 12.3.

ness of error is evil, and simplicity that does not turn aside from the way of faith is good. Holiness is odious if it falls into heresy, and if by disdaining to follow the beaten path, it is forced to wander over winding roads and dangerous pitfalls. Excessive purity plunged the Novatians, who are also called Cathari,[36] into the filth of heretical contamination, and excessive holiness cut off the Luciferians,[37] like infected branches, from unity with the body of the Church. For to claim a thing to be illicit, when it is allowed, and by so doing, boast that they are the defenders of morality, they are to be judged enemies of the Church, so that by externally chattering nonsense with one another like frogs in their swamps, by their violent objections they inwardly cause utter confusion.

(20) We can rightly compare this type of men to frogs or locusts, for as formerly these animals were a plague to the Egyptians, so now they devastate the Church. For Scripture says of locusts, "They covered the surface of the whole land, destroying everything." And then the text continues, "They devoured all the vegetation and all the fruit left on the trees."[38] Locusts, indeed, destroy the surface of the whole land, and devour the vegetation and the fruit on the trees, when detractors of any kind chew and tear into bits either our weak efforts, which are like the grass of the lowly, or the deeds of the perfect, which are here compared to the fruit of the trees, and then with the spiteful teeth of their corrosive envy devour them. Against such as these the Apostle says, "Do make a place for us in your hearts! We have wronged no one, ruined no one, taken advantage of no one."[39] And elsewhere in a reproachful tone he says, "But if you bite one another, if you ruin one another, take heed that you do not consume one another."[40]

(21) But since as men living in the monastery we are meant to be God's hunters, as Isaiah said, "I shall send my hunters and

---

36. Cf. *Can. Nic.* apud Rufinus, *Historia ecclesiastica* 1.6, 10.6; Augustine, *Haereses* 38.
37. The followers of Lucifer of Cagliari (+ c. 370), on which cf. M. R. P. McGuire, "Lucifer of Cagliari," *NCE* 8.845.
38. Exod 10.15.   39. 2 Cor 7.2.
40. Gal 5.15.

they shall hunt,"[41] after abandoning the goods of this world, shall we bare our teeth and snarl at one another, and like rabid dogs, tear one another to pieces with our jaws? Let us suppress our presumptuous pride and let oppressive holiness adapt itself to the capacity of our brothers. Whoever wishes to be holy, should be so privately in the sight of God, and not pride himself on being better than his weaker brother. A young dog whose duty it is to ward off strangers, should never neglect his charge and begin attacking the members of the family, lest instead of sleeping quietly in the house, he be put out and be forced to bay at the moon.

41. Jer 16.16, mistakenly identified here as Isaiah.

LETTER 147

Peter Damian to the clergy and people of the church of Faenza. At the death of their bishop, Peter of Faenza, the clergy of that city called upon Damian to visit them. But because of recent illness and the present press of work, he begged to be excused. He agreed with their decision not to proceed with electing a bishop until King Henry IV should arrive, and advised them to petition the pope not to appoint a bishop, but to allow the church to stand vacant under an administrator of their choice. If necessary, he would come to administer the sacrament of confirmation, or for other episcopal duties.

(Lent 1067)

 O MY HOLY AND REVERED BROTHERS AND SONS, the clergy and people of the church of Faenza, the monk Peter the sinner sends greetings in the Lord.

(2) When I learned of the death of sir Peter, your bishop of blessed memory, my spirit was suddenly disturbed, I was amazed at this unexpected turn of events, and my whole being was overwhelmed with grief and fraternal compassion. Yet, my son, the venerable abbot[1] whom you sent to me, found me in such a state of depression, not only because of recent illness, but also from certain difficulties I had experienced,[2] that it is impossible for me to visit you at this time. Wherefore, until I am able to come and be of service to you, I am sending this short letter to explain in a few words what, in my opinion, you should do.

(3) So far as I can gather, there was agreement among you, a

---

1. Lucchesi, *Vita* no. 205, tentatively identified him as Abbot Eleucadius of S. Maria Foris Portam.
2. Perhaps this is a reference to *Letter* 146, in which he speaks of his distress over affairs in Florence.

thing that has impressed me deeply, and you were incited to follow unanimously what together you determined to do, namely, not to elect a bishop until the arrival of the king. His visit, indeed, should remove uncertainty, and after all disagreements have been settled, reconcile both you and your church to live in peace and tranquility. Hence, you should request our lord, the pope, not to install a bishop for you at this time, but to allow your church to stand vacant for a while, deciding that you should remain under the tutelage of his good graces. But since by the mercy of God there are active, prudent, and learned clerics among you, one of these should be chosen, if that is your pleasure, a man deemed competent to act as administrator. On him you can lay the management and care of the whole diocese, and through him all necessary affairs of the church can be carried on. In the meantime, if you so ordain, and the occasion should arise, I will come and be at your service, and perhaps engage somewhat in confirming your children, or in other episcopal functions for the love of God and for your benefit.

LETTER 148

Peter Damian to Duke Godfrey of Tuscany and his wife Beatrice. He asks them to assist the abbot of St. John the Baptist in Valle Acereto, who has purchased a biblical lectionary, for which he is unable to pay. Their generosity will be rewarded by God, who will protect them in evil times. He would come to them in person, if not prevented by faltering old age. He encloses a letter to be delivered to the Empress Agnes by the next post they send to Germany.

(Lent 1067)

O SIR GODFREY, THE MARQUIS AND DUKE, and to her highness Beatrice, his wife, the monk Peter the sinner sends his prayers.

(2) This son of mine, the venerable abbot of the monastery of St. John the Baptist, purchased a biblical lectionary,[1] but because of his poverty he was unable to pay for it, and was compelled by necessity to beg me to give him the money. Since, however, I am presently unable to help him, I take the liberty of soliciting others, so that since he did not receive assistance from "us wealthy bishops," he might at least find some comfort from "you poor little folks."

(3) But if someone should say, "The world is enraged against us, war has broken out, and we have no time to offer gifts to God," let him remember that Joshua, the commander of the Israelites fought in the desert, while on the hilltop Moses prayed with his hands raised to heaven. But as Scripture relates, whenever Moses lowered his hands Amalek had the advantage, but when he raised them, Amalek was overwhelmed and Israel defeated him.[2] Hence the prophet says, "Lift up your hearts and

---

1. Cf. Lucchesi, *Vita* no. 23.
2. Cf. Exod 17.10–11.

your hands to God."³ One surely lifts up his heart and his hands to God, when he offers his prayers to God, and at the same time donates of his substance either for the equipping of the church, or to give help to the poor. Let us, therefore, put on the corselet of good works, and we need not fear the arrows of the wicked. And so, Solomon states in Proverbs, "Do not be afraid of the sudden terror or of the power of the wicked who are attacking you; for the Lord will be at your side, and he will keep your feet clear of the trap."⁴ But that we might know the source of such audacity, he immediately added, "Refuse no man a favor when it lies in your power to pay it. Do not say to your friend: 'Come back again; you shall have it tomorrow'—when you have it already."⁵ Therefore, do not trust in the force of arms, but in works of mercy.

(4) I would surely visit you at your command, if feeble old age did not impede my faltering steps. But let this brother see and judge whether I can be moved by a reasonable request. I humbly beg your excellency, moreover, that if you are sending someone to Germany, you might in your charity include the enclosed letter to my lady, the empress.⁶

---

3. Lam 3.41.
4. Prov 3.25–26.
5. Prov 3.27–28.
6. The present letter is important, since it demonstrates the actual transmission of two letters, indicating that Damian's correspondence was not just a literary exercise to escape the boredom of his hermitage. The enclosure is probably *Letter* 149 of this collection, not edited by Gaetani.

LETTER 149

Peter Damian to the Empress Agnes. The last of Damian's six communications to the empress, this long letter remained unedited until 1932. He deplores the many trips made by Agnes to the German court, and begs her to return permanently to Rome and to the religious life she had there undertaken. Many are saying that she will never return, and, for his part, he fears that the physical allurements of the court will weaken her former resolve. He refers autobiographically to his own experience, that nothing could persuade him even to walk past the house in Ravenna where he had been born, except on the occasion of the last illness of his sister, Rodelinda, who had been a second mother to him. This remark provides an opportunity of revising somewhat the rather somber picture of his youth, reported by John of Lodi. From this letter also, we can fix the date (1035) of his entry into the religious life at Fonte Avellana. Agnes should not pride herself on the nobility of her ancestors, remembering that the Empress Helena, the mother of the great Constantine, had been an innkeeper's daughter, and that Ruth of the Moabites, the ancestor of Christ, had been so poor that she lived off the few stalks of grain that the reapers had left behind. Both Pope Alexander and the archdeacon Hildebrand will be delighted at her return. He hopes to hear from Cardinal Bishop Lopertus, but for now may the Holy Spirit bless him.

(Lent 1067)

TO THE EMPRESS AGNES, the monk Peter the sinner sends his service.[1]

(2) As I daily grieve over your absence, I experience new sorrow that I am not myself, and what is more, that I am

---

1. This letter was edited for the first time by André Wilmart, "Une lettre de S. Pierre Damien à l'impératrice Agnes," *Revue bénédictine* 44 (1932) 125–146. It was later reprinted in G. Lucchesi, *Clavis* 144–148.

thoroughly disheartened. For where my treasure is, there will my heart be also.[2] For my treasure is undoubtedly Christ, and since I know that he is hidden in the temple of your heart, I think of you as the depository of heavenly fortune. And so, wherever you go, I never leave your side.

(3) But since in leaving us, you would never, I might say, have seized this opportunity unless I had given my consent, oh, that my tongue had either become totally rigid like that of Zechariah at the word brought by the archangel,[3] or, like Isaiah, a live coal from the altar had been placed on it by one of the seraphim.[4] And since according to Scripture, "the tongue has the power of life and death,"[5] it were better that it alone should suffer death by losing its power of speech, than by idle words to disturb the lives of so many good people. For since Isaiah said, "Woe is me, because I have held my peace,"[6] I can truly say, "Woe is me, because I have spoken." Moses, moreover, stood alone on the mountain with the Lord until he received the tablets of the Decalogue, which he was to deliver to the people. But as Scripture reports, "When the people saw that Moses was so long in coming down from the mountain, they confronted Aaron and said to him: 'Come make us gods to go ahead of us. As for this fellow Moses, who brought us up from Egypt, we do not know what has become of him.'"[7]

(4) Therefore, if this long delay of Moses wrought such harm on the people of God that it lost faith in him, cast a bull-calf of metal, and venerated idols,[8] how much damage will your long delay cause for the spiritual life of many, and for the loving expectations of those who are waiting for you? For, by the example of your leadership they had hoped to pass, not from one land to another, that is, from Egypt into the land of Canaan, but from earth to heaven, from this world to paradise. And so, if Moses, who was led to such heights of divine familiarity that he was deemed worthy of inaccessible conversation with almighty God, wrought such harm because he did not at once

---

2. Cf. Matt 6.21.
3. Cf. Luke 1.20, 22.
4. Cf. Isa 6.6.
5. Prov 18.21.
6. Isa 6.5.
7. Exod 32.1.
8. Cf. Exod 32.4.

return, how great must we reckon the obstacle that your delay presented to those who are following you as their leader and guide on the path to God, you who did not climb from the depths to the heights, but rather descended from heavenly contemplation to the level of the world, that is, to the royal court?

(5) Although I take it as certain that, as the angels who are sent as God's ministers never turn aside from the mission assigned to them, but, constantly carrying out their delegated duties, always fix their unalterable gaze on his face, so also you, wherever you walk and wherever you go, do not turn your eyes away from the sight of your heavenly spouse, that what was said of the mother of Samuel might also apply to the mother of the king: "Her face was no more changed."[9] For both Elijah and Elisha separately made the same statement, "As the Lord God of Israel lives, in whose sight I stand."[10] And it should be noted that no holy person says of himself that he sat down in the presence of God, as the Lord said to Moses, "But you yourself stand here beside me, and I will speak to you,"[11] because he profitably contemplates God, who, in attempting to free himself of the affairs of this world, does not lazily lie down and snore, but is up performing good deeds, his attention always directed toward God.

(6) Therefore, since many holy people have now lost heart in hoping for your return, and have given up because their repeated requests have ended in failure, they no longer expect you to come back. So return, my lady, return, and by the speed with which you carry out your promise, gladden the hearts of your loved ones who are saddened by your absence, lest those who yearn to see the fair vision of your angelic face be any longer discouraged by doubts concerning your future plans. And that you will not reject at least my use of prophetic words, along with Jeremiah I cry out, "Come back, virgin Israel, come back to your cities. How long will you continue to stray, my wayward child?"[12]—even though this journey of yours should not be ascribed to wanderlust, but rather to obedience and solid reasoning. And with the voice of the Roman Church I will say

---

9. 1 Sam 1.18.   10. 1 Kgs 17.1, 2 Kgs 3.14.
11. Deut 5.31.   12. Jer 31.21–22.

to you exactly what in Canticles the new universal Church cried out to the synagogue of old, "Come back, come back, Sunamite maiden, come back that we may gaze upon you."[13]

(7) Sunamite, in fact, may be translated to mean one who is captive and despised. But how is it proper to call you a captive and one despised? There is no doubt that you may rightly be thought of as despised, because you who were formerly distinguished by your royal attire, who will remember how you were surrounded by numerous fawning attendants, who were seen as one adorned with brilliant gems and as the centerpiece of a varied ritual, are now content with unseemly dark, gray dress, and find yourself deprived of earthly glory and of almost all attention by a host of servants. And how do we show that you might well be called a captive? But then I seem to remember what the Lord said through Jeremiah to the people of Judah, under siege in Jerusalem by the Chaldaean king, "I set before you the way of life and the way of death. Whoever will abide in this city will die by sword, by famine and pestilence, but whoever goes out and surrenders to the Chaldaeans, who now besiege you, will live; his soul will be to him as a spoil."[14]

(8) As it seems to me, he now abides in the city, who values the exile of this world as his heavenly fatherland, who causes his heart to be rooted in the love of earthly possessions. The Chaldaeans, however, are called captors, by whom are meant the holy apostles, the disciples of him who "ascended into the heights with captives in his train; he gave gifts to men."[15] The disciple of this master showed that he was following in his footsteps when he said in his second letter to the Corinthians, "Although we walk in the flesh we do not fight according to the flesh. The weapons we wield are not those of the world, but divinely potent to destroy strongholds, for demolishing the counsels of the body, and every high place that raises itself against the knowledge of God, and bringing into captivity every understanding in obedience to Christ."[16]

---

13. Cant 6.12. For the reading "Sunamite" (and not "Shulammite") see Sabatier 2.385.
14. Jer 21.8–9.   15. Eph 4.8.
16. 2 Cor 10.3–5.

(9) It is not out of place, therefore, to call the holy apostles Chaldaeans, since they destroy all that rears its head against the knowledge of God, and compel every human thought to surrender. Thus they turn the souls of men away from the Prince of this world,[17] who had captured them like rich spoils of war, and convert them to the service of Christ. Why, then, should we marvel that the title "captive" becomes you, since you were snatched by the apostles from the grasp of the world to become the spoils of God, and thus, in keeping with the precept of the old law, with shaved head and pared nails[18] you were brought as a new bride to the marriage chamber of the Redeemer? And to use another simile that becomes you, you were like that noble fish in whose mouth a silver coin was found,[19] caught by the hook of the heavenly fisherman and taken from the depths of the surging waves. Of these fisherman the Lord also spoke through Jeremiah, "I will send for many fishermen and they shall fish for them."[20] What a sorry fish it is, that is not caught in the nets of these fishermen, what an unhappy soul that is not captured by such victorious warriors. And so, whoever remains in the city, will die of famine, pestilence, and the sword, but they who surrender to the Chaldaeans, shall live. "The man who loves himself is lost," and on the other hand, "he who hates his soul in this world, will preserve it for eternal life."[21] And according to the Apostle, "Let us then go to him outside the camp, bearing the stigma that he bore. For here we have no permanent home, but we are seekers after the city that is to come."[22]

(10) We must, therefore, flee to the camp of the enemy lest we be forced to perish in the city, so that each one of us might uproot from our heart all hankering for this world, and arrive at the rights that accompany our surrender to the apostles. And lest we experience the destruction of the doomed city, but might save our life as a fugitive in exile, let us follow the command of him who said to Abraham, "Leave your own country and your kinsmen, and go to a country that I will show you."[23] In

17. Cf. John 12.31, 16.11.
19. Cf. Matt 17.23, 26.
21. John 12.25.
23. Gen 12.1.

18. Cf. Deut 21.12.
20. Jer 16.16.
22. Heb 13.13–14.

the writings of Zechariah, this same flight is suggested, and each faithful soul is urged to leave his own and flee into a strange land. For he says, "Away, away; flee from the land of the north, says the Lord, for I have scattered you to the four winds of heaven."[24] And then he goes on, "O Zion flee, you that dwell with the daughter of Babylon, because thus says the Lord of Hosts: After glory he has sent me to the nations that plundered you."[25] But if it is dangerous to remain in the city, how much more disastrous is it to return to the city walls you once deserted? Do you understand what I am saying? It is indeed a glorious thing to leave one's fatherland for the sake of God, but it is shameful to look back and retreat to the privileges one left behind,[26] since it was written of the sacred creatures, that "their feet were straight feet, and they did not turn back as they moved."[27]

(11) And so, once again I shall try to change your mind about your return, not by shouting at you, but by showing you my affection. And hence, the more quietly I speak, the stronger is my insistence, "Come back, come back, Sunamite maiden, come back, that we might gaze upon you."[28] And immediately the text continues: "What shall you see in this Sunamite maiden but the rank of singers in the camps?"[29] A chorus, to be sure, is a choir, an orderly rank of singers, while camps refer to military arrays and guards at their posts. Clearly, this variety is not at variance with any holy person who finds himself arrayed in the forces of the heavenly army, because anyone who is truly dedicated to God allies himself with his neighbors in fraternal charity, and fights implacably against the battle lines of our spiritual enemies. For when he joins his brothers in harmony, he sings sweetly to God. But while vigorously struggling with his passions, he never lets up in this hand-to-hand engagement. The minds and hearts of the saints are at once a chorus and an armed camp, for as they give praise to God in wholehearted fraternal love, they continue their restless fight against the forces of evil in the heavens,[30] armed with the corselet of virtue and the sword of faith.

24. Zech 2.6.
25. Zech 2.7–8.
26. Cf. Luke 9.62.
27. Ezek 1.7, 9.
28. Cant 6.12.
29. Cant 7.1.
30. Cf. Eph 2.2, 6.12f.

(12) All of this had been marvelously true of you while you were in the theater of war, while you were in training for spiritual combat, that is, while you were at the doorstep of the fisherman, and we saw you now and then, and were glad. But after you returned to the royal court, a nagging suspicion was at once aroused in me, that even though your holy purpose always remained firm and immovable in all its vigor, through the chinks in your armor, through sight and hearing, some gentle breeze at least would blow to move, if ever so lightly, the branches of hesitant and wavering thoughts. And since it is written of the tree planted beside a watercourse, that its foliage would never disappear,[31] even though the fruit of your good works does not fall to the ground from the verdant branches of your holy spirit, one must however fear lest the leaves of your fervent and genuine resolve should wither away.

(13) Moreover, if eyesight is of such importance even in dumb animals, that when Jacob exposed them to fresh rods, cut from various trees, they at once conceived with these rods in view, and thus afterwards the varicolored young corresponded to the different varieties of rod,[32] how much more certain it is that when human minds, endowed with reason, wish to distinguish what they perceive, they afterwards visualize in their imagination the images they acquired from their outer senses. And even though, through deliberation, these impressions never propose what one should do, still, as they frequently intermingle with our thoughts, they at times cause them to depart from their purity and innocence. Now, we also read of David that as he walked about on the roof of the palace, he saw from there a woman engaged in bathing, a woman who was undoubtedly Bathsheba.[33] He saw, in fact, and fell into sin; he opened his eyes, and in came the enemy. So death climbed in through his windows[34] and, as it is said elsewhere, his eye wasted his soul.[35]

(14) It is now exactly three decades, with the addition of about two years, since I exchanged my academic garb for a

31. Cf. Ps 1.3.
33. Cf. 2 Sam 11.2ff.
35. Cf. Lam 3.51.
32. Cf. Gen 30.37ff.
34. Cf. Jer 9.21.

monastic habit.³⁶ But no one could ever persuade me even to walk past the house where I was born, except only once someone wrote to me, I know not why, that late one night I should walk down the street and pass the door. A second time also, I was compelled to visit my elder sister of blessed memory, who had been a second mother to me, and was then desperately ill. But then, I admit, such a dim mist of modesty dulled my vision, that as I was in the house, I saw hardly anything of its furnishings.

(15) At the sight of secular things and worldly lifestyle the old conflict again erupts, so that the wild thorns of nettles and briars, that had lost their power to pierce or burn, now spread more destructively in the field of our soul. Dinah, you know, went out to visit the women of the country. Shechem, the local prince, saw her and took her, laid with her and dishonored her.³⁷ The Levite from the hill country of Ephraim, who would not listen to his father-in-law who urged him to stay with him, lost his wife while he was on his way. And when later he cut his wife's body to pieces, limb by limb, he incited all Israel to avenge this shameful and monstrous crime.³⁸ Shimei, son of Gera, was ordered to stay quietly at home, and under threat of death was forbidden to move from place to place. But when his slaves ran away, and he went out to find them, like any master would do, he was at once cut down by an avenging sword;³⁹ and as he exercised his rights over men in bondage to him, by his unfortunate action this foolish slave owner lost his own life. For since it is written, "Whoever commits sin is the slave of sin,"⁴⁰ the man who tries to find his slaves who have escaped, reverts to the servile condition of his past life that he had once despised.

---

36. This statement would date Damian's entrance into Fonte Avellana for about 1035, when he was 28 years of age. Here *clericalis cyclas* is understood to mean the garb of a learned clerk, teacher, or student, and not of a cleric in ecclesiastical orders. *Cuculla* is literaly a cowl, capuche, or hood, but can also mean a monastic habit. But see F. Dressler, *Petrus Damiani: Leben und Werk* 20, n. 24, where this text is seen to refer to Damian's ordination to the priesthood before he entered Fonte Avellana.

37. Cf. Gen 34.1–2.
39. Cf. 1 Kgs 2.36ff.
38. Cf. Judg 19.1ff.
40. John 8.34.

(16) And so, bride of Christ, if you would be free of the company of such slaves, let the noble character of your deeds be evident in your life, nor should you wish to boast of your family or the glory of your eminent ancestors. Roman history relates that Helena, the wife of Constantius the elder, whose son, the great Constantine, was created emperor in Britain after the death of his father, had been an innkeeper.[41] Yet she was possessed of such fervent faith, abounded in such love and pious devotion, and was so renowned for the innocence of her holy life, that now we see many basilicas erected in her honor throughout various kingdoms, a thing that is difficult or even impossible to find in the case of any other noble queen.

(17) Ruth, moreover, whose life was so poor and humble that she gleaned the stalks of grain left behind by the reapers, wielded the flail like the threshers, winnowed the corn she had found in the fields, and carried it on her shoulders to her mother-in-law.[42] And still from her came David, the ancestor of the king who rescued the whole world from slavery, and restored to it the rights of its ancient freedom. Now, since you too, like Ruth, came from the land of the Moabites, and then began your sojourn in the country of the Israelites, do not ever again return to the fields of your fathers, but from now on live alone with Naomi, who is called both beautiful and bitter.[43] "Do not call me Naomi," she said, "that is, beautiful, but call me Mara, that is, bitter, for the Almighty has filled me with bitterness."[44]

(18) All of this, in fact, seems aptly to apply to the holy Church, for it is both truly beautiful because of the charm of its spiritual virtues, and is always bitter for having to bear the pressures that assail it. This is why the bridegroom says to her in Canticles, "Your cheeks are like a pomegranate cut open, besides that which lies hid within."[45] A pomegranate, as we know, has a bitter rind, but its kernels are sweet indeed. And so, the

---

41. Cf. Ambrose, *De obitu Theodosii Imperatoris* 42 (CSEL 73.393).
42. Cf. Ruth 2.2, 17ff.
43. Jerome, *Nom. Hebr.* 34.7 (CC 72.102).
44. Ruth 1.20.
45. Cant 4.3.

holy Church endures the bitterness of external persecution that rages against it, but inwardly is beautiful, and retains its sweetness by the blamelessness of its appealing charity. She likewise says of the bridegroom, "My beloved is fair and ruddy";[46] fair because of his chastity, and ruddy from shedding his precious blood. You should therefore speak to the Roman Church in the words of Ruth to her mother-in-law, "Do not urge me to go back and desert you. Where you go, I will go, and where you stay, I will stay. Your people shall be my people, and your God my God."[47] And since the name "Ruth" has the meaning "hurrying,"[48] in keeping with the hidden sense of this word, do not delay any longer, but quickly provide solemn and festive joy for holy souls in all of Italy. And thus our lord Pope[49] will see his wishes fulfilled, and Hildebrand, your support and staff, who for me is but a reed,[50] like Jacob at the coming of Joseph,[51] will be revived at the sight of you.

(19) May the hand of Bishop Lopertus in his absence make the sign of the Cross over me, but through the presence of the Spirit may he bless me.

46. Cant 5.10.
47. Ruth 1.16.
48. Jerome, *Nom. Hebr.* 34.9 (CC 72.102).
49. Pope Alexander II.
50. Cf. 2 Kgs 18.21, Isa 36.6, Ezek 29.6.
51. Cf. Gen 48.2.

LETTER 150

Peter Damian to Baroncius, hermit, and later prior at Fonte Avellana. He gives his correspondent a bit of oft-repeated advice: Do not take a vigorous man's penance upon yourself. But if you do, be sure to discharge the obligation at once, else it will be your fate, like that of the monk in the story he relates, to suffer in purgatory for another's debt. Damian's belief in the dead returning to instruct the living is demonstrated by this letter.

(1067)

O SIR BARONCIUS,[1] my dear brother, the monk Peter the sinner sends the affection of fraternal charity.

(2) What I often emphasized when I was with you, I now write to you in my absence, and lest it get away like something floating by, I attach this slender cord of my writing. The point is this: in your unrestrained charity you should never agree to discharge the penance of someone who is strong and healthy. But if you do take this upon yourself, be sure to fulfill the obligation as quickly as you can. Moreover, since the canons forbid a priest to remit a fast of one day for a penitent, unless he immediately compensate for it by giving an alms of comparable value, how in good conscience can we bind ourselves to assume such a frightening obligation belonging to another, since we do not know how long we have to live?

(3) In fact, sir Martin, who lives in a Camaldolese hermitage, a man endowed with many virtues, especially with the gift of constant tears, is the source of the story I am about to tell you. "There was a monk," he said, "from a monastery in the area of Arezzo called 'In the Pines,' who was burdened with many sins.

---

1. Baroncius is identified as the recipient of this letter in three MSS: P1, G1, and Wi, all in the same tradition. In a document of February 1067, he is identified as the prior of Fonte Avellana. Cf. Lucchesi, *Vita* 1.34.

When a long and severe penance was imposed on him, in keeping with the magnitude of his faults, he asked a certain brother, who was a close friend of his, to help bear the onus of his expiation. This brother graciously accepted it, bore the part of the penance agreed upon, and assured his friend that he would not have to pay all of the debt. But while the former was relieved of part of the burden, and was freed of the obligation of living a more severe penitential life, the latter, after promising to pay the debt over a long period of years, sometime later became ill and suddenly met his death, which he had hoped would not occur in the foreseeable future. So far as anyone could judge, this brother had led a blameless life, and had a good reputation in the community.

(4) "But a few days later, he appeared in a dream to the penitent monk, and the latter at once asked him: 'Well, brother, how are things going with you? How are you?' The monk at once replied in a tone of complaint: 'It is not good at all, in fact, everything is most difficult, and that, because of you. For, while free of my own sins, because I loaded myself with your chains, and made myself responsible for another's obligation, and did not pay for it, I must undergo beatings and am forced to endure bitter suffering. Therefore, I entreat you, and beg with all the power that is in me, that you take care of yourself and help set me free. So, go and beseech the holy community of this monastery to pay the debt I had promised, and then neglected, and thus rescue me from the torments I now endure.'

(5) "When he awoke, the penitent related to the brothers what he had seen, and told them what he had heard, set forth his friend's request, and effectively begged their assistance. And what is more, when the brothers had at last satisfied the fixed amount of his penance by various practices of a special kind, the brother again appeared to the aforesaid monk, and with a serene and happy face showed him that he was rejoicing in heaven. When asked again how he was doing, he replied that through the prayers of his brothers he was not only rescued from his unfortunate sufferings, but had also recently been

brought to the holy company of the elect by the marvelous intervention of the hand of the Most High."[2]

(6) Blessed be the disposition of God's loving-kindness, that instructs the living even through the dead; and while chastising some, informs others how they may be freed from their chastisement. So, my brother, you have now heard this story; act with foresight and be on your guard.

---

2. *Poenitentiali Romano* cc. 43–44, used by Burchard, XIX, 9ff. (PL 140.980Dff.); *Poenitentiali Egberti* cc. 14–15, used by Regino II, 441–442 (PL 132.369C); Paul Fournier, "Études critiques sur le Décret de Burchard de Worms," *Nouvelle revue historique de droit français et étranger* 34 (1910) 103f.; Ryan, *Sources* no. 288.

INDICES

INDEX OF PROPER NAMES

Aaron, 29, 87, 153, 172
Abigail, 146
Abishag, 78–80
Abner, 36
Abraham, 46, 78, 147, 175
Absalom, 33, 37–38
Achan, 138
Achilles, 71
Achish, king, 112
Adelheid, queen of Italy, 13
Adeodatus, 29–30
Adonibezek, king, 55–56
Adraldus of Bremen, 26
Agnes, empress, x–xi, 13, 18, 21, 25, 53, 148, 169, 171
Alberic of Monte Cassino, 27, 40
Alexander II, pope, 10, 103, 171, 180
Amalek, 123, 169
Amasa, 36
Ambrose, saint, 7, 51, 122, 179
Ambrosius, hermit, 45
Anaclete (I), pope, 108, 118
Andrew, archpriest, 3
Antichrist, 111, 132
Apollos, 120
Appianus, 146
Arialdus, deacon, 49
Aristotle, 105
Arius, heretic, 5
Augustine, saint, 5, 41–42, 86, 105, 111, 165
Aurelius, bishop, 116–17
Auxentius, bishop of Milan, 51

Baal, 144
Barnes, Timothy D., 43
Baroncius, prior of Fonte Avellana, 17, 181
Bathsheba, 177
Beatrice, duchess, 114

Beatrice of Tuscany, 141
Bede, the venerable, 41
Benjamin, 50, 153
Bennett, C. E., 94
Berengar of Ivrea, 13
Bertholds of Reichenau, 103
Blum, Owen, vii–viii, 110–11
Boniface, pope, 108
Browe, Peter, 14, 24
Bruyne, D. de, 102
Burchard of Worms, 107–10, 118–19, 162, 183
Busch, Jörg W., 49

C< >, archpriest, 3
Carmi, 138
Cathari, 155, 165
Cencius, prefect of Rome, xii, 77, 150
Ceres, 62
Černik, Peter, 127
Cherethites, 28, 29
Cicero, 66, 72, 115, 164
Claudius of Turin, 29
Clement, pope, 115
Constantine the Great, emperor, 171, 179
Constantius, 179
Costandoni, Anselmo, 19

Damasus, pope, 118
Damianus, ix–x, 11–12, 97
Daniel, 67, 152
David, 6, 7, 28–29, 30–33, 36–39, 63–64, 78, 85–86, 88, 112, 123, 147, 152, 154, 159, 160, 164, 177, 179
Decentius of Gubbio, 92
Delilah, 83
Diana, 66
Dinah, 178

INDEX OF PROPER NAMES

Diogenes Laertius, 3
Doré, D., 50
Dressler, Fridolin, 19, 178
Drudo, 9

Elder, E. Rozanne, 103
Eleucadius of S. Maria Foris Portam, 167
Elisha, 50, 133, 173
Elkanah, 25
Ephraim, 27, 135, 178
Ephron, 46
Epiphanius, 5
Erlembald Cotta of Milan, 127
Erlembaldus, 49
Ermensinde, 21
Eusebius of Caesarea, 43
Eutropius, 146
Ezekiel, 31

Faustinus, bishop of Pontia, 116
Ferdinand I of Castile and Leon, ix, 19
Festus, 163
Fiedrowicz, Michael, 43
Fonte Avellana, 11, 45, 112, 171, 181
Fournier, Paul, 183
Fredelandus. *See* Stedelandus, emperor

Geerlings, Wilhelm, 51
Gehazi, 133
Gelasius I, pope, 10
Gennadius, 146, 162
Gera, 37, 178
Gilchrist, John, 104
Godfrey, duke of Tuscany, xi, 103–4, 112, 169
Godfrey of Lorraine, 141
Goliath, 29, 31, 119
Gozo, monk, 141
Gregory I, pope, 7, 8, 117, 151, 158–59
Grundmann, Herbert, 141
Guilla, countess, xii, 143

Hadericus, bishop of Orleans, 10
Hagar, 20, 77
Haggai, 106
Harro, bishop of Orleans, 10

Helena, empress, 171, 179
Heli, 128
Hemmer, H., 5
Henry III, emperor, 141
Henry IV, king, x, 148
Hermisindis, nun, 84
Hilary of Arles, bishop, 146
Hilary, pope, 43
Hildebrand, archdeacon, 11, 15, 148, 171, 180
Hippolytus of Rome, 43
Holda, 6
Horace, 94
Hubert, count, 145
Hugh of Cluny, 26
Humbert of Silva Candida, 155
Hymenaeus, 104

Iambi, 4
Innocent I, pope, 92
Ira the Jairite, 29
Isaiah, 24, 30, 34, 38, 85, 89, 113, 165, 172
Ishbosheth, 28
Ishmael, 20
Isidore of Seville, 4, 59, 62, 111

Jacob, 26, 46, 177, 180
Jannes, 104
Jemini, 37
Jeremiah, 22, 33–35, 69, 173–75
Jerome, saint, 4, 5, 28, 32, 50, 56, 78, 84, 86, 88, 92, 105, 113, 121, 123–25, 179–80
Jestice, Phyllis, 103
Jether, 36
Joab, 36, 39
John, chaplain, xi, 103, 104
John Gualbertus, xi, 103, 155
John, monk, 93
John of Lodi, xi, 77, 84, 171
John the Baptist, 40
John the Deacon, 117
John the Evangelist, 51, 89, 151
Jonathan, 139, 164
Joseph, 27, 46, 135, 161, 180
Joshua, 27, 111, 121, 135–36, 161, 169
Josiah, king, 6, 7, 144
Judah, 6, 79, 144, 174
Judas Maccabaeus, 154

INDEX OF PROPER NAMES

Judith, 146
Juvenal, 139

Keturah, 78

Laetus, monk, 137
Leclercq, Jean, 104
Leo I (the Great), pope, 118, 122
Leo IX, pope, 16, 104
Liupardus of Piacenza, 45–46
Livy, 146
Lokrantz, Margareta, 51
Lopertus, cardinal bishop of Palestrina, 148–49, 171, 180
Lot, 123
Lucchesi, Giovanni, 3, 9–10, 19, 21, 27, 51, 58, 102, 167, 169, 171, 181
Lucifer of Cagliari, 165
Luciferians, 165
Lucius, pope, 109

M< >, abbot, 55
Malachi, 152, 160, 161
Mambres, 104
Manasseh, 27
Manoah, 147
Marinus, x, 57–58
Marinus, monk, 15
Martin, hermit, 181
Martin the Bald, 68
Mary, 141
Maurus, monk, 140
Merob, 88
Meyer, Heinz, 4
Michael, archangel, 162
Michel, Anton, 157
Mittarelli, Johanne-Benedicto, 19
Moses, 28, 33, 73, 75, 86, 99, 100, 104, 108, 144, 153, 161–62, 169, 172–73
Muschiol, Gisela, 149

Naaman, 133
Naomi, 30, 179
Necho, pharoah, 6
Ner, 36
Nero, emperor, 163
Neukirch, Franz, 58
Nicholas, pope, 157
Nirenberg, David, ix

Noonan, J. T., 105
Novatians, 165
Nürnberg, Rosemary, 43

Obededom, 160
Odorannus de Sens, 105
Ornan, 32
Otto I, emperor, 13
Ozias, 146

Paul, apostle, 7, 34, 86, 104, 119, 120, 163
Paul, monk, 114
Pelethites, 28–29
Pelster, Franz, 109
Peres, 79
Peter, apostle, 13, 51, 100, 109, 119, 131–32, 148–49, 150–51, 156, 162
Peter Damian, vii–viii, 3, 10, 12, 21, 26–27, 40, 45, 49, 53, 55, 57, 73, 76–77, 84, 90, 97, 102–3, 112, 127, 143, 148, 150, 155, 167, 169, 171, 181
Peter, monk, 56
Peter of Faenza, bishop, 167
Peter, subdeacon, 117
Petronilla, 149
Philetus, 104
Pierucci, Celestino, 17
Pithom, 85
Plato, 3
Polybius, 146
Prosper of Aquitaine, 43
Pseudo-Isidore, 109
Pseudo-Jerome, 28–29, 32

Rahab, 79
Rainaldus, bishop of Como, 14, 21
Rainerius II, xii, 143
Rameses, 85
Ramos-Lissón, Domingo, 43
Regino of Prum, 108, 109, 183
Reindel, Kurt, viii, 3, 5, 29, 55
Resnick, Irven M., 127
Robinson, Ian S., 103
Rodelinda, xi, 171
Rodulfus, priest, 49
Romanus, monk, 15
Romuald, hermit, 61, 68
Romulus, 41

INDEX OF PROPER NAMES

Ruth, 30, 171, 179, 180
Ryan, J. Joseph, 10, 92, 107, 109, 115–18, 162, 183

Sabatier, P., 5, 7, 31, 80, 86, 102, 160, 174
Samson, 83, 113
Samuel, 63–64, 159, 173
Sarah, 147
Sardanapalus, 105
Satan, ix, 111, 138
Saul, 28, 64, 88, 159, 164
Scholten, Clemens, 43
Schwaiger, Georg, 43
Scipio, 146
Sellum, 6
Shechem, 178
Shimei, 36–37, 39, 178
Sibylla, countess, 61
Simon Magus, 50, 109
Solomon, 7, 31, 36–40, 70, 78–81, 89, 114, 127, 131, 134–36, 142, 164, 170
Stedelandus, emperor, ix, 19
Stephen I, pope, 3
Stephen, bl., 4
Stephen, chaplain, 19
Struve, Tilman, 19, 21

Suffena, countess, 145
Suntrup, Rudolf, 4
Sylvester, pope, 92, 118

Tebaldus, hermit, 102
Thales, 3
Theophilus of Alexandria, 43
Timothy, 12
Tudethchinus, chaplain, xi, 103–4

U< >, archpriest, 3
Uguzo, Marquis, 145

Vacandard, E., 92
Victorius of Aquitaine, 43–44
Violante, C., 49
Virgil, 59
Vitalis, priest, 49

Werner, Ernst, 4
Williams, Rowan D., 5
Wilmart, André, 171

Zechariah, 172, 176
Zeruiah, 36
Zeuxis of Heraclea, 66
Ziegler, Aloysius, vii

INDEX OF SACRED SCRIPTURE

Old Testament

Genesis
  2.16–17: 129
  3.17–18: 162
  4.7: 102
  11.2–3: 84
  11.4: 85
  11.9: 85
  12.1: 175
  16.2: 77
  21.12: 147
  23.16: 46
  25.1: 78
  30.37FF.: 177
  32.10: 26
  34.1–2: 178
  35.18: 50
  41.1–7: 162
  46.28–47.6: 45
  48.2: 180
  50.24: 46
  50.5: 46

Exodus
  1.11: 85
  4.3–4: 86
  4.10: 153
  4.14: 153
  4.15–16: 153
  7.11: 104
  10.15: 165
  13.19: 46
  17.10: 111
  17.10–11: 169
  22.22–24: 144
  25.37: 99

32.1: 172
32.4: 172
34.29–35: 153
35.5–8: 73
36.3–5: 74
36.6: 74
36–38: 30
37.23: 99

Leviticus
  27.28: 108

Numbers
  6.27: 160
  11.16–17: 28
  15.32–36: 139
  16.47–48: 87
  27.12: 33

Deuteronomy
  5.21: 131
  5.31: 173
  8.3: 137
  21.12: 175
  24.1: 77, 83
  25.2: 75
  25.2–3: 75
  28.17–18: 161
  28.20: 161
  34.1: 33

Joshua
  2.18: 79
  7: 138
  9.22: 121

17.14: 161
17.15: 135
17.16–18: 136
17.18: 27
18.3: 27

Judges
  1.6: 56
  1.7: 56
  3.15: 153
  13.22–23: 147
  15.15–17: 113
  16.20–21: 83
  19.1FF.: 178
  20.16: 50

Ruth
  1.1: 30
  1.16: 180
  1.20: 179
  2.2, 17FF.: 179

1 Samuel
  1.8: 25
  1.18: 173
  2.17: 128
  13.1: 28
  14.24–30: 139
  16.15: 159
  16.19: 30
  17.34: 29
  18.20, 27: 88
  19.22–24: 159
  21.10: 112
  25: 147

INDEX OF SACRED SCRIPTURE

2 Samuel
2.8: 28
4.5–12: 154
6.11–12: 160
8.18: 29
11.2FF.: 177
15.16: 38
15.18: 28
16.5FF.: 154
18.8: 32
18.8–9: 33
20.3: 38
20.26: 29
21.19: 29
21.21: 30
24.24: 32

1 Kings
1.3–4: 78
2.36FF.: 178
2.5: 37
2.6: 37
2.8: 37
2.9: 37
3.5: 63
6.7: 22
11.3: 38
13.8–9: 64
15.11: 64
15.24: 64
15.30: 64
16.1: 64
17.1: 173

2 Kings
3.14: 173
5.26: 133
5.26–27: 133
5.27: 133
6.16: 50
11.26–27: 64
12.13: 63
18.21: 180
22.18–20: 6
23.4–14: 144
23.29: 6
25.10: 135

1 Chronicles
2.55: 80
9.2: 121
21.25: 32
21.25–26: 32

2 Chronicles
1.5: 30
19.30: 47

2 Ezra
10.28: 121

Judith
8.12: 146

1 Maccabees
5.65–68: 154

2 Maccabees
2.4–5: 34

Job
21.13: 86

Psalms
1.3: 177
3.8: 85
5.7: 39
18.2: 152
18.6: 87
30.25: 89
44.3: 24
48.15: 86, 89, 125
56.5: 7, 114
57.7: 85
67.2–3: 17
69.4: 71
71.9: 124
72.9: 7
72.18: 86
82.6: 123
82.7–11: 123
82.13: 123
83.11: 164
83.12: 39
84.11: 39

87.7: 31
100.1: 39
101.10: 95
105.1: 7
106.38: 160
111.9: 132
117.1: 7
118.103: 67
120.6: 5
125.6: 99
131.9: 31
131.15: 160
134.6: 120

Proverbs
2.11, 16: 80
2.19: 80
3.25–26: 170
3.27–28: 170
4.5: 79
4.6–8: 79
5.18: 80
5.19: 80
5.20: 81
6.24–25: 78
7.4: 81
7.6–8: 81
7.9–10: 81
7.10–12: 82
7.16: 82
7.17: 78
7.18–19: 82
7.20: 82
7.26: 82
9.13–16: 81
10.1: 127
10.5: 128
11.4: 134
12.4: 83
18.21: 172
20.1: 136
21.17: 136
24.21–22: 70
24.27: 134
24.30: 134
25.18: 114
27.5: 142

INDEX OF SACRED SCRIPTURE

28.6: 134
28.16: 134
28.19: 135
28.20: 134
28.22: 134
29.1: 142
29.21: 136, 138
31.13: 31
31.19, 21: 31
31.22: 31

Ecclesiastes
5.9: 131
5.10: 131
5.11: 131
7.17: 164
9.10: 7

Canticles
1.2: 87
1.12: 24
1.15: 24
2.1: 20
3.7: 89
4.3: 179
5.10: 180
6.12: 174, 176
7.1: 176

Wisdom
2.6–7: 78
7.1–3: 40
12.15: 35

Sirach
2.16: 94
7.28: 83

9.8: 77
26.1–2: 78
34.21: 131
34.23: 131
34.28–29: 131

Isaiah
3.24: 85
6.5: 113, 172
6.6: 172
9.6: 30, 56
9.10: 89
11.1: 86
32.17: 22
36.6: 180
37.31: 47
40.3: 30
40.6–8: 54
40.31: 89
49.8: 7
49.18: 30
52.5: 128
53.5: 34
53.8–9: 34
61.10: 24
62.5: 24

Jeremiah
2.13: 69
9.21: 177
16.16: 166, 175
21.8–9: 174
31.21–22: 173

Lamentations
3.15: 89
3.26–28: 22

3.36: 35
3.37: 36
3.38: 35
3.41: 170
3.51: 177
3.53: 98

Ezekiel
1.7, 9: 176
16.10–11: 31
16.13: 31
29.6: 180

Daniel
1.17: 67
5.28: 79
12.3: 152

Joel
1.17: 85

Haggai
2.12–15: 107

Zechariah
2.6 176
2.7–8: 176
6.12: 84

Malachi
2.2: 160–61
2.7: 152
3.7: 142
3.9–10: 161
4.2: 5

New Testament

Matthew
3.16: 156
4.4: 137
5.3: 134
5.5: 98
6.1: 132

6.2: 133
6.21: 172
12.32: 163
12.36: 99
13.27: 50
13.28: 50

13.30: 50
17.23, 26: 175
18.6: 128
20.16: 88
22.14: 88
24.36: 5

INDEX OF SACRED SCRIPTURE

Matthew (continued)
  25.1: 54
  25.4: 100

Mark
  3.22: 113
  11.14: 162
  11.21: 162
  13.32: 5

Luke
  1.20, 22: 172
  1.35: 23
  1.78: 84
  2.10–11: 152
  2.14: 142
  2.9: 151
  6.20: 134
  6.25: 99
  9.62: 176
  10.1: 4
  11.21: 31
  12.10: 119
  12.49: 80
  15.2: 164
  16.12: 147
  20.35: 126
  22.28: 95
  22.29: 95
  22.49: 58
  24.32: 80

John
  2.20: 41
  6.33: 60
  6.54: 4
  6.61: 4
  7.16: 6
  8.34: 178
  10.2: 157
  10.27–28: 88
  12.25: 175
  12.31: 175
  12.32: 120
  12.35: 7

  13.27: 138
  14.6: 6
  16.6–7: 22
  16.11: 175
  19.39: 95

Acts
  3.19: 100
  4.34–35: 107
  8.9–31: 50
  8.23: 156
  25.11–12: 163

Romans
  2.24: 128
  6.4: 96
  8.32: 34
  12.3: 164

1 Corinthians
  1.4–7: 35
  1.11–13: 120
  1.20: 125
  1.21: 113
  1.25: 113
  3.11–13: 23
  3.13: 86
  4.3: 113
  5.8: 67
  6.10: 160
  6.13: 137
  6.15: 151
  7.1–16: 118
  7.2–3: 119
  9.27: 137
  10.4: 89
  10.27: 129
  16.21: 137

2 Corinthians
  2.14–16: 88
  3.6: 35
  6.2: 7
  6.14: 69
  7.2: 165

  10.3–4: 57
  10.3–5: 174
  12.2: 163

Galatians
  1.8: 51
  5.15: 165

Ephesians
  2.2: 113, 176
  2.19: 55
  4.8: 174
  4.28: 146
  5.5: 144
  5.27: 30
  6.12FF.: 176
  6.13–17: 58
  6.16: 23

Colossians
  1.24: 123

1 Thessalonians
  4.4: 58

1 Timothy
  2.4: 120
  3.4: 58
  3.15: 156
  4.3: 129
  4.4: 129
  4.12: 12
  4.13: 12
  6.8–9: 130
  6.10: 130

2 Timothy
  2.17–18: 104
  3.8: 104

Titus
  1.6: 58

Hebrews
  10.27: 87

10.38: 87
13.13–14: 53, 175

1 Peter
  2.9: 151
  4.15: 132
  4.16: 132

Jude
  1.9: 162

Revelation
  1.5: 151
  1.16: 154
  5.5: 35, 79

6.8: 89, 125
19.15: 50
22.11: 51

www.ingramcontent.com/pod-product-compliance
Lightning Source LLC
Chambersburg PA
CBHW032034290426
44110CB00012B/805